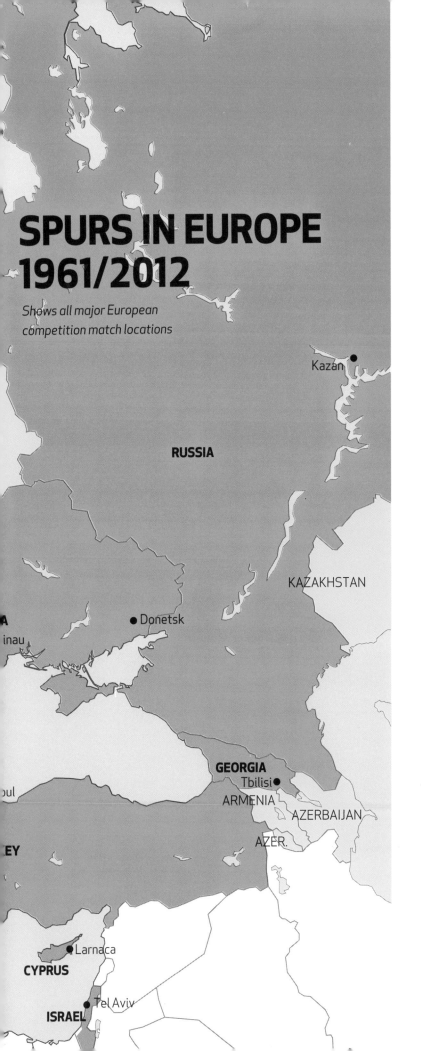

SPURS IN EUROPE 1961/2012

Shows all major European competition match locations

TOTTENHAM HOTSPUR

COMPLETE LIST OF EUROPI

1961-62 European Cup
v Gornik Zabrze, Poland
v Feyenoord, Netherlands
v Dukla Prague, Czechoslovakia
v Benfica, Portugal

1962-63 European Cup Winners' Cup
v Glasgow Rangers, Scotland
v Slovan Bratislava, Czechoslovakia
v OFK Belgrade, Yugoslavia
v Atletico Madrid, Spain, in Rotterdam, Netherlands

1963-64 European Cup Winners' Cup
v Manchester United, England

1967-68 European Cup Winners' Cup
v Hajduk Split, Yugoslavia
v Olympique Lyonnais, France

1971-72 UEFA Cup
v Keflavik, Iceland
v FC Nantes, France
v Rapid Bucharest, Romania
v UT Arad, R0mania
v AC Milan, Italy
v Wolverhampton Wanderers, England

1972-73 UEFA Cup
v Lyn Oslo, Norway
v Olympiakos Piraeus, Greece
v Red Star Belgrade, Yugoslavia
v Vitoria Setubal, Portugal
v Liverpool, England

1973-74 UEFA Cup
v Grasshopper Zurich, Switzerland
v Aberdeen, Scotland
v Dinamo Tbilisi, Soviet Union
v Cologne, West Germany
v Lokomotive Leipzig, East Germany
v Feyenoord, Netherlands

1981-82 European Cup Winners' Cup
v Ajax, Netherlands
v Dundalk, Republic of Ireland
v Eintracht Frankfurt, West Germany
v Barcelona, Spain

1982-83 European Cup Winners' Cup
v Coleraine, Northern Ireland
v Bayern Munich, West Germany

1983-84 UEFA Cup
v Drogheda United, Republic of Ireland
v Feyenoord, Netherlands
v Bayern Munich, West Germany
v FK Austria, Austria
v Hajduk Split, Yugoslavia
v Anderlecht, Belgium

1984-85 UEFA Cup
v SC Braga, Portugal
v FC Bruges, Belgium
v Bohemians Prague, Czechoslovakia
v Real Madrid, Spain

continued at back of book

THE GLORY GLORY NIGHTS

TOTTENHAM
HOTSPUR

Published by Vision Sports Publishing Ltd in 2012

Vision Sports Publishing,
19-23 High Street
Kingston upon Thames
Surrey
KT1 1LL
www.visionsp.co.uk

© Tottenham Hotspur FC
Text © Martin Cloake and Adam Powley

ISBN 978-1907637-66-7

This book is an officially licensed publication

The views expressed in this book do not necessarily reflect the views, opinions or policies of Tottenham Hotspur Football Club, nor those of any persons connected with the same.

Tottenham Hotspur FC
Bill Nicholson Way
High Road
N17 0AP
www.tottenhamhotspur.com

Publisher: Jim Drewett
Club liaison: John Fennelly
Historical consultants: Andy Porter and Bob Goodwin

Design: Doug Cheeseman
Additional Imaging: Jörn Kröger

Printed in Slovakia by Neografia

A CIP Catalogue record for this book is available from the British Library

THE GLORY GLORY NIGHTS

The Official Story of Tottenham Hotspur in Europe

by Martin Cloake & Adam Powley

TOTTENHAM HOTSPUR

Benfica depart
White Hart Lane
after training prior
to the European
Cup semi-final in
April 1962

CONTENTS

FOREWORD
GARETH BALE

❝ As you walk out of the Spurs dressing room at White Hart Lane you walk past an amazing picture of Bill Nick and Cliff Jones so it's impossible not to be aware of Spurs' great tradition. Playing in Europe is a massive part of that, it means so much to the club, the players and the fans. There's so much history at a club that was one of the first to take on the best in Europe, and the first in Britain to win a European trophy.

That's why it's been such a thrill for me to play for a team that is writing a new chapter in the club's European story. And playing in those European games is how anyone who pulls on the famous white shirt gets to really understand all that's said about Spurs in Europe and about why the glory glory nights under the floodlights are so magical. There's a real sense that European football is what makes this club special.

I'm told I made a place for myself in the story after those two unforgettable games against Internazionale in our Champions League run in 2010/11. People have been very kind, but I still say I'd rather we'd had a better result in Milan and I hadn't scored the hat-trick. But I couldn't fail to notice how much that fightback in the San Siro meant to the fans, or the fantastic atmosphere in the home tie. That second game was the sort of night we live for as players, just as much as the fans do. And once you've tasted that, you want more.

This club's European story began long before I was even thought of. So it's been a real pleasure to read the full story of all those games from the past. I've learned a lot as I turned the pages of this fascinating history, and I'm sure there's enough detail to give something new to even the most committed Spurs fan and historian. It's also been great to see how the current team fits in with the story and is seeking to add new achievements to what has already been a magnificent record.

It's also great to get so many different perspectives on the tale of Spurs in Europe – from the press reports that really give a sense of the times, to the memories of the players and of the fans who have travelled in such numbers and given generations of Spurs players such wonderful support. And I loved the pictures of all the gifts the club has been given by our opponents over the years and from all around Europe.

This is a marvellous book for all Spurs fans, and something that lives up to the high standards the club has set in Europe. Here's to another 50 years of glory glory nights. ❞

THE GLORY BOYS

In 1963, Tottenham Hotspur became the first British football club to win a European trophy, beating Atletico Madrid 5-1 in Rotterdam. In doing so, Bill Nicholson's team firmly established itself as one of the greatest sides of all time, just two years after becoming the first English side of modern times to win the league and FA Cup Double.

The story of Spurs in Europe is laced with romance and adventure, and with a pioneering spirit. After that historic first in 1963, in 1972 Spurs became the first British side to win two European trophies by lifting the first-ever UEFA Cup. Spurs fans were the first to fly to away games, and set the template for years of travel as fans of English clubs followed their teams across mainland Europe. By 1984, when Keith Burkinshaw's team lifted the UEFA Cup again, the only club to have won more European silverware was the great Liverpool dynasty of the 1970s and 1980s. Between 13 September 1961 and 6 March 1984, over 42 home European ties, Spurs remained unbeaten. After that loss to Real Madrid,

it would be 13 games and 23 years before Spurs lost a European tie at home again.

These are just some of the reasons why European football is so special at Spurs, a club which Nicholson once said was "nothing without European football". The 50th anniversary of that first European trophy win in 1963 presents a perfect opportunity to reflect on and enjoy one of football's most inspiring stories, and to appreciate the great games and the great players who have formed a part of it.

The first European tie at White Hart Lane against Gornik Zabrze from Poland's Silesian coalfields was an electrifying evening when the force of the team's performance was matched by the intensity of the noise from the crowd. And it was where the glory glory tradition from which this book takes its title was forged. The story of the Spurs team in Europe is also the story of Spurs fans, and it was a group of fans who set the template for the glory glory nights.

After the first leg in Poland, the Polish press had described Spurs as "no angels"

Right: The Tottenham Hotspur angels take to the pitch in 1961 and a famous chant is heard at White Hart Lane for the very first time

Below: Spurs return triumphant to Tottenham from Rotterdam in 1963. Jimmy Greaves (second right) shows off the Cup Winners' Cup along with (left to right) John White, Bill Brown, Ron Henry, Cliff Jones and Terry Dyson

"SPURS FANS DRESSED AS ANGELS PARADED AROUND THE TOUCHLINE, PROMPTING THE CROWD TO SING 'GLORY GLORY HALLELUJAH' – AND A FAMOUS TRADITION WAS BORN"

Steve Perryman (no 8) is congratulated by Alan Gilzean after one of his two goals against AC Milan in the 1972 UEFA Cup semi-final

after what it perceived to have been a robust approach. In response, a group of Spurs fans dressed as angels for the return, parading around the touchline carrying placards with slogans such as "Glory be to shining White Hart Lane". The humour of the response prompted the crowd to take up the chant of "Glory Glory Hallelujah", and one of the most famous traditions in football was born.

The other defining characteristic of Spurs in Europe is the adoption of the all-white strip, something which was allowed to slip for a few campaigns but which has now been firmly embraced. Opinion varies as to whether the all-white was a nod by Bill Nicholson to the great Real Madrid side that had dominated the early years of the European Cup, or more simply a tactic to ensure the players could see each other more clearly under the floodlights. Whatever the reasons, the all-white strip is *the* Spurs kit in Europe.

There are many great matches and great players in the story. In 1962, the legendary Benfica side featuring Eusebio came to White Hart Lane for what those who were there still say was one of the best matches ever played on these shores. Gianni Rivera's AC Milan fell

victim to two fine volleys from Steve Perryman and, in 1983, the Dutch master Johan Cruyff came off second best against the Crown Prince of English football, Glenn Hoddle. On that night, Hoddle firmly established himself as the King of White Hart Lane. That same campaign culminated in another unforgettable night as Tony Parks became the hero, saving two penalties in a nail-biting shootout to secure a second UEFA Cup win.

More recently, Spurs have written some new chapters, none more vividly than the night on which Gareth Bale helped destroy European champions Internazionale. That first Champions League campaign lit up the early stages of the competition, announcing Spurs as a major force in European football

Johan Cruyff appears to worship Glenn Hoddle during the 1983 UEFA Cup tie at White Hart Lane v Feyenoord

"A DEFINING CHARACTERISTIC OF SPURS IN EUROPE IS THE ALL-WHITE STRIP. OPINION VARIES AS TO WHY IT WAS ADOPTED; WHATEVER THE REASON THE ALL-WHITE STRIP IS *THE* SPURS KIT IN EUROPE"

Spurs players mob Graham Roberts after his equalising goal in the 1984 UEFA Cup Final v Anderlecht

once more and winning the club new friends after some lean years.

This book is part of a Spurs tradition too. In the foreword to the original version, published in 1986, club chairman Irving Scholar spoke of an uncle giving him a book called *Spurs Supreme* which commemorated the Double win. He said, "It recorded every game played that season, by way of reprinting at least one newspaper match report." And, said Scholar, "I must have read it at least 50 times over, never tiring of its content." His affection for that book prompted him to commission the original *The Glory Glory Nights*, a book which captured the imagination of a new generation of fans and inspired this new edition.

So this is the complete history of Spurs in European competition to date, put together in the style which has inspired successive generations of Spurs fans. Every match in a major European tournament is described, drawing on contemporaneous media reports to give a flavour of the time, and using the recollections of some of the great Spurs players who took part in the games.

What's noticeable is how the coverage has changed over the years. Where once

European competition was unusual, even exotic, now it is commonplace. And where once the only way of "seeing" the game, unless you were there, was through the pictures painted by Fleet Street's wordsmiths, now the reports are written in the knowledge that every minute of the action has already been watched by the reader. So the descriptive flourishes of the Sixties and Seventies have given way to the more personality-driven reports of modern times.

That may cause some to reflect a little sadly that the magic of Europe has lost its lustre. But despite the fact that European football is fast becoming a minimum financial as well as footballing requirement, leading to a situation where finishing fourth in the league is greeted with almost the same enthusiasm as a trophy win, the magic of European football remains as alluring as ever.

For the players, for the fans, for everyone associated with the club, there's something special about Spurs in Europe. This book is both a history and a celebration of the great players – in whatever shirt – and the great games that have woven one of football's most inspiring stories.

Gareth Bale and Peter Crouch celebrate after combining to score in a famous win over Inter Milan in the 2010 Champions League game at White Hart Lane

The 1960s

As one of football's true visionaries, Bill Nicholson was a manager willing to seek new horizons. After succeeding in the challenge of creating the best team in England, the Spurs manager turned his gaze to the continent, to pit his side against the finest foreign clubs. It would soon become apparent that European football was the ultimate test.

Hitherto, the European game had been viewed with suspicion and typically insular arrogance by the domestic football establishment. Chelsea had been warned from competing in 1955 by the Football League, and it took Manchester United's heroic but doomed campaign of 1957/58 to convince doubters as to the unique and captivating nature of floodlit football against exotic opposition, coupled with daring trips to far-flung locations.

The heartbreaking tragedy that befell the Busby Babes in the Munich air disaster in February 1958 denied one of English football's greatest sides the opportunity to realise its full promise, but it also helped imbue Manchester United and other British clubs with a sense of destiny. Far from being a distraction suitable only for foreigners to bother with, the European Cup became something of an obsession, the supreme test by which all domestic champions would subsequently be measured.

By the time Spurs qualified to compete for the 1961/62 European Cup, the all-conquering Real Madrid side of Di Stefano, Puskas and Gento had become the team all others aspired to beat. Real's 7-3 thrashing of Eintracht Frankfurt at Hampden Park in 1960 provided one of those landmark moments in football history when the game was elevated to something more than just a contest between 22 players.

Real were superseded by the brilliant Portuguese champions, Benfica, featuring the magnificent talents of Aguas, Coluna and the emerging Eusebio. Spurs more than held their own in such vaunted company and came desperately close to the ultimate triumph in their debut European season.

Having gained a taste for such adventures, Tottenham developed a hungry appetite for more. Nicholson soon came to realise how vital it was to measure his teams against the best sides of Spain, Portugal, Italy, Germany, Eastern Europe and beyond. "It's magnificent to be in Europe, and this club – a club like Tottenham Hotspur – if we're not in Europe we're nothing. We're nothing," he said, establishing a Spurs mantra, and emphasising how vital the arena became to the club's outlook. The European Cup Winners' Cup triumph in 1963, the first for any British side, established Tottenham as true pioneers and further elevated the club's standing.

Spurs suited European football. Their flowing play with the emphasis on sparkling skill and touch rather than physical effort and brawn was more in tune with the technically proficient culture of the Continent. The players felt at home, and turned on the style (as well as digging in when required). The White Hart Lane crowd responded in kind, packing the stands and terraces and providing an incessant roar that cowed opponents. The floodlights, the all-white kit, the emotional strains of "Glory Glory Hallelujah" made the 1960s a magical, memorable time. This was the era when the glory nights legend was born.

Left to right: Tony Marchi greets Eusebio prior to Tottenham's European Cup semi-final first leg in Lisbon v Benfica; Bobby Smith celebrates Spurs' 1963 Cup Winners' Cup victory v Atletico Madrid in Rotterdam; Alan Mullery, a key figure in the ill-fated 1967/68 Cup Winners' Cup campaign

CUP WINNERS' CUP
1962/63
GLASGOW RANGERS
SLOVAN BRATISLAVA
OFK BELGRADE
ATLETICO MADRID

EUROPEAN CUP
1961/62
GORNIK ZABRZE
FEYENOORD
DUKLA PRAGUE
BENFICA

1963/64
MANCHESTER UNITED

1967/68
HAJDUK SPLIT
OLYMPIQUE LYONNAIS

THE ROAD TO EUROPE

1961

Record-breaking Super Spurs had cut a thrilling swathe through English football by becoming the first side in 64 years to win the fabled Double. But even as Tottenham were earning their triumph in the 1960/61 season, thoughts were already turning to how they would fare in Europe.

The league title had been won with victory over Sheffield Wednesday. The subsequent defeat of Leicester City in the FA Cup Final showed the team was mortal, however. The 2-0 scoreline belied a win that was far from easy – "What a fearful fright these not-so-super Spurs were given," wrote Alan Hoby in *The Sunday Express*.

Now the European Cup beckoned and the opportunity to see what Spurs were really made of against the best in the world, not just England. In readiness for the opening tie against Gornik Zabrze of Poland, Nicholson visited three weeks ahead to scout not just the team but the location. It lived up to some Cold War stereotypes – a grim and daunting mining town with a sense of the unknown. "We were a very good side and we knew it. What we didn't know was how to play in Europe," Nicholson said. He and his team were about to find out.

Spurs celebrate
their historic Double
in May 1961; with
it came a place
in the 1961/62
European Cup

POLAND MINERS SHAME SPURS

Left: Legendary Polish striker Ernest Pohl celebrates scoring the third Gornik goal in Chorzow. The arena where the match was played is now called the Ernest Pohl Stadium, in honour of the man who remains the top scorer in the Polish league

Below: The original pennant handed to Spurs by Gornik. All the pennants pictured in this book are those Spurs received from other clubs

13 September 1961, preliminary round, first leg

GORNIK ZABRZE 4
TOTTENHAM HOTSPUR 2

Stadion Slaski, Chorzow, Poland *Att:* 70,000

As an introduction to the unique rigours of European football, this was a rude awakening. Gornik were hospitable hosts off the field but on it they provided anything but a warm welcome. Tottenham's inexperience was ruthlessly exposed and the Londoners were roundly criticised, not just for a humiliating defeat but for the manner in which they played.

"It was a match," Desmond Hackett reported in the *Daily Express*, "not far removed from being an evening of soccer shame for Tottenham." The visitors wilted in the face of a fierce Polish onslaught. They succumbed to a 4-0 deficit and, while two late goals rescued the tie, this was a performance far removed from the silky soccer with which the team had made its name.

Little about the match was familiar. Among a feverish 70,000 crowd Spurs found next to no support – according to the *Daily Mail*'s Ian Wooldridge, just a single Tottenham fan, student David Mummery, had made the trip. Mummery witnessed an uncharacteristic

Spurs display, littered with mistakes and ill-tempered reactions. The Polish fans vented their anger at what they perceived as over-physical tactics from Spurs.

The focus of their ire was Dave Mackay, who was roundly booed for a full-blooded tackle on Jan Kowalski that forced the left-half out of the game 16 minutes into the second half. By then, Gornik had established command, their fluid attack causing havoc in the Spurs defence. A brace from the teenage Jerzy Musialek, another from the outstanding Ernest Pohl and an own goal from Maurice Norman left Spurs in real danger of exiting the competition at their first attempt. In the end it was Mackay's determination that saved the day, as Cliff Jones and then Terry Dyson finished off moves instigated by Tottenham's marauding midfielder in a desperate 20-minute face-saving action.

Brown, Baker, Henry, Blanchflower, Norman, Mackay, **Jones***, White, R. Smith, Allen,* **Dyson**

JONES' HAT-TRICK TEARS THE POLES RIGHT APART

20 September 1961, preliminary round, second leg

TOTTENHAM HOTSPUR 8 (10)
GORNIK ZABRZE 1 (5)

White Hart Lane *Att:* 56,737

The return tie against Gornik was one of those glittering occasions in Tottenham's stellar history, and played a large part in defining the unique character of Spurs in Europe. It is a game that has gained almost mythic status.

No one who was there will ever forget it. Tottenham dazzled, amazed and delighted in a manner few other British club sides have ever matched. The crowd of 56,737 provided a deafening, frightening fusillade of noise that reduced the Poles to quivering wrecks.

The build-up to the game has provided as many legends as the action itself. In response to the accusations from the Poles that over-physical Spurs were "no angels", the group of home fans dressed as heavenly characters paraded around the pitch before kick-off, leading the vast choir in the first rendition of "Glory Glory Hallelujah". Nicholson, meanwhile, had ordered the tallest, burliest men among the groundstaff to line up in the tunnel to help intimidate the Poles.

The mind games worked. Gornik were overwhelmed by a tidal wave of Spurs attacks and supporter fervour. Danny Blanchflower started the rout with a penalty in the ninth minute, before Jones brought the teams level on aggregate with a header. The Welshman completed a brilliant first-half hat-trick, with Pohl giving the visitors a glimmer of hope in between Jones's second and third strikes.

Bobby Smith increased the advantage before half-time and again in the 72nd minute with a header, before Dyson's coruscating finish and John White's strike a minute from time completed the eight-goal haul.

It had been scintillating, breathless stuff. It was, as Clive Toye vividly observed in the *Daily Express*, "a savage destruction... won in the first ferocious 45 minutes of a night of emotion at White Hart Lane that had the huge bawling crowd screaming with joy".

Brown, Baker, Henry, **Blanchflower,** *Norman, Mackay,* **Jones 3,** *White,* **R. Smith 2,** *Allen,* **Dyson**

Hubert Kostka, the Gornik goalkeeper, is well beaten by a header from Bobby Smith, Tottenham's centre-forward (out of shot), for the home side's fifth goal. Looking on is Terry Dyson, Tottenham's outside-left

SPURS v GORNIK ZABRZE
LOOKING BACK WITH **BILL NICHOLSON**

Bill Nicholson flew to Warsaw three weeks before Tottenham's first European Cup match to look at what the team could expect. Even the experienced boss who had previously taken his side to Eastern Europe for friendlies was surprised at the differences. At a time when the Cold War was at its height, journeys behind what was dubbed the "Iron Curtain" carried a sense of intrigue and daring – and some welcome surprises as to the hospitality extended.

"There were no quick spying missions to that part of the world in those days," Nicholson recalled over 20 years later. "I remember flying into Warsaw and the train journey down to Katowice took four hours. It was a very depressed place. You had to feel sympathy for the people. It was a cold mining area. Everything was grey. They tried their best for us.

"I remember going to the stadium and seeing women on their hands and knees with scissors cutting every blade of grass. The pitch was in immaculate condition. There was a pattern running from corner to corner of the ground. It was an example of how they were determined to put on their best face.

"However, it was obvious in some cases that the best in Poland was just not good enough. The hotel standards were a prime example. It was supposed to be one of the best in that part of Poland. I was not happy, though, and we had a bit of an 'up and downer' about it.

"But to show how wonderful those people were, when we returned with the team the whole hotel had been given a face lift. The whole place had been painted, the

restaurant area had been vastly improved, there had been a general spring cleaning of all the rooms and the curtains were replaced. It was not exactly the Ritz, but it was still a great deal better than before."

It was not only off-the-pitch factors that were a great surprise to those Tottenham pioneers. The playing style of the Europeans was very different. Nicholson actually had a league game of Gornik's watched and said:

"We knew nothing of them. The league game did not tell us anything that was remotely useful either. We knew that they had a good player in Pohl, but we were not expecting anything more unusual than a normal English league game.

"What a shock we got. We had practised normally. We worked very hard and we were convinced that our European preparation was as thorough as it could be. We had decided that we would adopt the same sort of principles and philosophies that had helped us to win the Double.

"We were convinced that we had nothing to worry about unduly [but] we did not know how to play games over two legs.

"We had to learn quickly. At 4-0 down in the first leg we were in danger of being tossed out of the competition at the first time of asking. We'd tried to play our normal attacking football. We threw caution to the wind and paid the price. They hit us hard.

"It made us realise that some teams on the continent prepare for the European ties very differently. They played a much more containing game. We had to learn to eradicate the other teams' strengths without losing our own strengths. Gornik did it to perfection and, but for our ability to play outstanding football, we would have been out."

Watching the game from the Gornik dugout, Nicholson had feared that his side would be caught in the "whirlwind" effect. He said: "It is so easy when goals are going in to be swept away.

"It happened to Gornik at White Hart Lane. They were crushed 8-1. They were not that bad, but they were caught in a domino effect. When one goal goes in it is difficult to halt the flood.

"It was an amazing start. Maybe we learnt more in that 90 minutes than we had learnt in 90 years before. Europe was certainly a different place."

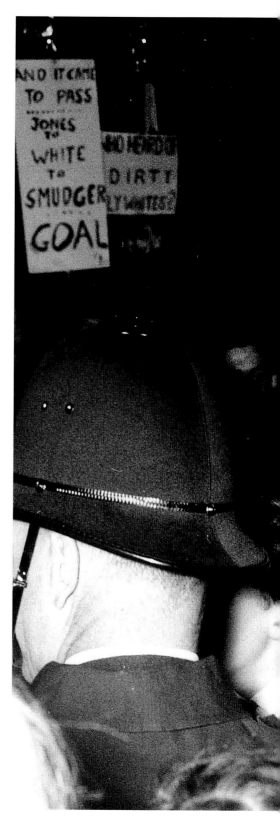

POST-MATCH **REACTION**

From the Spurs programme, 30 September 1961: "Harking back to our match with KS Gornik, it was thrilling to hear the old-time 'Tottenham Roar' at full blast, but though our

Euphoric scenes as Bobby Smith is mobbed by fans after the final whistle v Gornik Zabrze at White Hart Lane. To the left are appropriately worded banners carried by the 'Tottenham angels'

supporters were obviously out to do their best to help the team 'wipe the slate clean' as soon as possible, their vocal enthusiasm seems to have worried some members of the Press. 'Hate' and 'fanaticism' have been suggested as the reasons for such prolonged enthusiasm, but those who know the true Spurs supporters know fans who appreciate good football, as was witnessed by the spontaneous ovation given to Gornik when Pohl hit that tremendous goal.

But what's the use of supporters if they do not support, the more so in such an important game when support is even more necessary? We, at any rate, were proud of our supporters, and of our players who made it such a memorable evening."

SPURS v GORNIK ZABRZE
IN PICTURES

Top: Les Allen heads for goal, with Bobby Smith ready to pounce
Bottom: Terry Dyson and Les Allen celebrate Tottenham's fifth goal on the night

Main picture: Spurs players celebrate a famous floodlit win on the night the all-white kit is worn for the first time in a European tie at White Hart Lane

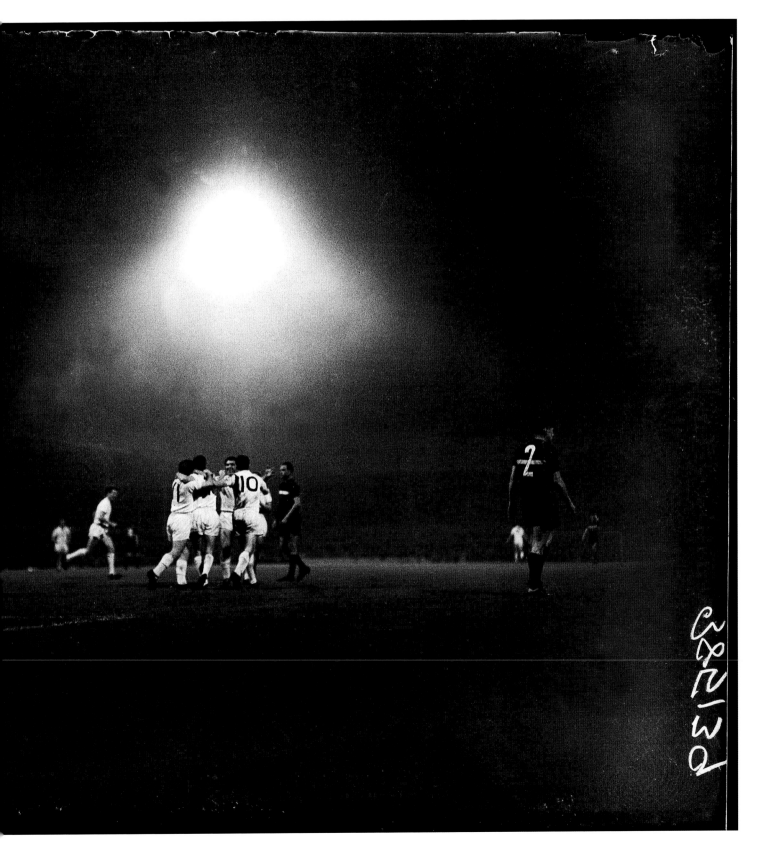

Terry Dyson celebrates scoring the first goal in Rotterdam. Young Frank Saul, who scored twice on the night, runs in to make certain

European Cup Soccer

DYSON & SAUL PUT SPURS ON WAY TO LAST EIGHT

Splendid Fighting Display Leaves Manager Nicholson Unimpressed

1 November 1961, first round, first leg

FEYENOORD 1
TOTTENHAM HOTSPUR 3

Feyenoord Stadium, Rotterdam, Netherlands *Att:* 61,719

As on their travels to Poland, Spurs once again faced a partisan first-leg crowd. Again they played an opposition brimming with flair. And once more, the north Londoners fell below their own exacting high standards. This time, however, they proved victorious, illustrating that, just a matter of three games into their campaign, Spurs were learning how to cope with the distinct and demanding tests of European football.

It was the 18-year-old Frank Saul who stole the show, scoring twice to reward the 1,000 Tottenham supporters who had made the trip across the North Sea to Rotterdam. Saul was a fringe player who would go on to make just 129 appearances in his nine years at the club, but when his limited opportunities came he rarely let the side down.

His contribution in this game was telling. After Spurs had weathered a vigorous test in the opening spell, the visitors took the lead against the run of play just before half-time as Terry Dyson nodded home from close range. Saul belied his tender years to keep his cool and score twice in the second half. The first came on 48 minutes, when he headed in from a John White cross. Twenty-three minutes later Saul was fed by Cliff Jones and finished with a marked degree of composure.

Feyenoord had at least gained some reward for their endeavours with Reiner Kreijermaat's pulverising drive from 35 yards just past the hour, but the Dutch were left to rue their luck when Rinus Bennaers, "a tiny 31-year-old car salesman who plays soccer for pocket money" as reported by Ian Wooldridge in the *Daily Mail*, twice hit the bar late on. Spurs had survived, but only just. "We muddled through. That's all you can say," said Bill Nicholson. "Our mistake? There were so many I don't know where to start." Bill Nick was clearly in the mood to demand significant improvement.

*Brown, Baker, Henry, Blanchflower, Norman, Marchi, Jones, White, **Saul 2**, Clayton, **Dyson***

Mackay taken off, roars back to stop Dutch

15 November 1961, first round, second leg

TOTTENHAM HOTSPUR 1 (4)
FEYENOORD 1 (2)

White Hart Lane *Att:* 62,144

If Feyenoord had displayed traditional Dutch qualities of enterprise and flair on home turf, they revealed another side to their game in north London. This was no footballing master class – more a lesson in how to emerge broadly intact after the sternest of physical challenges that rekindled long-smouldering suspicions about foreign teams.

"Having watched these brawling, mauling Dutchmen strongman their way through a depressing second half," fumed Desmond Hackett in the *Daily Express*, "I came to the firm decision that if this is the Common Market of European football, we are better off out of it." Thankfully, Spurs were not out of it. While the hosts were not able to fully impose their natural game, Tottenham did enough to resist Feyenoord's physical approach.

Nicholson got something of the response he had demanded after the stuttering display in the first leg, with Blanchflower orchestrating matters from his midfield position early on. It was Feyenoord who took the lead on the night, however, when Bennaers beat Brown from close range with nine minutes gone. Three minutes later, any nerves were calmed when Mackay hooked the ball back for Dyson to head in.

Mackay was to be a central figure to the encounter. Just moments after Tottenham's equaliser, he was knocked senseless in a collision with Feyenoord's towering defender Hans Kraay. Mackay, for once, came off worse and was taken off. Lesser men would have called it a night, but with typical determination Mackay re-entered the fray, his all-white kit spattered with blood.

"What am I doing here? Let me get back," he roared. His re-emergence revitalised both players and the crowd – "they must have heard the cheers halfway down the Seven Sisters Road," wrote *The Guardian*'s Eric Todd. With that, Spurs' progress was assured.

*Brown, Baker, Henry, Blanchflower, Norman, Marchi, Jones, White, Saul, Mackay, **Dyson***

Dave Mackay is down but not out. Despite concussion, he returned to the fray after being knocked flat in a collision with Feyenoord's Hans Kraay, who also receives treatment

European Cup Soccer

NICHOLSON PLAN ALLOWS DUKLA ONLY ONE GOAL

Spurs' Blanket-Defence Success: Semi-final Within Reach

14 February 1962, second round, first leg

DUKLA PRAGUE 1
TOTTENHAM HOTSPUR 0

Stadion Dynama, Prague, Czechoslovakia *Att*: 38,000

Spurs had reached the quarter-finals growing in confidence and appreciation for the finer points of European football. They received a mid-season boost with the record signing of Jimmy Greaves – a signal of intent that the best side in Britain was laying down a challenge not just to British clubs but the cream of Europe.

While Greaves sat out the away meeting with Dukla Prague, his new team-mates produced a cautious, largely defensive display that negated the Czechs' home advantage. Hitherto any defeat would have been viewed as a setback, but attitudes towards the competition were maturing. In keeping the score down to 1-0, the team, press and even the demanding Nicholson seemed pleased. "I am well satisfied," he told *The Daily Sketch*'s Laurie Pignon. "The plan worked as I expected, especially in the first half…"

Playing Tony Marchi as an extra centre-half on a snow-covered pitch gave Spurs a four-man defence. Not everyone was happy with the tactic: Pignon reported that one purist Spurs director muttered, "I wouldn't like to see it every week", but it was effective. Dukla found Tottenham's rearguard tough to break down and only had Rudolf Kucera's 59th-minute goal to count for their dominance.

Indeed, Spurs were unfortunate not to end the match on level terms. Bobby Smith thought he had equalised nine minutes later, but he was ruled offside. As tensions rose and the tackles increased in intensity, a series of spats broke out and both Smith and Jones were cautioned for reacting to bad challenges. Smith even resorted to throwing a snowball at one assailant. But with Spurs holding firm and Bill Brown pulling off a series of fine stops, a highly satisfactory, professional display gave Tottenham the platform for completing the job at the Lane.

Brown, Baker, Henry, Marchi, Norman, Mackay, Medwin, White, R. Smith, Blanchflower, Jones

Bill Brown, surrounded by his well-marshalled defence, sees off another Dukla Prague attack

The second leg story—attack, attack, death before defeat

SPURS SWITCH TO GLORY

White's genius splits Dukla giant defence

26 February 1962, second round, second leg
TOTTENHAM HOTSPUR 4 (4)
DUKLA PRAGUE 1 (2)
White Hart Lane *Att*: 55,388

Tottenham brought the frozen weather back home with them, but their performance was one of white-hot intensity. On a rock-hard frozen surface, Spurs reproduced their Gornik-demolishing form to book their passage into the semi-finals.

Leading the charge were Mackay and Smith, who scored two apiece. For Smith in particular it was sweet satisfaction. He had lost his place earlier in the season and with the signing of Greaves both he and Les Allen found their status under threat. His physical presence allied to his considerable skill, however, made him the ideal man for the big European occasion, his power, finishing and burly presence proving valuable weapons.

Dukla had tried to bully Spurs in the first leg but had little answer in the return. Within 15 minutes they were two down on the night. First, a Blanchflower free-kick was flicked on by White for Smith to score. Five minutes later, White fed Mackay who controlled with his left before smashing home with his right.

The visitors rarely troubled Bill Brown but snatched a shock aggregate equaliser within seconds of the restart via Josef Jelinek. There was to be no panic from Spurs, however. Relying on the brand of football that had won them the Double less than a year before, the team passed, dribbled and dazzled their way back into the lead, scoring twice more. In the 55th minute White was once again the provider as he crossed for Smith to powerfully head home before Mackay completed the scoring just 60 seconds later with a second barnstorming finish.

The crowd roared their approval and belted out "Glory Glory Hallelujah". As Peter Lorenzo noted in *The Daily Herald*, "Spurs' magnificent, controlled football sustained at a breathtaking pace was enough to make anyone forget the arctic chills."

Brown, Baker, Henry, Blanchflower, Norman, Marchi, Medwin, White,
R. Smith 2, Mackay 2, *Jones*

Bobby Smith, recently restored to the Spurs attack and bang on form, scores Spurs' first goal in the home leg

Nicholson switches Greaves to right wing in his first European Cup-tie

NOW SPURS NEED THREE!

Benfica go flat out—snatch quick goals

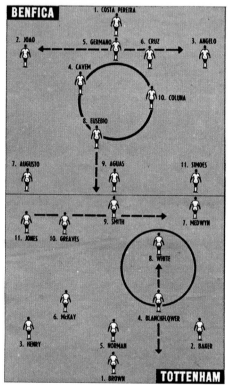

21 March 1962, semi-final, first leg

BENFICA 3
TOTTENHAM HOTSPUR 1

Estadio da Luz, Lisbon, Portugal *Att: 70,000*

The histories of many football clubs are littered with hard-luck stories – the "ifs and buts" that can make the difference between epic triumph and heartbreaking failure. Often they disguise individual failings, or the human errors that are part and parcel of the sport. But Tottenham's dramatic defeat in Lisbon still rankles as an injustice.

What looked like two perfectly good goals for Spurs were disallowed by Swiss referee Daniel Mellet. The first controversy came in the sixth minute when Greaves burst through and scored but the strike was ruled out for offside. The second came five minutes from time when Greaves and Smith combined only for the Yorkshireman to be again ruled offside – despite the fact that two Benfica players were on the goal line.

It felt like a mugging amid the hostile, deafening surrounds of the spectacular Estadio da Luz. Nicholson was typically blunt, pointing to a generally poor performance from his re-arranged side in which Blanchflower had looked out of sorts in an unfamiliar inside-left berth. Greaves, making his European debut and Cliff Jones missed excellent chances to compound the sense that Spurs had not merited a draw.

But the feeling of injustice was tangible. Reigning champions Benfica had set the sternest of tests, racing into a 2-0 lead through strikes from Simoes and Augusto within 20 minutes. Smith reduced the deficit in the 54th minute, only for Augusto to grab his second 19 minutes later. Even if just one of the ruled-out Tottenham goals had stood, however, the prospects for the return would have been so different.

"Spurs have become hardened to this toughest-ever world soccer contest," wrote a sympathetic Hackett in the *Daily Express*. "We shall do them at Tottenham, just wait and see," glowered Mackay. The stage was set for one of the most dramatic, memorable and epic matches in Tottenham history.

*Brown, Baker, Henry, Marchi, Norman, Mackay, Greaves, White, **R. Smith**, Blanchflower, Jones*

Top left: Cliff Jones in an aerial battle during the European Cup semi-final first leg at Benfica's stadium, the Stadium of Light

Top right: Spurs warm up prior to the game with the reigning European champions

Above: Tactical preview, 1962-style. The predicted line-ups show a Benfica team that features future Ballon D'Or winner Eusebio in a withdrawn free attacking role and Blanchflower held back on the right

Facing: The match as billed in *France Football* magazine highlights the contrasting attributes of Spurs captain Danny Blanchflower and Benfica's José Aguas

COUPE D'EUROPE
2e DEMI-FINALE

LA CLAIRVOYANCE DE
◄ DANNY BLANCHFLOWER
TOTTENHAM
CONTRE
L'ENTHOUSIASME DE
JOSÉ AGUAS
BENFICA ▼

5 April 1962, semi-final, second leg

TOTTENHAM HOTSPUR 2 (3)
BENFICA 1 (4)

White Hart Lane *Att:* 64,448

Below left: Benfica train at White Hart Lane under the tutelage of their Hungarian manager Béla Guttmann

Below right: Danny Blanchflower shakes hands with Benfica captain José Aguas

Opposite: Fans offer sympathy to Blanchflower and John White, after they failed to find the goal that would have forced extra-time on the night

If a game of football can be measured by the superlatives heaped upon it by the hard-nosed gentlemen of Fleet Street, then Tottenham's second-leg showdown with Benfica must surely rank as one of the greatest in the sport's history. This was no ordinary game. It stands as one of the most glorious failures any club has ever produced.

The *Daily Mirror*'s Bill Holden described it simply as a "titanic struggle". After the excitement of the opening exchanges had given way to the main act, the *Daily Mail*'s Ian Wooldridge called it the "the most thrilling and heart-aching hour's football I have ever seen". Wooldridge's counterpart at the *Express*, David Miller, dubbed it "the most electrifying ninety minutes of European football I have seen on an English ground" – and this comment came 20 years after the event. Miller's praise strikes at the heart of what this game symbolised: a generation on and people were *still* talking and writing about it.

The 64,448 packed into White Hart Lane who created a cauldron of noise would hold the memory as long as they lived. With the second half shown live on ITV, millions more witnessed the mighty tussle between two outstanding teams from the edge of their seats. In the end the holders would cling on to their advantage. But they arguably never faced as great a test as the one Tottenham Hotspur provided.

The night began for Spurs in disastrous fashion, as Benfica's redoubtable skipper José Aguas, who also hit the woodwork, stunned the home spectators with a 15th-minute opener to give his team a 4-1 aggregate lead. The silence was only momentary, with the crowd and the Tottenham players combining as one to hammer the Portuguese into submission.

On 23 minutes came the turning point and yet more controversy when Greaves was released by Smith and finished with expert ease. Referee Aage Poulsen whistled for a goal, only for his fellow Dane, linesman Hensen, to incorrectly signal offside. Enraged by another cruel injustice, Spurs attacked like men possessed. Ten minutes before half-time came the breakthrough as Smith lashed home a chance created by White.

Spurs needed two goals to draw level. They reduced the deficit to one when Blanchflower, coolness personified, scored from the spot in the 48th minute. Thereafter it was a massacre, albeit without the goals to show for it. Chances were missed, while Spurs hit the woodwork three times, most despairingly when Mackay's 20-yard drive struck the crossbar in the final minute. And with that, Tottenham's European dream was over.

Shattered Spurs players were distraught. "This is twice I have been done in the European Cup," fumed Greaves, reflecting on his disallowed goals over the two legs. His

European Cup Semi-final
MAGNIFICENT SPURS GO DOWN FIGHTING

manager was more sanguine and self-critical. "My men played too quickly," Bill Nicholson told the *Mail*'s Roy Peskett. "They were too hurried. Their enthusiasm ran away with them. They lacked a little control and one or two players did not quite do what we had hoped. If we had kept our heads the result might have been different."

To Benfica's enormous credit, they had withstood the most exacting of tests. They went on to retain the cup, beating Real Madrid 5-3 in the final, a testament to their collective brilliance and the superb management of Béla Guttmann. The Hungarian, one of the great coaches of the game, was full of praise for Spurs. "It was the hardest game of my life… [Spurs] are one of the best teams in Europe. One day soon, with one or two changes, they will win the European Cup."

President of FIFA and the grand old man of English football, Sir Stanley Rous, reciprocated, casting Benfica as "masters of the game". Even Alan Hardaker, the aptly named secretary of the Football League who had been so opposed to European football in the 1950s, was in a generous mood – though he missed the salient point. "It was a wonderful game. It was the best advertisement for league football for a long time." The truth was that this magnificent encounter amply illustrated just how wonderful European football could be.

Brown, Baker, Henry, **Blanchflower,** *Norman, Mackay, Medwin, White,* **R. Smith,** *Greaves, Jones*

Referee says 'Yes,' linesman says 'No'—so ends European Cup crusade

ONE GOAL FROM GLORY

Benfica stagger off after 90-min blitz

HERE IT IS—GOAL THAT ENDED A DOUBLE DREAM

All the months of hope and worry for Spurs are smashed in one split second of shooting. Here is the goal, by Aguas, that made Spurs' task almost impossible and gave Benfica a 4–1 lead in the semi-final second-leg at Tottenham.

By IAN WOOLDRIDGE: Spurs......2, Benfica......1

Benfica win 4—3 on aggregate.

THE seven-month crusade is over. But in the emptiness of the morning after let us pay tribute to the team that finally triumphed over Tottenham. Benfica, champions of Portugal, survived 90 minutes of football hell that would have destroyed almost any other team on earth.

For 65 of those minutes they withdrew into a red fortress round their own penalty area and withstood the greatest pounding that Spurs have ever mounted.

In the end, staggering with weariness and mottled with bruises, they were too exhausted to do more than fall on the necks of their opponents.

This to me is the true picture of the most exciting finale I have ever seen to a football match, truer indeed than to try to make an international incident of the fact that a Danish linesman named Hensen will be blamed forever by Tottenham's fans.

But that man probably robbed Spurs of the chance of a replay in neutral Brussels.

In the 23rd minute Jimmy Greaves waltzed on to a short flicked pass from Bobby Smith and slid it smoothly past the careering body of Costa Pereira. It looked a perfect goal.

Aage Poulsen, hysterical Londoners unleashed the greatest roar of this ear-shattering night, he was already striding back to the centre spot.

But Hensen, a slim, erect, isolated figure on the far touch-line, had his magenta flag pointed skywards. This was fortune's vengeance on Spurs.

Poulsen strode back, listened intently, thrust his way out from a bouncing encirclement of wildly protesting Tottenham men and ruled Greaves offside.

That was the turning point.

Tottenham had started with the seemingly impossible burden of a two-goal deficit from Lisbon. Their fate seemed certain when, in a 15th minute of sudden shock, Jose Aguas, the great clear-brained captain of these 11 Portuguese men of war, strode through a great gap to score the first goal of the night.

It was from that even worse position that Spurs broke out to set seige to Benfica's goal in the most thrilling and heart-aching hour's football I have seen.

JON'S SPORTING TYPES

Glory, glory, Benfica

Look what Spurs miss

SPURS have failed the final hurdle to the European Cup Final. But they were in it long enough to prove what a fantastic money-spinner it is.

Their eight ties brought them about £80,000. If they had reached the final they would have got a further £20,000 for winning, or £10,000 as runners-up.

The players drew about £40 last night, bringing their European Cup bonus to £200.

SPURS

	Brown	
Baker		Henry
Blanchflower	Norman	Mackay
White		Greaves
Medwin	Smith	Jones
Simoes	Aguas	Augusto
Cruz	Coluna	Eusebio
Angelo	Germano	Cavem
	Pereira	Joao

BENFICA

The Benfica team were on a £700 semi-final bonus.

Last night's 65,000 crowd raised the total attendance for Spurs' eight ties to 508,067—344,087 of them at the four White Hart-lane matches.

● All tickets for the European Cup final at the Olympic Stadium, Amsterdam, on May 2 have been disposed of.

● The stadium holds 60,600, with seats for 44,600 at 35s, 25s, and 15s. It costs 6s. to stand.

Recklessly

They simply forced their way through flesh and blood and bone to hammer on the great door that Benfica had slammed in their faces.

In the 35th minute came their first reward. Bobby Smith, flinging his huge frame recklessly at anybody who dared to block his path, drove in a superb White cross.

Now it was half-time. For Spurs it was a battle more to beat the clock than to beat Benfica. Instead of 90 minutes they had now only 45 minutes left to score three goals for victory, two for survival.

Just two minutes into the second half the nerves of 65,000 were truly on the tightrope. Danny Blanchflower had cut that deficit again.

Coluna, nominally inside left but now withdrawn almost on to his own goal-line in desperate defence, backed into the advancing John White. As Blanchflower moved up to take the penalty I would not have been in his boots.

Yet he did it as if he had been set to prove some theoretical point. He moved in with a corkscrew run, and as Pereira flung himself far to the right of his goal, Blanchflower's penalty burst into the net six yards wide of his falling body.

Desperately

And so the scene was set for the finale. For 55 of the remaining 45 minutes Spurs stormed on and on. Chances came, Jones, for the second time, blazed a preciously carved chance over the bar.

Greaves, his sharpshooting blunted on a night when it was never more desperately needed, missed two slim openings.

And all the while the clock ticked on.

In the end, perhaps appropriately, it was Mackay who drew the last great gasp from a crowd now silenced by tension.

From 20 yards he unleashed a shot that climbed towards the roof of Benfica's net—glanced the top of the bar and pitched into the crowd.

The match was over. Tottenham turned and embraced their enemies.

A magnificent gesture — for during 180 minutes in two countries Benfica, holders of the European Cup, had proved themselves only fractionally a greater football team than Tottenham Hotspur.

HOW THEY COMPARED

	Spurs	Benfica
Corners	5	4
Fouls conceded	7	17
Offside	5	4
Shots	24	13

GREAVES CALLS IT CUP ROBBERY No. 2

By ROY PESKETT

JIMMY GREAVES, whose "goal" for Spurs in the 23rd minute was disallowed for offside, protested after the match: "I thought it was a good one. I ran between two Benfica players before shooting."

Then the England inside forward added ruefully: "This is twice I have been 'done' in the European Cup."

Spurs manager Bill Nicholson also thought it was a good goal. But he gave this verdict on the game:

"My men played too quickly. They were too hurried. Their enthusiasm ran away with them. They lacked a little control, and one or two players did not quite do what we had hoped.

"If we had kept our heads the result might have been different. Losing that first goal was vital, but we had our chances."

Real? No

Nicholson's summing-up of the European Cup Final : " I think Benfica will beat Real Madrid."

Benfica coach Bela Guttman admitted he had been very worried. He said :

"It was the hardest game of my life. I thought Spurs would equalise in the last ten minutes."

The Danish referee, Aage Poulsen, said of that last, all-attack spell by Spurs, when they always looked likely to equalise : "I allowed one minute extra because of time-wasting by Benfica."

But Guttman also criticised the referee. He said : "I blame him that we gave away more free-kicks than Spurs. How many fouls didn't he give against Tottenham ? "

Guttman ended with this tribute : "Spurs played better here than in Lisbon. They attacked more. They are one of the best teams in Europe. One day soon, with one or two changes, they will win the European Cup.

Sir Stanley Rous, president of FIFA, praised Benfica. "Everyone is a ball artist. They can play the ball from any angle. They are masters of the game."

● BEFORE the match, Guttman said he was resigning as Benfica coach at the end of the season.

" They have won two championships and the European Cup. What more is there for me to do with them ? "

A goal? Scorer Jimmy Greaves thought it was. So did Cliff Jones, seen turning away here. But the verdict was offside.

They tried to upset me—but it failed!

Blanchflower

DANNY BLANCHFLOWER (Spurs captain): "I thought Benfica were trying to worry me when I went to take the penalty. That was why there was so much fuss. There was a time when they might have worried me—not now.

It was a hectic sort of game and we did not get any of the breaks after giving away a goal in the first-half that could have been offside.

My impression was that one linesman kept his flag up all the time and the other fellow did not raise his.

☆

Benfica's goalkeeper saved them. He grabbed balls on the 18-yard line. I thought we were going to get. I think Real Madrid will beat them six times out of ten.

CLIFF JONES (Spurs outside left) : "You cannot give a team like this four goals—you could not do it to Crewe Alexandra. Benfica played better here than in Lisbon."

EUSEBIO (20-year-old Benfica inside right), who cried with joy after the match : I am so happy to be in the final for the first time that I don't know what to say. I hope that in this year against Real Madrid I can win the same medal as all my colleagues."

GASTAU SILVA (Benfica director) : The referee was very bad. The goals Simoes scored should have been allowed and the penalty against us was never a foul."

COLUNA (Benfica inside left) : "We only tried to defend ourselves. That was our main idea. Tottenham fought very well. The half-line is one of the best I ever played against in the world. Mackay is an extraordinary player.

The penalty against me was never a foul. I went for the ball and the charge was fair.

PEREIRA (Benfica goalkeeper) : "Tottenham are one of the best teams in Europe. This was the hardest game we have ever played.

The penalty was never a foul. White just threw himself to the ground and Coluna charged in very fairly and correctly."

And this was the sequel to the Greaves "goal" : a fan running on to the field to protest and being taken off.

SPURS v BENFICA
LOOKING BACK WITH **JIMMY GREAVES**

It is half a century since the night that Tottenham's glorious Double-winning side was beaten in the first European crusade – but for Jimmy Greaves the memories would remain as clear as if they had happened yesterday. He was convinced that in the heat of the night Tottenham had been robbed. The passing of the years would do nothing to detract from that view.

Tottenham were 3-1 down from the first leg in the Stadium of Light in Lisbon, but they believed that in the 23rd minute their chance of reaching the final was shattered. Greaves remembered it all. A Danish referee called Aage Poulsen. A pass from Bobby Smith and a clinical finish. The ball was in the net.

In 1986, reflecting on events in 1962, he also remembered the anger. "I was sure that it was a good goal. I don't think that anyone will ever be able to change my view of that. There were defenders all around me.

"Bobby slotted the ball through and I went between at least two defenders before shooting past Costa Pereiera, the Benfica goalkeeper. I really thought that goal would put us through to the final.

"The disappointment of that defeat was immense. I felt a little guilty because I missed some great chances after that, but I don't think it was meant to be my year."

While Greaves might have understandably felt frustrated, and was self critical in his analysis of the campaign, it had been a remarkable year for the east Londoner. He had arrived at Tottenham in December 1961 to great fanfare, carrying the record price tag of £99,999 Spurs paid to AC Milan.

It is a well-worn tale that the fee reflected Bill Nicholson's wish not to burden him with the label of becoming a £100,000 player. Expectations were still huge, however. Greaves lived up to them with immediate effect, scoring 30 goals in five months, but in his limited opportunities in Europe, he couldn't quite make a scoring impact – though not for want of trying.

"We were done a couple of times in the European Cup that season. It was a great education for us though. It helped us in the years to come. We learned to handle defeat and disappointment.

"Maybe it made us into a better side. We had learned the differences between playing in England and playing in Europe. We were no longer the innocents abroad."

It was a night of disappointment for Bill Nicholson who described Benfica as one of the best sides he had come across in Europe.

"They were a team of artists. They were the masters that season. They had the great players. They had Coluna and Eusebio. They were an outstanding collection. They proved to be the base for Portugal's best years in European football. They were the backbone, too, of the 1966 World Cup team."

Top: Jimmy Greaves's contentiously disallowed goal v Benfica at White Hart Lane. The linesman (just visible beneath the goalkeeper's left arm) puts up his flag, just as Greaves tucks the ball away

Left: How the press reported Greaves's "cup robbery"

THE ROAD TO EUROPE
1962

Bill Nicholson's greatest Spurs team fell just short of winning the long-sought-after Double in consecutive seasons, narrowly missing out on the 1961/62 league title to Ipswich Town – managed by Nicholson's former team-mate Alf Ramsey – but beating Burnley at Wembley 3-1 to become only the second side to lift the FA Cup two seasons on the trot.

In the final, Jimmy Greaves caught the eye, scoring an exquisite opening goal. Bobby Smith added a second, becoming only the second player to score in consecutive Wembley finals (Manchester City's Bobby Johnstone was the first in 1955 and 1956) and Danny Blanchflower slotted home a penalty to seal the win. *Sunday Times* correspondent Brian Glanville described Spurs' performance as one of "poise and fluency" and with an attack "so eager for the kill [it] does not pardon vulgar error". The win secured a place in the following season's Cup Winners' Cup. After coming so close in the epic battle against Benfica, this was almost certainly the legendary team's last chance to prove they could win a trophy against the best Europe had to offer, and in doing so become the first British side to lift a European trophy.

Spurs' goalkeepers Bill Brown and John Hollowbread lead the training run at Red Army Stadium, Belgrade, April 1963, where they played OFK Belgrade in the European Cup Winners' Cup semi-final

Spurs players sportingly applaud their Rangers counterparts off the field after the conclusion of their Cup Winners' Cup tie at Ibrox

31 October 1962, second round, first leg

TOTTENHAM HOTSPUR 5
GLASGOW RANGERS 2

White Hart Lane *Att*: 58,859

For all the talk of pitting the best England had to offer against the cream of Europe, the first game of the campaign threw up the best Scotland had to offer – Rangers of Glasgow. In a game which the *Daily Express*'s Desmond Hackett described as played in "a moving spirit of nobility and pride", and amidst "a whirlpool of noise", the two sides served up football "at its proudest peak". John White nodded home a Jimmy Greaves cross after four minutes, but Rangers pulled level nine minutes later. Then Greaves and White combined again, the Scotsman heading in another. Les Allen grabbed a third before an own goal by the home side's Bobby Shearer made it four for Spurs. Rangers pulled one back – and it was only half-time. The intensity did not drop after the break, but when Maurice Norman stormed forward on 80 minutes to ram home a shot, Spurs had a commanding lead.

Brown, Baker, Henry, Blanchflower,
Norman, *Mackay, Medwin,* **White 2,**
Allen, *Greaves, Jones* [*Shearer og*]

11 December 1962, second round, second leg

GLASGOW RANGERS 2 (4)
TOTTENHAM HOTSPUR 3 (8)

Ibrox, Glasgow, Scotland *Att*: 80,000

It took Jimmy Greaves just eight minutes to wrap the tie up in front of 80,000 packed into Ibrox. Bobby Smith, recalled to the first team, turned provider for the striker who replaced him, switching the ball for Greaves to run on to and outpace the Rangers defence and score what the *Daily Mirror*'s Ken Jones called "a brilliant right-foot goal". Rangers would not roll over, equalising just after half-time. Within three minutes, however, Spurs were ahead again through Smith. On 74 minutes Rangers equalised, but that man Smith popped up to snatch the winner four minutes from time. In this England v Scotland face-off, it was the Anglo-Scot combination of Greaves, Smith and man of the tie White who made the difference. And Spurs, who had little left to prove as far as entertaining went, had also displayed some steel in a hard-fought battle.

Brown, Baker, Henry, Blanchflower,
Norman, Mackay, Medwin, White,
R. Smith 2, *Greaves, Jones*

Six-goal blitz by Spurs

Goalkeeper Viliam Schroif and right-back Urban of Slovan Bratislava turn round in dismay as Jimmy Greaves scores a fourth goal for Spurs in the Cup Winners' Cup third-round tie

5 March 1963, third round, first leg

SLOVAN BRATISLAVA 2
TOTTENHAM HOTSPUR 0

Tehelne Pole, Bratislava, Czechoslovakia
Att: 15,000

In a performance bluntly described by *The Times'* anonymous correspondent as "pathetic", Spurs fell victim not only to a cloyingly muddy pitch but also to a Czech side full of "speed, craft and imagination". Spurs were "out-thought and out-manoeuvred" by a side playing the deep-lying centre-forward favoured by many teams from eastern Europe at the time, and stymied by their own tactic of deploying centre-forward Frank Saul at outside-right with a brief to switch to a defensive role if necessary. Goalkeeper Bill Brown performed heroics to keep the score respectable, but mistakes by the defence either side of half-time gifted the Czechs a two-goal lead. John White was frozen out of the game, Jimmy Greaves, Bobby Smith and Cliff Jones reduced to ploughing lonely furrows in the mud. The second leg was still to come, but a place in the semi-finals looked in serious doubt.

Brown, Baker, Henry, Marchi, Norman, Mackay, Saul, White, R. Smith, Greaves, Jones

14 March 1963, third round, second leg

TOTTENHAM HOTSPUR 6 (6)
SLOVAN BRATISLAVA 0 (2)

White Hart Lane *Att:* 61,504

Nine days after the battering in Bratislava, Spurs destroyed the pride of Czechoslovakia. On 31 minutes, Dave Mackay brought a John White pass down with his chest and thudded home. On 44 minutes, Jimmy Greaves waltzed through to equalise on aggregate, and on the stroke of half-time Bobby Smith powered home a header. Second-half goals from Greaves, Cliff Jones and White wrapped up a performance Bill Nicholson described as one of "pure power". The crowd, too, played its part on a spectacle the *Daily Express*'s Clive Toye dubbed "the raging tide of Tottenham", with Slovan manager Anton Bulla saying after the game, "I envy Spurs their supporters. We have never played before such a crowd." Just as Gornik Zabrze had found, beating Spurs away only served to increase the Lilywhites' determination to impose their will. The semi-final beckoned.

*Brown, Hopkins, Henry, Marchi, Norman, **Mackay**, Saul, **White, R. Smith, Greaves 2**, Jones*

Big match verdict:

A BRAW, BRICHT NICHT — FOR SPURS !

By PETER LORENZO

N⁰ questions, no arguments, Spurs proved themselves cocks of the North, South, East and West—as far as British football is concerned—at White Hart Lane last night. This tremendously tough, tense game was billed as the first round of the European Cup-winners' Cup.

Spurs . . . 5

White (2), Allen, Shearer o.g., Norman

Rangers . . 2

Henderson, Millar

Les Allen leaps to score Spurs' third goal.

Willie Henderson 'walks' the ball in for Rangers

Dave Mackay tackles, and falls. Rangers' Bobby Shearer (left) goes flying.

Right: Spurs fans are in good heart during the all-British European tie at White Hart Lane

Greaves sent off as Spurs win

Left: Bobby Smith bears down on goal in Belgrade, in an example of a photograph sent "down the wire", in the press parlance of the time

Inset: As pictured in the club programme, Bill Brown celebrates a great away result

24 April 1963, semi-final, first leg

OFK BELGRADE 1
TOTTENHAM HOTSPUR 2

Red Army Stadium, Belgrade, Yugoslavia *Att: 45,000*

This was the kind of tie that gave European games the shroud of mystery that fuelled the romance of a game finding its feet on a wider stage. A first leg played deep inside the Eastern Bloc, at the height of the Cold War. The setting, an imposing Communist-era stadium in Belgrade. The opponents, a side emerging from the shadow of Red Star and Partizan, its two city rivals, to enjoy its own golden age. The first leg was a sensation.

Spurs were superb, crushing an extremely capable side so thoroughly that they were whistled off by a partisan 45,000 crowd that rose to acclaim the London side on the final whistle. But even this achievement was eclipsed by the controversial red card served on Jimmy Greaves, who became the first Spurs player to be sent off for 40 years. Greaves had never been sent off before in his entire career, and *Daily Herald* reporter Peter Lorenzo said, "I didn't see anything that merited such drastic action." Hungarian referee Lajo Aranjosi said Greaves had kicked OFK's centre-half. "I told Greaves that this wasn't gentlemanly," he said. Greaves at first refused to leave the pitch, before Tony Marchi persuaded him to go. Bill Nicholson was furious about the decision and Spurs were down to 10 men. This team, however, was not one to fold at a setback.

Spurs were a goal ahead, thanks to a strike from John White who scored on 26 minutes after a free-kick. The kick was taken in fractious circumstances, the Belgrade players jostling Bobby Smith after he was bundled over. OFK equalised on 36 minutes. In the 55th came the sending off. Then, 10 minutes from time, Terry Dyson snatched an opportunist goal to seal a performance of grit and guile to set Spurs up for the second leg.

Brown, Baker, Henry, Marchi, Norman, Mackay, Greaves, J. Smith, R. Smith, **White, Dyson**

Mackay drives Spurs into final

1 May 1963, semi-final, second leg

TOTTENHAM HOTSPUR 3 (5)
OFK BELGRADE 1 (2)

White Hart Lane *Att:* 59,736

The performance in Belgrade was a triumph, the return at White Hart Lane was less of a swashbuckler, more the kind of performance a great team needs to dig out when it counts. In the preceding games, John White, Jimmy Greaves and Bobby Smith had shone. Now it was time for leader of the band, Danny Blanchflower. The *Daily Express*'s Desmond Hackett put it succinctly as he opened his report: "A quiet, unflappable football professor called Blanchflower steered Spurs through a sea of stormy soccer into the final of the European Cup Winners' Cup last night."

In what Hackett described as "a harassing and adventurous journey" in which "Spurs were too easily rattled by the well-drilled moves of OFK", Blanchflower conducted a performance in which the Spurs defence, for once, outshone the attack. But this was Spurs, the team described by writer Julie Welch as "the greatest footballing machine this country has ever seen", so even a defensive

masterclass oozed excitement and goals. Dave Mackay "smashed up the Yugoslav attacks", Bill Brown marshalled his defence, Ron Henry, Peter Baker and Maurice Norman excelled. Up front, Bobby Smith played "one of his best and most effective games of the season". But Blanchflower pulled the strings.

On 29 minutes he sent Mackay away with a superb pass. OFK hit back on 35 minutes. The players grew jittery. The fans got nervous. And then there was Blanchflower. He sucked the energy from the gathering storm, reclaimed the centre of gravity, and slotted a pass to White. White stroked the ball into the box, Mackay chested down, Cliff Jones stabbed it in. On 49 minutes, Smith headed a third. Spurs became the first English team to reach a European final.

Brown, Baker, Henry, Blanchflower, Norman, Marchi, **Jones,** *White,* **R. Smith, Mackay,** *Dyson*

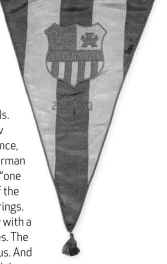

Bill Brown sees off an attack led by OFK Belgrade's Skoblar, the Scottish goalkeeper helping secure safe passage for Spurs towards the Cup Winners' Cup Final

15 May 1963, Final
TOTTENHAM HOTSPUR 5
ATLETICO MADRID 1

Feyenoord Stadium, Rotterdam, Netherlands *Att:* 40,000

Spurs not only notched up another achievement that no other team can ever match, but they put domestic football back on the world stage a full decade after the Magical Magyars of Hungary had dismantled the myth of English superiority. But in the run-up to the game, few had expected victory, let alone one so emphatic. Because the odds seemed stacked against Spurs.

Atletico were the holders and, under the management of José Villalonga, were seriously challenging the great Real Madrid team of the era for the position of Spain's top team. On the morning of the game, Dave Mackay failed a fitness test. While Danny Blanchflower was still the captain, it was Mackay's drive and energy that was increasingly at the heart of Tottenham's success, and Bill Nicholson was despondent at the loss of his most consistently effective player.

The final was played in Rotterdam's Feyenoord Stadium in front of a crowd of 40,000, including 4,000 Spurs fans. Many of them had travelled as part of an extraordinary airlift operation organised independently by fans themselves, a tale detailed more fully in the "Rotterdam Airlift" section (see page 42). Many more travelled under their own steam at a time when travel to Europe was nowhere near as cheap and convenient as it is today. Spurs were on the brink of making history again, and this was not a game to be missed.

Before the game, Nicholson was unusually downbeat, the loss of Mackay weighing on his mind as he went through how good each

Below: Spurs striker Jimmy Greaves on target in the Cup Winners' Cup Final

Right: Danny Blanchflower is triumphantly chaired by his team-mates

Atletico player was. Blanchflower stepped in, reminding those in the dressing room that they were more than capable of giving the Spaniards a few things to think about.

Spurs took to the pitch and, as is so often the case in the crunch games, an unexpected hero emerged. For, as the *Daily Telegraph*'s Donald Saunders wrote, however much the victory was "a triumph of team work… one name will immediately spring to mind. For this was Terry Dyson's game."

Along with fellow winger Cliff Jones, Dyson tore Atletico to shreds. He scored two, made two and, said Saunders, "by his example of tireless devotion to duty he inspired the other forwards, who had been out of touch for several weeks, to click back into top gear".

It was a nervy opening, but on 16 minutes Jones centred for Jimmy Greaves to score. Seventeen minutes later, Dyson chipped to Bobby Smith who laid it off for White to slam into the roof of the net. But two minutes after half-time, Atletico pulled one back from a penalty after Ron Henry had punched the ball away from goal. The Spanish side looked set to overrun Spurs, pouring forward relentlessly. Then Spurs broke the siege, Dyson picked up the ball on the left and curled a sweet shot into the top of the net.

Greaves added a fourth from a Dyson centre. Then came Dyson's crowning moment. He picked up the ball and drifted in from the left touchline. Exchanging passes with Tony Marchi, he pushed on, gathering pace. Atletico's defenders backed off. Dyson carried the ball 25 yards, checked, looked up and, without breaking stride, unleashed a 20-yard shot high into the top-left corner.

At the final whistle, Mackay raced from the bench to embrace Smith. The 4,000 Spurs fans stayed long and late to cheer the first British team to win a European trophy. And as the players savoured the victory in the dressing room, they heard Leo Hearn, one of the world's most experienced referees, say, "You could send this side anywhere in the world and be proud of them."

*Brown, Baker, Henry, Blanchflower, Norman, Marchi, Jones, **White**, R. Smith, **Greaves 2, Dyson 2***

SPURS v ATLETICO MADRID
THE ROTTERDAM AIRFLIFT

Some 4,000 Spurs fans travelled to Rotterdam in an unprecedented display of support. Trains and ferries were booked solid, but many went by air in an operation which prompted *The Tottenham and Edmonton Weekly Herald* to observe: "The Berlin Airlift had nothing on this. Never before has an English team had so much fantastic support for a game on the Continent."

These were the days before travel abroad was commonplace, and those 4,000 people opened a new chapter in football history. Aubrey Morris was the extraordinary man who organised it all.

Born into a family of Jewish bakers in 1919, Morris had already lived a challenging life. He'd fought against the Blackshirts in the battle of Cable Street, organised support for Republican Spain, been evacuated from Dunkirk, stood as a candidate for the Communist Party, learned The Knowledge and plied his trade as a London cabbie, and built up a thriving travel business organising trips to destinations across Europe. In 1960 he organised the first charter flight for fans when he took a planeload of Tottenham supporters to Sunderland for an FA Cup tie.

Alongside his colleague Sid Silver, and with the help of family and friends, Morris began to organise more and more ambitious trips, including a trip to Lisbon for the 1962 game against Benfica. More than anyone else he was responsible for ensuring that Spurs were well-supported whenever they played abroad.

Before his death in 2008, Morris spoke to the authors about the airlift. His firm, Riviera Holidays, operated from an office in Bishopsgate. "It was like a little hothouse in there," Morris said. "I got 33 aircraft to fly from Southend and Gatwick... Argonauts, Elizabethans, Dakotas, DC3s. We had all sorts of people from all walks of life. We even had schoolchildren coming in and putting their £8 10s down. We had a real mix of people.

"In Rotterdam we had 60 coaches lined up. My son Michael and I missed the last goal because we had to go out and see that everything was alright."

Albert Lee, a committee member of the Spurs Supporters Club, was one of the fans who travelled. "We arrived in Rotterdam about

midday and spent about five hours in the town soaking up the atmosphere with locals and Madrid supporters. There was no football violence then.

"When we arrived at the ground all we could see was the blue and white of the Spurs. Thousands had come by plane, but many more came by ferry. I would say about 90 per cent were ordinary working-class people."

Morris said he was driven to organise those European trips by "a feeling that something special was happening. [And] in a business sense, I thought it was an opportunity". It certainly was. In 1965 Riviera was bought out by Thomson Holidays and Morris became the firm's managing director, gaining recognition as a pioneer of the package holiday. It all started from what journalist Geoffrey Goodman described in his obituary of Morris as "the brilliant idea to pioneer a cultural revolution in the old-style world of football".

The airlift was a remarkable feat of organisation and helped set in place a strong tradition of English fans travelling to support their team. And it was a key part of the changing social landscape of the 1960s. As Morris said then, "All those fans travelling abroad. Ordinary working people. Think what this can do for the future. Just imagine."

SPURS SUPPORTERS' CLUB

European Cup Winners Cup Final
ROTTERDAM, 15th MAY, 1963

In the event that our team plays Atletico Madrid at Rotterdam the following trips have been arranged. The arrangements include the flight outward and return and all coach travel from Central London to ground and return, airport taxes included. A ticket for the match is guaranteed to all travellers, but is not included in the price stated.

Coaches will leave Tottenham at approximately 7 a.m. and supporters will arrive in Rotterdam at approximately 11 a.m. Those travelling on Excursion 'A' and 'B' will arrive back at Tottenham soon after midnight. Those taking the two-day Excursion 'C' will arrive back at Tottenham during the late evening of 16th May.

EXCURSION 'A' — Constellation, D.C.4 and Viking Flights from Southend, Gatwick and Luton Airports to Rotterdam ... **£8.10.0.**

EXCURSION 'B' — Vanguard, D.C. 6B., Viscount and Hermes Flights from London Airport to Amsterdam (coach to Rotterdam) **£10.0.0d.**

EXCURSION 'C' **2-DAY TRIP** — Viscount and D.C.4 Flights from Southend Airport to Rotterdam, Lunch, Dinner, Bed & Breakfast on 15th and Lunch on 16th May. Medium Class Hotel **£13.0.0d.** Superior Class Hotel **£14.10.0d.**

As aircraft availability is very limited, applications for places will be accepted in order of receipt in this office. For that reason also, and to streamline administration, applications must be accompanied by remittances for **full payment**—preferably by post.

RIVIERA HOLIDAYS Ltd., 282 BISHOPSGATE, LONDON, E.C.2
Phone : BIShopsgate 9317

Return to—
RIVIERA HOLIDAYS LTD. (SP), 282 BISHOPSGATE, LONDON, E.C.2.

I wish to book .... places on Excursion 'A') please delete
                                                    Excursion 'B' } excursions
                                                    Excursion 'C') inapplicable

and enclose my remittance for £......................... being ....

places @ £............ ... . each.

NAME.. Day 'Phone No...............
(block capitals)

ADDRESS...

(block capitals)
The names and addresses of your companions should be written on the reverse of this form.

Will you still wish to go to Rotterdam if Spurs do not play ?   YES/NO

The Turnpike Press Ltd. (T.U.), 81 Turnpike Lane. N.8.

Top: Spurs fans en route to Rotterdam for the 1963 Cup Winners' Cup Final. Pioneering football package tour operator Aubrey

Morris is bottom left, with moustache

Centre: Morris with a party of Spurs supporters in Lisbon in 1962

SPURS v ATLETICO MADRID
LOOKING BACK WITH **TERRY DYSON**

Terry Dyson's entry into the record books, for the Tottenham victory in the European Cup Winners' Cup Final states merely that he scored two of the five goals. But on that exciting night in May 1963 it may have been a piece of defensive work from the winger Dyson that turned the final against Atletico Madrid Tottenham's way. For after Jimmy Greaves and John White had put Tottenham into the lead in the famous Feyenoord Stadium, Madrid pulled a goal back.

Dyson recalls: "We suddenly went two goals up, but then the penalty by Collar changed the whole face of the match. From being in a clear lead we were battling to survive.

"For 10 minutes Atletico threw everything they had at us and we were fortunate to hang on. Then in another attack the ball broke free to their full-back Rivilla."

It was at that moment that Dyson made his most important intervention of the evening. He said: "Dave Mackay was not playing in the game because of an injury but when the full-back broke through I wondered what Mackay would do.

"I remembered that he got so many of his injuries by lunging in, just throwing himself at people. So I decided to try the same. I launched myself in just as the player shot.

"The ball hit me on the knees and it really did hurt but it was worth it. In that moment I think that the match changed. If the ball had gone in and made it 2-2 who knows what might have happened?"

Within minutes of that Mackay-type tackle, Dyson was the Spurs hero at the other end. "I remember John White putting the ball inside the full-back and I kept thinking how close he was to me.

"I rushed the cross a little bit and was disappointed. I thought that it was much too close for the goalkeeper."

In ideal conditions the cross was too close to Madinabeytia, but in the pressure of a European final the Spanish goalkeeper flapped at the ball, turning it into the net.

Dyson said: "My great memory was of the goalkeeper crying when the ball went into the net. From that second there was no doubt that we were going to win the game."

The goal floored Atletico and Dyson crossed soon afterwards for Greaves to score his second and Tottenham's fourth. Then Dyson wrapped up the match with a spectacular goal.

Dyson said: "I played a one-two with Marchi and no one came to me. I kept going towards goal and when I looked up I could not even see the keeper so I just shot and in it went."

For Tottenham it was the fitting memorial to the Double side. They felt that the 3-1 cup final success against Burnley the season before had not done them justice. There was a need to leave a greater mark in the history books and this was it. No one could take from them the fact that they had become the first British side to win a European competition.

Dyson said: "I have never experienced anything like that. It was a totally different occasion. We had won the Double and then won the cup final the following season.

"But it was strange; it seemed as though the cup final success was an anti-climax. We knew that we were a good side, but we had not produced it in the final. This, however, was different. It was probably our best team performance."

In the village hotel outside Rotterdam the team celebrated in style as well. "We went into the nightclub there and let our hair down with the supporters.

"We knew most of them anyway. They were the same people who travelled the country with us during the season and they were the same ones who had gone into Europe with us. That was the way it should have been."

Dyson was delighted to see that even Bill Nicholson joined the celebrations that night. "It was about the only time that Bill came out with the team. I don't think that I ever saw him looking so pleased."

It is not surprising that Bill looked so proud. Dyson recalled his last words before the team went out that night. He said: "Bill took myself and Cliff Jones to one side and said: 'This will be your night. Take on the full-backs as often as you can.'"

He was not wrong.

SPURS v ATLETICO MADRID
IN PICTURES

Left: The players parade the trophy on the pitch in Rotterdam while man of the match Terry Dyson hugs Peter Baker (right)

Above: Dutch cartoonist Dik Bruynesteyn's distinctive caricatures from the Cup Winners' Cup Final programme

SPURS v ATLETICO MADRID
IN PICTURES

These previously unpublished colour photos, taken by life long Tottenham fan Charles Whitmore, are a candid and personal view of the trophy homecoming

Top to bottom: Delighted crowds watch the players' bus set off from Edmonton town hall; the now legendary angels prepare to worship their

heroes; the players' bus passes, those on board include Dave Mackay with his children and Cliff Jones filming events for posterity on cine film

Right: Fans get their hands on the trophy through the gates of White Hart Lane after the victorious players returned to Tottenham from Rotterdam

SPURS v ATLETICO MADRID
IN PICTURES

TOTTENHAM HOTSPUR F.C.

Back row, L to R : Baker, Norman, Brown, Blanchflower, Henry, Mackay
Front row, L to R : Jones, White, Smith, Greaves, Dyson

Left: Issued at the start of the 1963/64 season, a commemorative team picture produced by Typhoo tea

Below: A signed photographic print issued by the club to mark the European victory

Right: Tony Marchi leans out of the club offices holding tightly on to the precious silverware

EUROPEAN CUP WINNERS CUP FINAL
Tottenham Hotspur 5   Atletico Madrid 1
ROTTERDAM MAY 15th 1963

TOTTENHAM HOTSPUR FOOTBALL CLUB
EUROPEAN CUP WINNERS CUP CHAMPIONS

LEAGUE DIV. 1
CHAMPIONS
1950-51   1960-61

F.A. CUP WINNERS
1901 · 1921 · 1961
1962

FEYENOORD STADIUM
15th MAY 1963 | SPURS 5 v ATLETICO MADRID 1

THE ROAD TO EUROPE
1963

As holders, Spurs were automatically invited to defend the European Cup Winners' Cup for the 1963/64 campaign. It was a welcome return to the European stage, but participation in such a showpiece competition obscured an emerging trend. On the home front in the previous season, Spurs had missed out on the trophy haul that had been a feature of the early 1960s, as form in both domestic league and cup slipped.

Injuries and absences were key to the gradual decline in the middle of the decade, with both Blanchflower and then Mackay badly missed – Mackay with a double leg break, Blanchflower to eventual retirement. Those losses were put in stark perspective by the heartbreaking death of John White, killed by lightning on the Crews Hill golf course in the summer of 1964. In a football context, the sudden absence of three players integral to the smooth running and supreme performance of the team was a serious blow to the club.

That was for the future, however. No one was to know what lay in store, but the chance for a last European hurrah for the Double side came with a short-lived but eventful experience in the Cup Winners' Cup – albeit against very familiar opponents.

Dave Mackay,
Bill Brown, Jimmy
Greaves and Terry
Dyson peer out into
the fog in search of
Manchester United
players. This "Battle
of Britain" match
was postponed
because of the very
poor visibility

Manchester United try nine-man defence plan

MACKAY BUSTS BUSBY WALL

3 December 1963, second round, first leg

TOTTENHAM HOTSPUR 2
MANCHESTER UNITED 0

White Hart Lane *Att: 57,447*

So much for the exotic delights of foreign opposition. For Tottenham's opening round in defence of their crown, they were drawn to face the English FA Cup holders. Even so, facing Manchester United in another "Battle of Britain" had a tantalising allure. Spurs and United were two of the nation's more glamorous sides and produced some memorable encounters during the swinging 1960s. The European meeting was to be a topsy-turvy classic of its kind.

This was not quite the fully functioning United side in which the Best, Law and Charlton triumvirate would wreak glorious havoc at home and abroad, but Matt Busby's reshaped team were the emerging force and provided the most testing of opposition. In the opening leg at White Hart Lane, Spurs dominated possession and territory but found it hard to break United down.

It looked as if the match was heading for frustrating stalemate for the Londoners,

until Dave Mackay seized the initiative in the 67th minute. With all the physical purpose and energy that made him such a favourite among colleagues, management and fans, he drove into the heart of the visitors' back line, collected the ball after a neat back heel from Cliff Jones and rifled home from a tight angle.

It looked as if that would be the only reward for Spurs, until an under-hit back pass from United's right-back Tony Dunne enabled Terry Dyson to nip in. The hero of Rotterdam smashed a shot beyond Dave Gaskell before anyone had a chance to react. Even the crowd were stunned momentarily, before the importance of Dyson's late strike hit home. Spurs were to take a two-goal advantage to Old Trafford. It should have been enough, but was the last joy of a brief European campaign.

Brown, Baker, Henry, Marchi,
Norman, **Mackay,** *Jones, White,*
R. Smith, Greaves, **Dyson**

Terry Dyson offers a sporting hand to United keeper David Gaskell as Spurs faced English opposition in European competition for the first time

Mackay carried off, Spurs go out 4-3

10 December 1963, second round, second leg
MANCHESTER UNITED 4 (4)
TOTTENHAM HOTSPUR 1 (3)
Old Trafford, Manchester, England *Att:* 59,597

The scoreline tells a misleading story – for this was no capitulation on the road that led to a slim aggregate defeat, but a tale of the Double side bowing out of Europe with pride intact.

"They have never given a better example of the majestic poise and assured skill which make them the finest team of the generation," wrote former Arsenal centre-half Bernard Joy in *The Evening Standard*. For, while Spurs ultimately suffered a demoralising defeat, the circumstances did them huge credit.

Two minutes after David Herd had given United a sixth-minute lead on the night, Tottenham received a dreadful blow when Mackay broke his leg in a clash with United's Noel Cantwell. It was to prove costly as this, combined with another fracture less than a year later as Mackay attempted a comeback in a reserve match, effectively robbed him of 18 months of football. There were mutterings in subsequent years about the degree of intent in the late Cantwell's challenge, but at

the time he was cleared of blame. Cantwell himself was magnanimous in victory, claiming of Tottenham that "no team has played better with 10 men" – for, in the last years before the introduction of substitutes, Spurs had to play a man short for over 80 minutes.

They did so in superb style, defending manfully but without sacrificing attacking intent. With all the verve that had made Super Spurs so admired, Tottenham took the game to United and created chances of their own. Even after Herd's second in the 53rd minute, Tottenham's response was immediate, as Greaves's header from a White cross restored advantage to Spurs. It was not to continue, though, as two goals from Charlton, the last a brilliant strike two minutes from time, finally settled an unforgettable tie.

Brown, Baker, Henry, Marchi, Norman, Mackay, Jones, White, R. Smith, Greaves, Dyson

United's David Herd dives in to score the first goal of the night as Ron Henry and Tony Marchi look on helplessly

THE ROAD TO EUROPE
1967

A convincing 2-1 victory over Chelsea in the first-ever "Cockney Cup Final" not only prompted choruses of "Knees Up Mother Brown" among the Tottenham support, but it also took the team back into Europe. Jimmy Robertson and Frank Saul grabbed the goals, while Alan Gilzean and Alan Mullery dominated in attack and defence. It was also a special day for Dave Mackay, who lifted his third FA Cup in seven years, this time as skipper – a feat made all the more remarkable because of the Scotsman's double leg fracture between the second and third victories. This was a team rebuilt after the break-up of the great Double side, and the shocking death of John White. Spurs topped the table in October, but then fell away to eventually finish third. The FA Cup became the team's sole target, and it looked as if another great chapter of European glory beckoned. The achievement moved Mackay. He said: "They say I'm a tough guy, but my eyes began to cloud over… as I moved up the steps to the Royal box to collect the trophy." It was, he said, his "supreme moment". Once more, Europe beckoned.

A new generation of Spurs players get their hands on the FA Cup in 1967. Left to right: Pat Jennings, Terry Venables, Alan Mullery, Jimmy Robertson and Cyril Knowles

STUNNED SLAVS BURN THEIR BANNERS AS ROBERTSON, GREAVES FORGE 2-0 LEAD

Strolling Spurs on easy street

HAJDUK TOTTENHAM
SPLIT, 20. SEPTEMBRA 1967.

IGRALIŠTE HAJDUKA - POČETAK U 15.30 SATI

20 September 1967, first round, first leg

HAJDUK SPLIT 0
TOTTENHAM HOTSPUR 2

Stadion Stari plac, Split, Yugoslavia *Att: 25,000*

Spurs turned up on the Dalmatian coast in the doghouse after suffering heavy away defeats in the league against Arsenal and Manchester United. They redeemed themselves with a determined and intelligent performance in the 70-degree heat against a backdrop of exploding rockets set off by a fiercely partisan crowd.

Spurs snatched the lead within just four minutes, Jimmy Robertson slotting Jimmy Greaves's low pass home after Frank Saul had sparked a break. Staying compact, Spurs then dug in to repel wave upon wave of attacks. The team, said Geoffrey Green in *The Times*, "gave every ounce today as they enticed Hajduk into their defensive net". The reporter was less complimentary about the Bulgarian referee, describing him as "an official who must have learnt the rules from a book unknown to the original lawmakers". Matters weren't helped by the cacophony of whistles being blown in the crowd, with Greaves and Alan Gilzean

frequently pulling up thinking the referee had blown for offside "only to find it was some joker up on the open terraces," wrote Green.

But character ran deep through this team, and it stuck to the task. Mike England "was a colossus in the air," reported Green, Phil Beal "stuck to the insidious, clever [Miroslav] Vardic like a leech" and Alan Mullery "was always at hand to cover and to pick up a loose ball to start a counter attack". Three minutes before the end, Greaves took a Mullery pass on his toe, sprinted 40 yards past three tackles and smashed a left-footed shot into the top corner. Spurs had been expected to struggle. Now, with two away goals, it looked like game over. Vardic, who had pledged to shave his beard off if his side lost, was left to contact his barber.

*Jennings, Kinnear, Knowles, Mullery, England, Beal, **Robertson, Greaves**, Gilzean, Venables, Saul*

Top: Jimmy Robertson, (no 7), runs away after scoring the first goal in Split

Inset: Cyril Knowles throws flowers into the crowd before the game; the gesture was reciprocated at the end of the game by the firing of fireworks and rockets

27 September 1967, first round, second leg

TOTTENHAM HOTSPUR 4 (6)
HAJDUK SPLIT 3 (3)

White Hart Lane *Att:* 38,623

Split score three but Spurs safe

Many European games have illuminated White Hart Lane, but this one saw the famous old ground plunged into darkness in the second half, as 11 of the lights on each one of the four floodlight pylons went out. And Spurs almost saw their own hopes extinguished, despite racing into a 3-0 lead courtesy of goals from Jimmy Robertson, Alan Gilzean and Terry Venables. Jimmy Greaves went close on numerous occasions and Cliff Jones, in for Frank Saul to give the side more aerial power, was on the hunt for goals. "Once," said the *Daily Telegraph*'s Bryon Butler, "he flung himself at a centre so hard that he hit the back of the net, bounced off and then, somehow, managed to get his foot caught in the netting."

Spurs finished the first half thinking the job was done, and began the second half without the intensity they had displayed before. Hajduk's forwards had been awful, failing to hold the ball up or take any pressure off their defenders, let alone threaten Pat Jennings in the Spurs goal. Then, nine minutes before the end, they scored twice in a minute.

Miroslav Vardic finally showed what he was capable of, finding space on the right to fire home. Then Džemaludin Musovic stabbed home a rebound after Ivan Hlevnjak had hit the bar. Three minutes later Robertson made it four for Spurs, but still there was a twist to the tale. Cyril Knowles handled in the box and Hlevnjak converted the penalty with the last kick of the match.

Despite those last minutes of madness in the gathering darkness, Spurs had saved the match and the tie. Winners by 6-3 on aggregate, Spurs had nevertheless had a warning that every game in Europe had to be played out until the last minute.

*Jennings, Kinnear, Knowles, Mullery, England, Beal, **Robertson 2**, Greaves, **Gilzean, Venables**, Jones*

Alan Mullery and Cliff Jones rise together to meet a cross, but neither hit the target

29 November 1967, second round, first leg

OLYMPIQUE LYONNAIS 1
TOTTENHAM HOTSPUR 0

Stade de Gerland, Lyon, France *Att: 10,997*

No one predicted a riot when Spurs, never a physical or cynical side, went to Lyon. But a riot is what ensued as players and fans fought on the pitch for eight disgraceful first-half minutes.

In the first 15 minutes of the game the entire Spurs defence, plus forwards Cliff Jones and Terry Venables, were booked. Yet, said the *Daily Mail*'s Brian James, no tackle was "delivered with more than ordinary firmness. Such tackling is allowed in England. The world, as represented here by Czech referee Krnavak, does not." In turn, Spurs' players were angered by the body-checking and shirt-pulling of their opponents. Jimmy Robertson was sent tumbling with the ball 20 yards away.

Jimmy Greaves and Alan Gilzean were punched in the face. The atmosphere was combustible. In the 33rd minute, it exploded.

Lyon forward Andre Guy was tackled by Alan Mullery. Both fell. As they rose, Guy kicked Mullery in the face. The Spurs players sprinted to their team-mate's rescue. Lyon's players piled in from all over the pitch, aiming kicks and blows. Dozens of fans from the 10,000 strong crowd vaulted a fence to join the fray on the pitch. For eight minutes recurrent flashes of violence flared as the officials struggled to restore order. When they did, Mullery was sensationally sent off (along with Guy), the blood still trickling down his face.

Spurs carried on, having to be calm now in the face of continuing provocation. They were quicker and cleverer than Lyon, but could not find a way through. On 75 minutes, Fleury Di Nallo put the home side ahead.

Bill Nicholson was furious. "The match was a disgrace," he said. "This Lyon side played more like Rugby League than Football League." Spurs, however, were expected to right the injustice in the return.

Jennings, Kinnear, Knowles, Mullery, Hoy, Mackay, Robertson, Greaves, Gilzean, Venables, Jones

---

LOOKING BACK WITH **ALAN MULLERY**

Alan Mullery has still got the "chip" in one of his front teeth to remind him of the attack by Andre Guy, hard man of Olympique Lyonnais, the French Cup holders.

It was one of the most ferocious matches Mullery ever played in. In fact nothing compares with the night of European madness against Olympique Lyonnais and a fighting Frenchman, Andre Guy.

"The funny thing was, he was such a good player," recalled Mullery, who went on to a management career with Brighton, Charlton, Crystal Palace and QPR after his playing days with Spurs.

"But he was an absolute animal. I went into the tackle and he turned round and kicked me full in the mouth.

"There's a lot of people in the game who have said that I had a big mouth, so when an Adidas boot came my way it was odds-on my mouth would catch it!

"I retaliated. I punched him. And both of us got sent off. It was what you'd expect playing on foreign soil."

But it didn't end there. Far from it. As the players marched off at half-time a fight broke out in the tunnel.

Mullery added: "He went off first, dashed around the corner and hid. He then pounced and laid into me. Bill Nicholson had to pull us apart. Our manager slung me into our dressing room, but four yards away there was virtually a free-for-all with a 10-a-side punch-up as that fellow Guy stood outside our dressing room door shouting abuse.

"I've never experienced anything like it, and Bill Nick was so furious he said we will tear this team apart in the second leg back at White Hart Lane. It's the only time I can recall Bill saying something like that.

"Unfortunately I was banned from the game and we went out on the away goal rule. Certainly, the intimidation in the first leg in Lyon cost us the tie.

"We were one of the few sides in those days regularly in Europe and we had a big reputation. They were a physical team and they decided to 'tank in'.

"But we had a few people in our team who could look after themselves, even though we were not an over-physical team."

Mullery recalled the style of play Spurs adopted at the time in Europe. "I can't remember going away from home to defend. We always felt we were good enough to win home or away and we always played the same way… 4-2-4. It meant a tremendous amount of work for the two midfield players, myself and Terry Venables."

Lyons win an adding match after five-goal second half

Spurs out of Europe

13 December 1967, second round, second leg

TOTTENHAM HOTSPUR 4 (4)
OLYMPIQUE LYONNAIS 3 (4) *Spurs lost on away goals*

White Hart Lane *Att:* 41,895

Bill Nicholson had been furious with Lyon after the first game, having not only seen the disgraceful scenes on the pitch but after receiving an elbow in the eye himself at half-time as combat continued in the tunnel. Spurs had returned from that game with five players injured, but after elimination on away goals, Nicholson was honest – and scathing – about his own players. "This was diabolical," he said. "We just made a series of mistakes from beginning to end. The last goal was the finish. I felt Jennings should have got back for it. Even then there were two blokes standing by the far post doing nothing."

Admittedly, Tottenham fielded an inexperienced defence. But, wrote the *Daily Mail*'s Brian James, "even those who were left could and should have held that lead". The lead he referred to was the 2-0 scoreline Spurs had at half-time, both goals coming from Jimmy Greaves – the first a scorching drive in the 20th minute, the second a penalty just before half-time.

Then, in the 54th minute, Fleury Di Nallo pulled one back to give Lyon the away goal that meant Spurs needed to win by two clear goals. A minute later, Spurs restored the lead they needed as Cliff Jones dived amid a flurry of flailing feet to head home. Spurs led 3-2 on aggregate. But five minutes later Angel Rambert cut in from the left and drilled a shot past Jennings.

On 70 minutes Alan Gilzean chested down a cross from Jimmy Robertson and slammed home. Then, with 10 minutes to go, Pat Jennings was rooted to his spot as a cross came over for Mohamed Bouassa to bundle in.

Nicholson and Spurs' 1960s European adventures were over. The next seasons saw him start to build another great team – but in a changing world which would challenge the approach he passionately believed in.

Jennings, Kinnear, Knowles, Bond, Hoy, Mackay, Robertson, **Greaves 2,** *Gilzean, Venables,* **Jones**

Jimmy Robertson and Cliff Jones dive in on the Lyonnais goal but their efforts ended without reward

IN CONVERSATION WITH
TERRY DYSON & CLIFF JONES

Cliff Jones and Terry Dyson were key figures in Spurs' early European campaigns – two men who helped set the template of the glory glory nights. It's half a century since those famous first matches but many of the duo's memories of that famous era are as fresh as ever.

What made the glory nights so glorious?
Cliff Jones The 1960s at White Hart Lane were just unbelievable. There would be over 60,000; we'd be dressed in white, Bill, Danny and the boys, the Tottenham Angels… The air always seemed to be crisp. They were just very special nights.

Terry Dyson It was brilliant. We came out from the West Stand and the ground was packed; they had to lock the gates a couple of times, people couldn't get in.

It's the Gornik game and its atmosphere that fans still talk about even today.
TD I couldn't believe the atmosphere. I've spoken to so many people about that night and no one will ever forget it. We ran out and the noise, well, it was electric – incredible. A nice evening, spot of rain and we murdered them. We played really, really well – and that was the start of it.

It didn't get off to the best of starts with defeat out there, though?
CJ We went into it as if we were playing a normal league match. Gornik were a top side – the Polish national team more or less, and we were down and out. We pulled a couple back, but it hadn't been a good performance. We realised we couldn't go away and go four goals down – you can't always pull them back.
TD Bill had gone to see them play and told us he'd be disappointed if we didn't win out there. So we thought we'll be all right. We were 3-0 down at half-time. Bill said, "For

crissakes, give us a chance back in England, don't let them score any more." They scored another after half-time, but I got one and so did Cliff.
CJ We always seemed to get the away leg first and that was an advantage. Bill responded to the first Gornik game and set the team up differently. He brought in Tony Marchi and made us more defensively minded then he would do for a normal league game. He realised we needed to keep it nice and tight and bring them back to London. Not many teams would live with us at home. Bill set us up like that, knowing we could always pull one, maybe even two goals back at home.

It was Terry who paid the price for that more conservative approach.
TD We then beat Feyenoord, I scored in both ties and then Bill left me out. He wanted to bring a sweeper in and had to leave out one of the forwards and he chose me. There were no places for subs then of course. Naturally I was very disappointed.
CJ Bill would stick the extra man in defensive midfield and we played a lot tighter. But it worked. I had sympathy for Terry because he was a big part of the side.

It must have been a quick learning experience for Bill and the players?
CJ We would do whatever Bill told us and Bill set us up to play that way.
TD As he used to say when we were on the way to win the Double, "Forget that cup game, now we concentrate on the next league

game." When Europe came along, he treated it the same way – one game at a time.

He wanted to test the team, I think. To see how good we really were. We were the best in England but he wanted to see what we were like against the best in Europe. And we wanted to test ourselves.

So did Bill go in for a lot of preparation and tactical detail?
TD He'd go out and scout them and tell us a bit about their players. With the success we'd had before, though, we were confident about playing anybody. The beauty of our game was that we played pretty much the same way as we did at home. Bill changed that a bit when he brought in a sweeper. It was revolutionary for the time.
CJ I was an instinctive type of player – I never really thought a great deal about how I would play, it came to me naturally and that's the way I approached it; others were different: Danny Blanchflower, when we went out on to

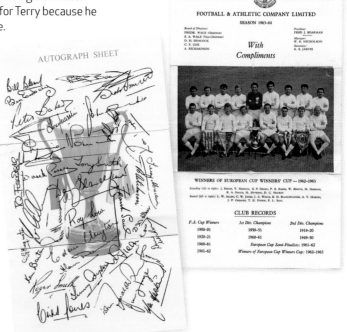

TERRY DYSON
Spurs career:
209 apps, 55 goals
Europe:
9 apps, 8 goals
European honours:
Cup Winners' Cup
Winner 1963

CLIFF JONES
Spurs career:
378 apps, 159 goals
Europe:
19 apps, 7 goals
European honours:
Cup Winners' Cup
Winner 1963

the field, would take over the management and make changes. He was allowed to do that because Danny could read the game perfectly. The players would have team meetings. Very rarely would I say anything. Bill would ask if anyone wanted to say something and it would be Danny who would. We were never deep thinkers beyond obviously wanting to win the game.

TD Bill was superb – how he never got knighted I don't know. He and Danny both believed that even if we were playing badly we all would want the ball. If you were a good enough player you always wanted the ball. You might do some bad things with it, but you'd do some good things as well.

Did foreign players and teams present different challenges?

CJ Players were the same all over the world – they all just wanted to kick you! Well, perhaps they tried to kick us a bit more in Europe.

TD There were some great foreign players but there were some bloody awful ones as well. They didn't really have a different style, as such.

Did your European experiences have a bearing on your overall game, your domestic football?

TD I think it did have some effect on us for the league game on the Saturday – back then, we would stay over for another night with different, food, surroundings, strange bed and all the travelling. Not fatigue, as such, just an effect.

CJ The more the boys played together, though, the more we understood each other's game and it gave us confidence. We knew we could compete with anybody. Success breeds success.

Bill would say, "You play the way you train" – train with effort and method and you play accordingly. We worked on a lot of dead-ball situations, working in threes in the box, in pairs, interchanging. He always had something that kept us interested. Fitness was the other side, even to the extent we brought in a weight trainer.

We were in Russia on tour in 1959 and saw the Bolshoi ballet. Bill was impressed with the fitness of the ballet dancers and was told a lot of it was down to weight training. We'd never heard of it then, so when he got back to London he got Bill Watson the weightlifter to train us, to give us that extra bit of power and reaction. We just went up another gear. They say about how hard players are trained today. They would never have trained with more method or harder than we trained.

So Europe suited Spurs?

TD Teams gave you a little bit of room, a lot of them sat back and gave us space which we exploited. Don't forget we played with five or four forwards, not like today!

CJ In Europe Bill would sometimes want me to release the ball earlier. When you're facing people like Eusebio you had to be aware of them. But Bill was more concerned with the way we played. He knew that if we played to our ability and with effort then we'd be in with a shout regardless of who we faced.

> **"BILL NICHOLSON AND DANNY BOTH BELIEVED THAT EVEN IF WE WERE PLAYING BADLY WE ALL WOULD WANT THE BALL. IF YOU WERE A GOOD ENOUGH PLAYER YOU ALWAYS WANTED THE BALL"**
> TERRY DYSON

You were in with a shout against the very best, and so nearly overcame Benfica; what a tie that was.

CJ It just didn't work out for us. When we played them in the second leg, the crowd were amazing and lifted us, but we felt the crowd were so intense, it translated itself to the pitch. Where normally the ball would be played through Danny or John White, they were being bypassed due to the urgency, which was coming through from the fans.

We put Benfica under a lot of pressure and Bobby Smith was very effective because he was physical as well as skilful and European sides weren't used to that, particularly goalkeepers; Bobby didn't half give them some stick. But the Benfica keeper Costa Pereira and the centre-half Germano gave Bobby as good as they got, and to a certain extent I think that's why they were successful against us.

TD We were so unlucky. Greavesie got two goals that should have stood. Dave Mackay hit the bar in the last minute. But that's how it was. We would have beaten Real Madrid, they weren't the side they had been previously and so we were all very disappointed. To be fair, Benfica had most of the national side in their team.

It was a heady time for the fans, they were really entertained, weren't they?

CJ I remember we had a little routine in the warm-up when Dave Mackay would chip balls into a sack held by one of the staff. It became a feature for the spectators. He was a very skilful player, as well as hard and strong.

Mackay made quite an impression the next season at Rangers, in the European Cup Winners' Cup.

CJ They called it the Battle of Britain and it certainly was, but a comprehensive win for us.

IN CONVERSATION WITH
TERRY DYSON & CLIFF JONES

We beat them 5-2 at home then we went up to Ibrox. We talk about atmosphere but I tell you, when we came out to face 80,000 at Ibrox, it was just unbelievable, a lot like Gornik. You couldn't hear yourself think. They'd been whipped into a frenzy. We'd been told they were on £200 a man to beat us – a lot of money in those days. We were on a normal win bonus of £4. Bit different, eh?

TD We got a bonus for winning the final, it wasn't a lot – not like they get now. No image rights on our contracts! [laughs]

CJ In the first few minutes at Ibrox Greavesie scored and there wasn't a sound. We thought, "Hang on, what's going on here, has it been disallowed or something?" The crowd were completely silent.

Rangers had a very good team with most of the Scottish international side. Their full-back Bobby Shearer was one hard nut. We had Dave Mackay. The crowd were just waiting for Mackay and Shearer to tackle each other. And when it happened? It was like a clash of trains at full speed! They both went for it and my, the crowd went potty. But Dave came away with the ball and with his chest puffed out – gotcha!

So you reached the final. A lot's been said about the pre-match talk in the dressing room. What are your recollections?

CJ Bill never wanted to get too complacent – he wanted us to be aware of the opposition. Then Danny would chip in and say, "Yeah but what about us and how good we are, eh?" It worked. That's where Danny and Bill were so good, they worked as a team. Bill was the main man, he ran the club from boot room to board room. He gave us values, leadership. But when we went out onto the field Danny took over. Bill and Danny would disagree but there'd always be a handshake after.

TD Bill was very thorough, and would point out what their defenders were good with, but then Danny would say, "Don't worry about them, let them worry about us." They had a good relationship.

And the game itself?

TD Bill had changed tactics again and brought me back; I'd been playing well in the league so I was restored to the European side. I was lucky really. I scored goals in big games. We were 2-0 up and Ron Henry conceded a penalty. They scored and we were under the cosh for 10 minutes. We were very lucky. I got this ball played up to me, flicked it round one side and ran round the other, I was marching on and put a cross in. It started swinging in towards the keeper and I thought, "Oh, he's got this," but he pushed it into the net.

That changed the game. I crossed one for Greavesie and I got another. They were backing off, I was about 25 yards out; I couldn't see the keeper so I just hit it and it flew in. A great goal that was.

CJ That was Terry's night – he's probably told a few people that? [laughs]

He's being modest.

TD Ah well, it changed things and then I got my second goal. Bobby said, "You've got to retire now, it will never be better." I said, "Nah, I'm just coming into my prime." [laughs]

CJ Terry would always say, "Remember Rotterdam." He was brilliant that night. He got two great goals and had a blinder. It was his night. He's such a great infectious character. Afterwards we'd be training in a five-a-side game or an actual match even, and someone would say, "C'mon Terry, for Christ's sake do something" and he'd go, "Oi! Remember Rotterdam!"

> **"TERRY WOULD ALWAYS SAY, 'REMEMBER ROTTERDAM'. HE WAS BRILLIANT THAT NIGHT. HE GOT TWO GREAT GOALS AND HAD A BLINDER. IT WAS HIS NIGHT. HE'S SUCH A GREAT INFECTIOUS CHARACTER"**
> **CLIFF JONES**

To be fair he could never top that. It was a great night for Tottenham and a great night for British football. We became the first British side to win a European trophy. It's always that way when someone does something first, like Bannister breaking the four-minute mile, Hillary climbing Everest, they count – that includes winning the Double for the first time and winning the first European trophy. Special.

Can you describe how that special victory felt?

TD You don't think about it at the time. After you think that you and the team played well, you're just delighted because it was a final. Same as in the FA Cup Final. You think, "Brilliant, it's a kid's dream." But it wasn't just me, the whole team played very well, Cliff on the other side, he was terrific. We were the two wingers and murdered their full-backs.

CJ You could say that Terry on one side, myself on the other, we caused a lot of problems. And if Dyson says that he's gotta be right, eh? [laughs] We had right laughs with him, Bobby and Archie Stokes, Les Allen, they all used to like a little bet – Walthamstow Dogs was a very popular place then.

The team spirit of that time seems great. You must have bonded by going on European adventures?

TD We didn't all have the same interests, but we all got on. They were good lads. Trips abroad brought us closer together. We took the mick out of each other, had laughs, and we all thought a lot of each other. I roomed with Les Allen. Bill Brown and Dave Mackay, Ron and Pete together, Cliffie and John White, Bobby and Maurice, and Danny was on his own. He was the perfect captain; he mixed well with the boys but was a good liaison between us and Bill.

CJ John was my best mate, bless him. We just bonded well, he was a special player and a special character.

Cliff Jones (second left) and Terry Dyson (fourth left) embark on Spurs' first game in Europe, away to Gornik Zabrze in Poland

What were the places you visited like?
CJ You could never get a decent cup of tea, I remember that! It was all quite a unique experience. I was never too keen on flying.
TD We were very lucky, really. Nowadays people go abroad all the time, but then people didn't do things like that. We saw parts of the world we'd never have seen if we hadn't been footballers. We were able to have a look round the cities we were in. We were let out as long as we didn't do anything silly, go and have a couple of drinks if you want to and see you in the morning.

We travelled with the media and we were closer to the supporters than they are today. When we won the Cup Winners' Cup we stayed just outside the city and were sat in this bar and loads of Tottenham fans came back and joined us, it was like a little nightclub.

If you had got another crack at the European Cup, would you have won it?
TD We'd have had a good chance – we were one of the best sides. Mackay broke his leg; we'd lost John, Danny had to finish and that broke the team up.
CJ We felt we could beat anybody, particularly at home.

So how did it feel to see the modern Spurs in the Champions League?
TD Some of it bores me. It's not the "Champions" League – you can finish fourth and still get into it.
CJ The signs are there for more. We got a taste of it. In the game against Inter Gareth Bale was giving Maicon a 10-yard start and he slaughtered him.

It must have brought back memories, seeing a fellow Welshman in the all-white kit tearing down the wing?
CJ It was wonderful. I see Gareth and I say to him, "Hey, you're the new Welsh wizard, but I was the old Welsh wizard!" I remind him of that. He goes, "All right, Cliff." [laughs] There are promising days ahead. But they are never going to be like the old glory nights. The whole period, the start of the Swinging Sixties, the Beatles just coming in to change the face of music, England winning the World Cup in 1966, and Spurs at White Hart Lane – it was just unbelievable, a very special time.

The 1970s

The greatest managers do not succeed just once, they build on their achievements by renewing and recreating that success. Spurs in Europe in the 1970s is the story of Bill Nicholson's third great team. Comparing this team with the Double-winning side rather misses the point – this Spurs side deserves recognition in its own right. During the decade, the club played in four finals in as many years, winning three. The timing was all the more important because of the success of the neighbours from Highbury in emulating the Double achievement in 1971, albeit with considerably less flair.

It was in the 1970s that Spurs really established their reputation as a cup team, and when the European character of the club was cemented. The Double winners may have bestrode the heights in 1962 and '63, but the class of the early Seventies were in Europe year in, year out. In the league, Spurs finished third, sixth, eighth and 11th between 1971 and '74. They lifted three cups, although two of those victories – the League Cup wins against Aston Villa and Norwich – were lacklustre affairs.

For the record, Spurs also won the short-lived Anglo-Italian League Cup Winners' Cup in 1971, beating Torino 2-0 in the second leg at White Hart Lane, 3-0 on aggregate.

Spurs of the early Seventies had artistry, but the team's success was due just as much to grit and determination, and was arguably a greater achievement than that of the "Team of the Century", as the Double side had been dubbed. There is much to enjoy, especially in the forging of a formidable European reputation.

Highlights include the club's record win in Europe, an epic UEFA Cup semi-final against AC Milan in which Steve Perryman turned in a striking performance, and the goalscoring exploits of Martin Chivers and Alan Gilzean – still first and second respectively in the club's list of European goalscorers. And of course there was the victory over Wolverhampton Wanderers in the first-ever UEFA Cup Final, the first European final to be contested between two English clubs. In Europe, Tottenham Hotspur could not drop the habit of notching up firsts.

But at the end, there is the tinge of sadness. An awful night in Rotterdam in 1974 was to prove Tottenham's last foray into Europe for eight years. It signalled the end of a great team and led to the start of a decline that ended with relegation and a rebuilding of the club. And, hardest of all, that night hastened the departure of the club's greatest-ever manager – Bill Nicholson.

Nicholson had seen the game he loved change and he was growing increasingly disillusioned with the way it was going.

"Money took over. It became such an influence, people became frightened of losing," he said. "Defence became exaggerated and the goals fell away. There were no free attacking matches and the game was spoilt as a spectacle." So when the great man asked, "What have they done to my game?" in the aftermath of Rotterdam, he was, as ever, seeing the bigger picture.

Welcome then, to Spurs in Europe in the 1970s.

Left to right: Martin Chivers in action v Wolves in 1972; Alan Mullery picks up the UEFA Cup the same year; Ralph Coates after scoring v Leipzig in 1974

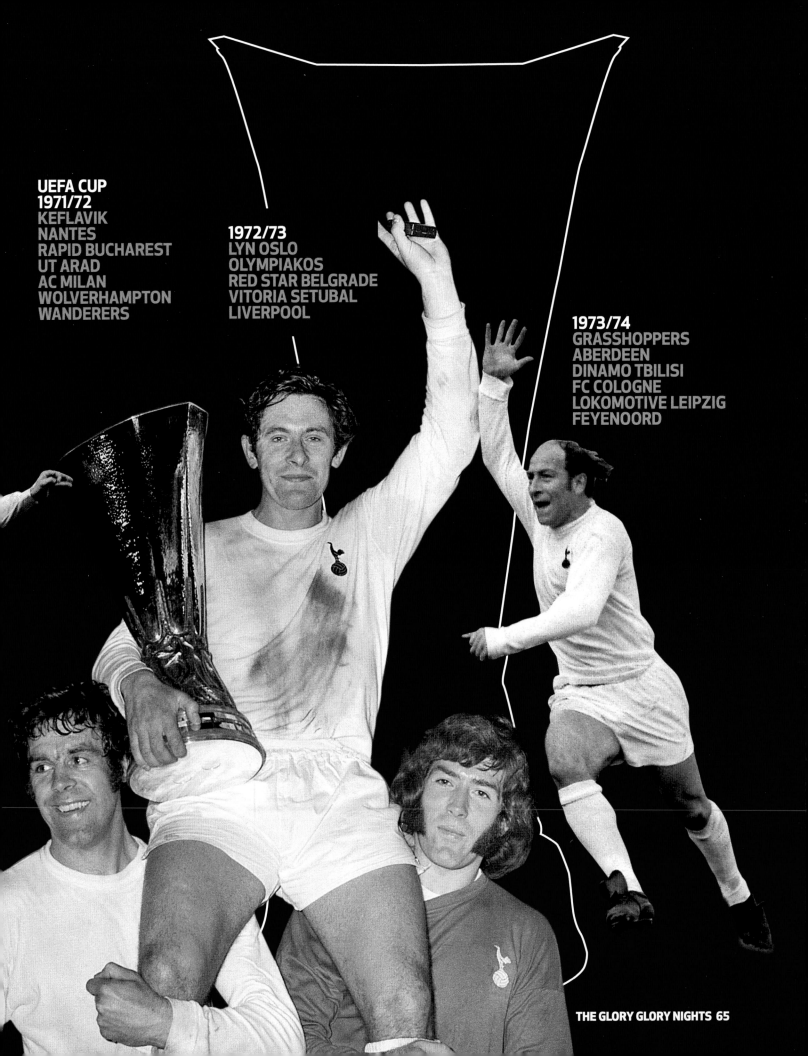

UEFA CUP
1971/72
KEFLAVIK
NANTES
RAPID BUCHAREST
UT ARAD
AC MILAN
WOLVERHAMPTON
WANDERERS

1972/73
LYN OSLO
OLYMPIAKOS
RED STAR BELGRADE
VITORIA SETUBAL
LIVERPOOL

1973/74
GRASSHOPPERS
ABERDEEN
DINAMO TBILISI
FC COLOGNE
LOKOMOTIVE LEIPZIG
FEYENOORD

THE ROAD TO EUROPE
1971

Spurs returned to Europe after three years thanks to a League Cup win over Aston Villa. The measure of the success was that this was the third trophy-winning side Bill Nicholson had fashioned. The turning point had come in January 1970, when an FA Cup defeat by Crystal Palace spurred Nicholson to axe his established stars and refresh the team. That Palace performance was the end for Jimmy Greaves, who was packed off to West Ham in exchange for Martin Peters. Alan Gilzean, Cyril Knowles and Joe Kinnear all learned their lesson from Greaves's fate and fought their way back. Now they played alongside youngsters such as Steve Perryman as Spurs began to establish a reputation as a cup team. The League Cup had once been dismissed, but now the winners qualified for the new UEFA Cup. Spurs took their chance, thanks to two goals from Martin Chivers, the second a great strike which saw him turn under pressure to slam a left-foot shot home. Nicholson was full of praise. "If I had a drink handy I would get everyone to propose a toast to Martin Chivers," he said. It was the club's ninth major trophy. Spurs were back in European competition.

With Spurs hoping to soar to new heights, one fan turned astronaut prior to the UEFA Cup Final at White Hart Lane in 1972

SPURS HOT IT UP WITH NINE GOALS

14 September 1971, first round, first leg

KEFLAVIK 1
TOTTENHAM HOTSPUR 6

Laugardalur Stadium, Reykjavik, Iceland
Att: 11,000

The *Daily Mail*'s Brian Scovell described it as "the most one-sided encounter they've had in these parts since the British Navy took on the Icelandic fishing protection vessels in the Cod War a year or two back". Spurs battered the Icelandic amateurs with Alan Gilzean scoring on just seven minutes. Among the 11,000-strong crowd were 200 Spurs fans who saw their team thrash what Scovell described as "embarrassingly naïve" opposition. Spurs eased up in the second half, but still managed to score three more. The home side managed to reply, Olafur Juliusson stabbing home a rebound after a Jennings save. Ralph Coates and Alan Mullery (2) also got on the scoresheet, with Gilzean grabbing a hat-trick. Late on, substitute Graeme Souness played the only 14 first-team minutes of his Spurs career on this night.

Jennings, Kinnear, Knowles, **Mullery 2** *(Souness), England, Beal,* **Coates** *(Pearce), Perryman, Chivers, Peters,* **Gilzean 3**

28 September 1971, first round, second leg

TOTTENHAM HOTSPUR 9 (15)
KEFLAVIK 0 (1)

White Hart Lane *Att:* 23,818

Another hat-trick, this time from Martin Chivers, helped Spurs to an aggregate 15-1 win – one goal short of the record score by a British side in Europe that had been set by Leeds United. And Keflavik got off lightly – Tottenham's forwards "squandered a succession of chances" according to Steve Curry of the *Daily Express*. Steve Perryman, Ralph Coates, Cyril Knowles, Alan Gilzean and Phil Holder also got themselves on the scoresheet but, said Curry, "if the game has made Spurs fans aware of the jewel they have in big Martin Chivers, then it will have served a useful purpose". Bill Nicholson said after the game: "It is a good thing for football in general to have sides like this playing in European football. It is all part of the game's goodwill. And Keflavik played with great sportsmanship." And yet only 23,818 turned up to White Hart Lane to watch this one.

Jennings, Evans, **Knowles,** *Mullery (Pearce), England, Beal,* **Coates, Perryman, Chivers 3,** *Peters (Holder),* **Gilzean 2**

Alan Gilzean slides in to score of one of Spurs' nine goals v Keflavik at White Hart Lane

Jimmy Neighbour watches Martin Peters challenge for a high ball during the testing goalless tie in France

20 October 1971, second round, first leg

NANTES 0
TOTTENHAM HOTSPUR 0

Stade Malakoff, Nantes, France *Att*: 20,033

In the previous round the opposition had been poor. This time, on a winter night in western France, it was Spurs who were lacking. David Miller in the *Daily Telegraph* said, "Tottenham's near-million-pound team gave one of their worst-ever displays" and concluded that "seldom will [they] survive such a roasting without punishment". The French side played with four strikers whose rapid movement gave the Spurs defence all sorts of problems. Nantes' players were sharper and faster. Phil Beal found himself drawn back to help cover his defence, while Alan Mullery, Martin Peters, Alan Gilzean and Martin Chivers seemed to have lost the ability to pass the ball. Pat Jennings pulled off a great save early on and somehow Nantes could not find the net. But in the last half hour they tired and Spurs might have snatched something. The tie was on a knife edge.

Jennings, Kinnear, Knowles, Mullery, England, Beal, Neighbour, Perryman, Chivers, Peters, Gilzean (Morgan)

2 November 1971, second round, second leg

TOTTENHAM HOTSPUR 1 (1)
NANTES 0 (0)

White Hart Lane *Att*: 32,630

Martin Peters, captaining the side in the absence of Alan Mullery, put Spurs ahead on the quarter hour, but a crowd of just over 32,000 had to endure a nervous night as the home side failed to convert a host of chances. Such was the Lilywhites' dominance in the first half that, wrote Geoffrey Green in *The Times*, "Jennings might well have laid himself a table and helped himself, cross-legged, to a bottle of aperitif". As the pattern continued into the second half with Spurs still failing to kill the tie off, Green discerned that "waves of impatience rose from the crowd as both teams began anxiously to stammer and stutter". The score stayed at 1-0, and Spurs were through. But Tottenham had so far failed to shine in the competition, and tough opponents awaited in the last 16. "Tottenham will have to find something deeper within themselves," judged Green.

*Jennings, Evans, Knowles, Pratt, England, Beal, Neighbour, Perryman, Chivers, **Peters**, Gilzean (Pearce)*

Spurs beat hate war

8 December 1971, third round, first leg

TOTTENHAM HOTSPUR 3
RAPID BUCAREST 0

White Hart Lane *Att:* 30,702

Spurs went ahead after 20 seconds. A long throw from Martin Chivers bounced in front of Martin Peters and, as Romanian keeper Rică Răducanu stood motionless, Peters thrust his head forward to nod home. Răducanu was more animated on 36 minutes, protesting there had been a foul in the build-up to Chivers bagging a second. As the game restarted Răducanu was still gesticulating angrily as a back pass came towards him. The 6ft 5in keeper seemed to ignore the ball, and only when Alan Gilzean sprinted for it did he move to gather it. According to Chivers, Răducanu "acted like a complete nutter throughout the game", and the *Daily Mirror's* Ken Jones labelled him "a comedy goalkeeper". Chivers gave Spurs a 3-0 lead but, said Jones, "they may have cause to regret the chances they squandered". Rapid had a habit of scoring against good teams at home.

Jennings, Evans, Knowles, Coates (Pearce), England, Beal, Gilzean, Perryman, Chivers 2, Peters, Neighbour

15 December 1971, third round, second leg

RAPID BUCAREST 0 (0)
TOTTENHAM HOTSPUR 2 (5)

Stadionul Giulesti-Valentin Stanescu, Bucharest, Romania *Att:* 12,000

This was the Battle of Bucharest. The Romanians set up in a 4-2-4 formation and married a physical approach with waves of attacks. Spurs held on until half-time with the score still 0-0. Substitute Jimmy Pearce opened the scoring on the hour. Three minutes later he tangled with Ion Pop after the Romanian kicked him. Both were sent off. In the end, said Geoffrey Green in *The Times*, Spurs "took control against a fading opponent to round off a coldly efficient performance". Chivers, who scored a beauty from a tight angle six minutes from time, said: "After the game there were bodies lying everywhere in the treatment room." Bill Nicholson said: "I have never seen a dirtier team or a more vicious attack on a team of players than that. It was so bad Bucharest have refused to hand the film of the game over to the BBC."

Jennings, Evans, Knowles, Coates, Collins, Beal, Pratt, Perryman (Naylor), Chivers, Peters, Gilzean (Pearce)

Top left: In the Battle of Bucharest, Martin Peters and Alan Gilzean evade a Rapid player's studs

Top right: Bill Nicholson attempts to diffuse a confrontation during the acrimonious tie

Spurs players salute the crowd prior to the quarter-final tie in Arad, another Romanian club, although this was a friendlier tie than the previous round

7 March 1972, fourth round, first leg

UT ARAD 0
TOTTENHAM HOTSPUR 2

Stadionul Francisc von Neumann, Arad, Romania *Att:* 20,000

Spurs returned to Romania but UT Arad were something of an unknown quantity. By the end of the first leg, however, according to Brian James in *The Times*, Arad "were shown to be neither sophisticated enough nor possessed of sufficient stamina to deter a Tottenham team growing fast to the state of resolution and discipline that not only wins matches in Europe, but also competitions". Spurs used two lines of four to squeeze the play, leaving Arad "to struggle along pointless avenues," said James. Roger Morgan grabbed a goal on 12 minutes, then just before half-time a standard routine saw Mike England head home after Alan Gilzean flicked on a corner at the near post. In the second half, strangely, Arad changed their shirt colour from cream to red, but the change did not affect the black-and-white fact of Tottenham's dominance.

Jennings, Evans, Knowles, Pratt, **England,** *Beal, Gilzean (Collins), Perryman, Chivers, Peters,* **Morgan**

21 March 1972, fourth round, second leg

TOTTENHAM HOTSPUR 1 (3)
UT ARAD 1 (1)

White Hart Lane *Att:* 30,253

Spurs came into the return leg after losing an FA Cup tie against Leeds United, and with Martin Chivers banned after picking up too many yellow cards. They almost allowed a poor Arad side to become the first team to win a European tie at White Hart Lane. Despite presenting almost no attacking threat, Arad stole into a 63rd-minute lead thanks to Flavio Domide. Spurs wasted chances, until, nine minutes from time, Alan Gilzean headed home. In the *Daily Express*, Norman Giller described Gilzean as "graceful as a Nureyev on grass", saying that "perhaps in his final season", Gilzean had "stitched the few magnificent moments into this not very memorable match". Bill Nicholson also praised Terry Naylor, deputising for the injured Phil Beal in defence. Spurs were through to the semi-finals, but the home crowd had jeered them before Gilly came to the rescue.

Jennings, Evans, Knowles, Coates, England, Naylor, **Gilzean,** *Perryman, Pratt, Peters, Morgan*

5 April 1972, semi-final, first leg

TOTTENHAM HOTSPUR 2
AC MILAN 1

White Hart Lane *Att*: 42,064

Italian giants AC Milan were drawn to face Spurs in the semi-final, with coach Nereo Roçco's team including the great Gianni Rivera and, in goal, a certain Fabio Cudicini, whose son Carlo would eventually play for Spurs. Bill Nicholson had to recall Alan Mullery from a loan spell at Fulham, so depleted were his playing resources. Mullery had been suffering from a recurring injury and the loan had been arranged to get him match fit. But Nicholson had no choice but to bring him back and throw him in for a huge test.

On 25 minutes things looked bad for Spurs when Milan took the lead through Romeo Benetti, who seized on a half-clearance by Terry Naylor to strike an opening goal described by the *Daily Mail*'s Jeff Powell as "full of skill and power".

With that away goal counting double and the Italians renowned as masters of the defensive game, Spurs faced an enormous challenge. They needed goals to have a chance at the San Siro.

But there was another side to the Italians, too, and they showed it in bucketloads. Spurs were "shamefully brutalised by the hatchet men of Milan", fumed Powell, branding the Italians "a downright disgrace" and saying "coach Nereo Roçco stands accused as an accomplice to the soccer crimes his team

committed". Referee Mariano Iglesias was, said Powell, "so out of touch he awarded 38 free-kicks against Tottenham, 22 against Milan". In these circumstances, he said, "only a hero would have gone looking for goals in the face of the cynical chopping".

But Spurs had not one, but two heroes on a night that drew 42,000 to White Hart Lane for what was to prove one of the greatest nights in the club's history. One was Mullery who, said Powell, "gave Spurs renewed drive and direction" to "force surprising cracks in one of the world's greatest defences". Mullery broke up the Italian attacks and harried their midfield, refusing to buckle under intimidation. The other hero was Steve Perryman, whose two cracking volleys gave Spurs the win. The first came on 33 minutes, a 20-yard rocket after Alan Gilzean and Martin Peters combined to lay it into Perryman's path. The second was driven low into the right-hand corner of the net on 67 minutes, shortly after Riccardo Sogliano was sent off for the latest in a series of assaults on Mullery. Spurs had kept their cool in the face of intense provocation, held the line and breached what some still say was the finest defensive line ever assembled.

Perryman remembers: "Being one goal down at home, bearing in mind we had to go to the San Siro to face a hostile crowd, was far from ideal. We were fully aware that the Italians would relish a defensive job of holding on to their lead, particularly an away goal.

"I'm not exactly noted for my goals. Certainly not for scoring from outside the box. But that was the only way through their well-drilled defence. They were shocked by my goals. It was just my night, perhaps my best in Europe – certainly for scoring."

Chivers also remembers how vital those goals were, saying: "Bill always emphasised he wanted 20 goals a season from the midfield trio of Perryman, Mullery and Peters. Steve was a great defensive midfielder… but if he never scored another goal that season it didn't matter because those two great goals gave us an excellent chance of reaching the final."

*Jennings, Kinnear, Knowles, Coates (Neighbour), England, Naylor, Gilzean, **Perryman 2,** Chivers, Peters, Mullery*

Below left: Alan Mullery shakes hands with AC Milan's legendary captain Gianni Rivera before the semi-final at White Hart Lane

Above: Mike England rises above a group of AC Milan players during the 2-1 home win

Right: Spurs players mob double goal-scorer on the night, Steve Perryman

SCORCHER STEVE IS THE SPURS ACE

STEVE'S DOUBLE CHEERS SPURS

19 April 1972, semi-final, second leg
AC MILAN 1 (2)
TOTTENHAM HOTSPUR 1 (3)
San Siro, Milan, Italy *Att:* 68,482

Mullery's magic
SPURS IN FINAL

Above: Alan Mullery scores the crucial goal in the San Siro

Right: Bemused AC Milan Goalkeeper Fabio Cudicini and his defence can only stand and watch as Mullery turns to celebrate his superb strike

On a tense night in Milan Spurs showed they had the character and the ability that had been doubted earlier in the run. Alan Mullery was again the star of the show. After just seven minutes he cracked a 20-yard curling shot into the top corner of the net, with Steve Perryman turning provider after his goalscoring heroics in London. Then Mullery masterminded a rearguard action that beat the Italians at their own game in their own backyard. Tottenham, said the *Daily Mirror*'s Harry Miller, "were stretched to the limit of their strength and character to hold on". But they did, only conceding in the 68th minute when Phil Beal brought down Alberto Bignon and Gianni Rivera converted from the spot.

Nicholson withdrew John Pratt and sent on Terry Naylor to shore up the defence. On the vast terraces, bonfires burned. Miller thought they "seemed like a funeral pyre for Milan's hopes". But there had been one more twist in what had been an extraordinary tie.

In the 61st minute, Beal and Romeo Benetti scuffled in the Spurs penalty area. Belgian referee Pierre Loraux booked them. But he wrote down the names of Perryman and Milan's Giorgio Biasolo, having got the shirt numbers of the respective players the wrong way round. After the game he insisted he had been right, even when it was pointed out that Perryman had dark hair while Beal was fair. And that Biasolo had been substituted six minutes before the incident and was not on the field! In his autobiography, Chivers says Perryman accepted the card "with good grace", knowing that Beal was already on a yellow.

At the final whistle, the Spurs players were held in the centre circle for 15 minutes as the crowd exhausted their supply of missiles.

*Jennings, Kinnear, Knowles, **Mullery**, England, Beal, Coates, Perryman, Chivers, Peters, Pratt (Naylor)*

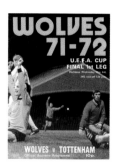

3 May 1972, Final, first leg

WOLVERHAMPTON WANDERERS 1
TOTTENHAM HOTSPUR 2

Molineux, Wolverhampton, England *Att:* 38,362

The first leg of the first all-English European final, and one between two teams whose histories were replete with the romance and thrill of European nights under the floodlights, was a subdued affair. In *The Times*, Geoffrey Green said: "For nearly an hour, the game was bankrupt and it seemed that we were heading for a stalemate." And in the *Daily Mail*, Jeff Powell said: "There was no escaping the ordinary feeling of a league game."

The general sense of anti-climax was shared by some of the players too. "We wanted a foreign team but it wasn't to be," remembers Martin Chivers. "Our wives and girlfriends were also disappointed. The club had promised to pay for them to travel to the final and I don't think they were expecting a return train ticket to Wolverhampton."

But this was, after all that, a final, and it was Chivers who was to step forward to cement his place in Spurs history on this night. Twelve minutes into the second half, he rose to meet a long free-kick from Mike England. The Wolves defence seemed momentarily transfixed, and Chivers headed Spurs into the lead. "Wolves," observed Green, "were victims of their own realism, which proved a poor guide, as they swung the ball about in long passing. Tottenham's strength lay in their collective effort."

Collective effort was certainly not lacking, but on 87 minutes another moment of individual brilliance put Spurs in the driving seat. Wide on the touchline, Chivers flicked the ball infield off the side of his foot. Wolves' John McAlle closed it down but was dispossessed by Alan Mullery. He laid the ball back to Chivers, who cut inside as Mullery went wide and Alan Gilzean moved square. Chivers opened up, driving forward at full stretch, and unleashed a scorching shot without breaking stride that flew past Phil Parkes and into the net.

Chivers said he took the shot knowing that the Spurs fans massed behind the goal "would hold onto it for 30 seconds or so if I missed". It was, he said, "the best goal I ever scored for Spurs in my life".

It was vindication for Chivers, who says he had retreated to the toilets at half-time to avoid another rollicking from Nicholson and his assistant Eddie Baily. Chivers felt the duo were on his back too often, while many fans shared the view that Chivers was lazy when the going got tough. A few days before the final Chivers had played for an England team badly beaten by West Germany and his stock was low. Now, said Powell, he had "not only reduced Wolves to outsiders... but also reaffirmed his right to lead the England bid for Nations Cup revenge". What a difference a game makes.

Mullery was, again, one of the team's most influential players, Green picking out his "spirit and drive in midfield".

Wolves had pulled level through a quickly taken free-kick in the 71st minute, a set piece controversially allowed by Tofik Bakhramov.

Left: Martin Chivers's two goals against Wolves. The first a header, the second a superb long range strike

The referee was no stranger to controversy. When running the line at Wembley in the 1966 World Cup Final, he had judged Geoff Hurst's effort to have crossed the line.

Spurs looked to have settled for the draw when Ralph Coates was withdrawn for John Pratt. But Chivers's second goal meant Spurs were now in a commanding position. The club had never lost a cup final, and never lost a European tie at White Hart Lane. Surely another European trophy was within the grasp of the north Londoners?

Jennings, Kinnear, Knowles, Mullery, England, Beal, Gilzean, Perryman, **Chivers 2,** *Peters, Coates (Pratt)*

COCK-A-DOODLE SPURS

Meet the men from White Hart Lane . . .

● BACK (left to right): Pat Jennings, Ray Evans, Cyril Knowles, Martin Chivers, Mike England, Peter Collins, Martin Peters, Alan Gilzean, Terry Naylor, Phil Beal.
● FRONT: Joe Kinnear, Jimmy Neighbour, Ralph Coates, Steve Perryman, Alan Mullery, John Pratt, Tony Want, Jimmy Pearce, Roger Morgan.
Picture: Carlton Photographic

Above: Double goal-scorer on the night, Martin Chivers

Left: The Spurs team as pictured in the Wolves match programme

17 May 1972, Final, second leg
TOTTENHAM HOTSPUR 1 (3)
WOLVERHAMPTON WANDERERS 1 (2)
White Hart Lane *Att*: 54,303

White Hart Lane was crammed to capacity as Spurs walked out to play their 26th cup tie of a marathon 68-game season. In the end, the night would belong to Alan Mullery, the player whose see-saw season epitomised the peaks and troughs of Tottenham's progress. At one stage his career at Spurs seemed over, he was plying his trade in the Second Division, and just two weeks before this final he had retired from international football. And yet in the latter stages of the first-ever UEFA Cup, he had led Spurs to the brink of yet another first, leading his team across frontiers of both geography and achievement. It was fitting that it was his goal that won the cup.

Spurs started at pace, determined to make sure of victory rather than hang onto it, but also mindful that a gruelling 90 minutes might have been beyond their tiring legs and hearts. Mullery and Steve Perryman held the middle, while Martin Peters buzzed energetically behind Martin Chivers and Alan Gilzean as Spurs probed for an opening. On the half hour Peters floated a free-kick. The ball went over Chivers's head and there was Mullery, throwing himself full length to send a diving header flashing into the Wolves net. Mullery later revealed it was a deliberate move they had practised in training but couldn't get right.

The place erupted, but Mullery was out cold, having landed face first in the goalmouth and knocked himself out. As the celebrations

continued, Mullery was helped from the pitch to get patched up. He soon returned to continue marshalling his troops, but in the 41st minute he played a part in Wolves' equaliser. Danny Hegan's shot bounced off Mullery and fell to David Wagstaffe, who slammed it past Pat Jennings to level.

At half-time Spurs changed their approach, deciding to keep it tight rather than press for another goal. They soaked up the pressure, although Wolves found it hard to muster much threat. Spurs' marathon season, wrote Norman Giller in the *Daily Express*: "had drained them of energy and initiative". Bernard Joy in *The Evening News* said that, in that second half: "Spurs had their worst 45 minutes in the competition." When Wolves did threaten, the Spurs defence matched them, with one magnificent save by Jennings from a John Richards effort standing out.

At the final whistle thousands of fans swarmed onto the pitch. They engulfed captain Mullery as he carried the cup in his arms around the pitch on a second lap of honour after his exhausted team-mates had retreated to the dressing room. Giller opened his report by saying: "Alan Mullery's astonishing season ended last night with him displaying the UEFA Cup in a one-man victory parade around White Hart Lane."

The triumph meant Tottenham Hotspur was the first name engraved on the new trophy. They were the first British club to win two European trophies. And the victory meant that Bill Nicholson had won more trophies than any other manager in the Football League. Since he took charge Spurs had played in three FA Cup Finals, one League Cup Final and two European finals. They'd won the lot, and they'd taken the league too. That made seven trophies in 14 years at a time when the game was far more competitive than it would become. It made Spurs London's top dogs just a year after Arsenal seemed to be eclipsing them. And it meant that Spurs would be back where Nicholson always said they belonged the following year – in Europe.

*Jennings, Kinnear, Knowles, **Mullery**, England, Beal, Gilzean, Perryman, Chivers, Peters, Coates*

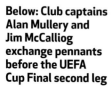

Below: Club captains Alan Mullery and Jim McCalliog exchange pennants before the UEFA Cup Final second leg

Above: Mullery puts his head where it hurts and scores with a crucial cup-winning header

Right: Skipper Mullery clings onto the UEFA Cup, in the inaugural year of the competition

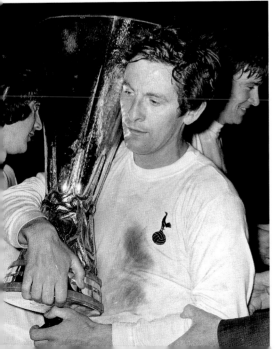

SPURS CLINCH IT AGAIN

SPURS v WOLVES
IN PICTURES

Above: The Spurs crest that used to take pride of place on the dressing room wall. It can be seen in the picture opposite

Right: A rare shot from inside the home changing room, as the players and management celebrate with the UEFA Cup

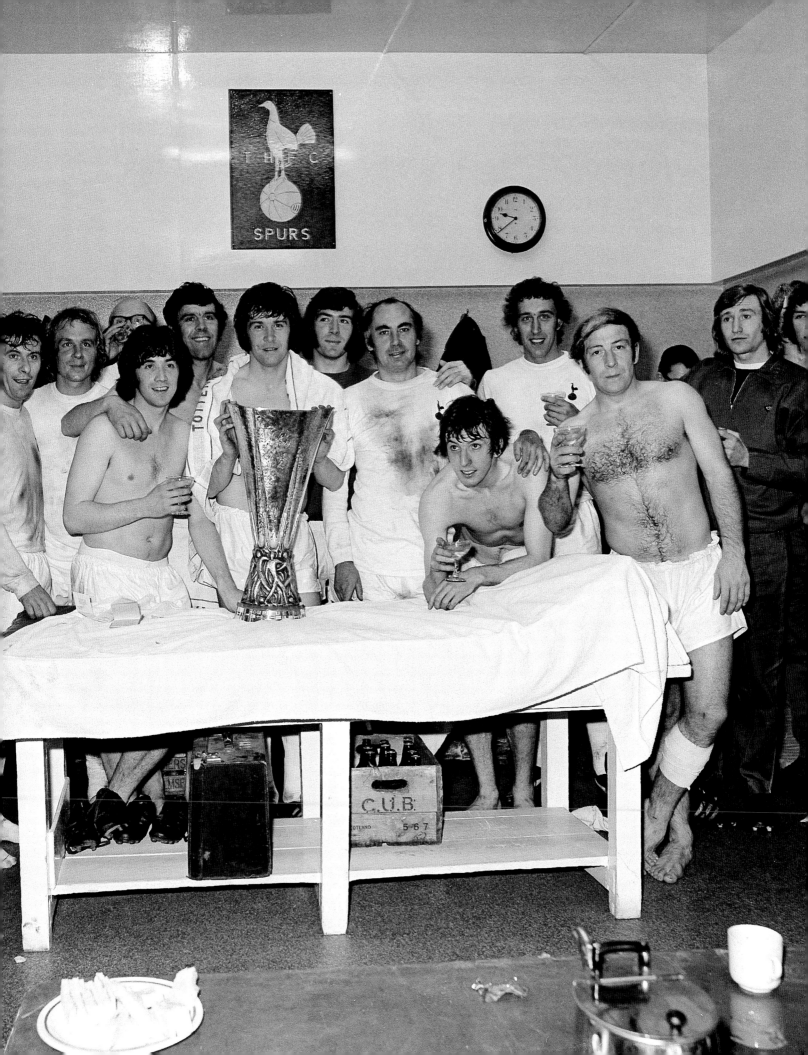

SPURS v WOLVES
IN PICTURES

Left: Alan Mullery is chaired around White Hart Lane by delirious fans on what proved to be his final appearance in a Spurs shirt

Top: Joe Kinnear, Phil Beal, Alan Mullery, Pat Jennings, Alan Gilzean and Cyril Knowles meet the Mayor of Haringey at a reception for the cup winners

Above: The proud squad at the start of the 1972/73 season with the UEFA Cup and the Anglo-Italian League Cup Winners' Cup

THE ROAD TO EUROPE

1972

The UEFA Cup Final victory over Wolves had another happy benefit besides the obvious priority of securing a trophy. It meant that, after a domestic season that promised much but ended with nothing to show for a punishing schedule, Tottenham Hotspur were able to return to European campaigning to defend their title.

It also provided a fillip in the effort to win further honours at home. Bill Nicholson looked forward with renewed confidence, telling Bernard Joy "the side that wins the UEFA Cup very often goes on to take the League Championship, as Leeds and Arsenal did". Nicholson even ventured that "any club that is in the European Cup and feels confident… ought to withdraw from the FA Cup". It might come as shock to read that one of the game's purists was prepared to "devalue" the FA Cup as long as 40 years ago. Such comments are more readily associated with the ultra-professionalism of the modern age and the obsession with the Champions League places. But it was a clear sign that managers of English clubs were putting greater store in taking on Europe's best rather than focusing on the more familiar home comforts.

The post-match scenes in Setubal, Portugal, in March 1973. Fans spill onto the pitch to congratulate Pat Jennings and the Spurs team after the tie was won on away goals

CHIVERS MAKES IT A SIX-HIT SPECIAL

Alan Gilzean scores one of his two goals, out of Spurs' six in Oslo, but, as the 6-3 scoreline hints, it was an erratic performance against a team of Norwegian amateurs

13 September 1972, first round, first leg

LYN OSLO 3
TOTTENHAM HOTSPUR 6

Ullevaal Stadium, Oslo, Norway *Att:* 10,770

If the scoreline suggested a comfortable Scandinavian stroll, the reality was different. In a performance veering from precision finishing to sloppy defending, Spurs only confirmed their superiority over their plucky amateur opposition in the final eight minutes, when two goals from an otherwise muted Martin Chivers restored a sense of reality to the contest. Before then the Norwegians had taken the lead just eight minutes after kick-off through Jon Palmar Austnes. Suitably stirred, Tottenham equalised within seconds of the restart via Martin Peters, took the lead with John Pratt's 25-yarder on 24 minutes, and then added two more from Alan Gilzean in the 38th minute. Oslo responded in the same crazy 38th minute through Trygve Christophersen and from the same source again in the 58th minute to give Spurs a needlessly uncomfortable second half, before Chivers's late intervention.

*Jennings, Evans, Knowles, **Pratt**, England, Naylor, **Gilzean 2**, Perryman, **Chivers 2**, Peters, Pearce*

27 September 1972, first round, second leg

TOTTENHAM HOTSPUR 6 (12)
LYN OSLO 0 (3)

White Hart Lane *Att:* 21,109

Spurs made it 15 unbeaten European games in succession with an easy victory. On home turf the Lilywhites had few of the jitters that had characterised the lacklustre performance in Oslo. The Norwegians did well to hold out for 20 minutes, before Chivers picked up where he left off and added two more goals to his burgeoning European tally. His first was a close-range finish after Alan Gilzean's shot had been spilled by goalkeeper Sven Olsen. Thirteen minutes later Chivers met John Pratt's cross at the far post and flicked home. Gilzean fed Ralph Coates to score Spurs' third eight minutes into the second half, and five minutes later Jimmy Pearce impressed with a right-foot volley. Chivers completed his hat-trick on 71 minutes, before Coates ended Oslo's misery with his second seven minutes from time. Oslo were, as Harry Miller noted in the *Daily Mirror*, "punchdrunk from the power of English football".

*Jennings, Kinnear, Knowles, Pratt (Holder), England, Beal (Naylor), Gilzean, Perryman, **Chivers 3**, Pearce, **Coates 2***

..SO-SWEET SPURS
Old glory days are back again

Left: Ralph Coates is on target, scoring one of Spurs' four goals v Olympiakos at White Hart Lane

Below: Martin Chivers lets fly in the return leg in Athens but Spurs lost the match 1-0

25 October 1972, second round, first leg

TOTTENHAM HOTSPUR 4
OLYMPIAKOS PIRAEUS 0

White Hart Lane *Att:* 27,815

Spurs recorded a convincing win that all but secured the tie, but Olympiakos were no pushovers. Their honest application impressed, not so some less sporting shirt tugging and assorted indiscretions which were missed by referee Alfred Delcourt, "stricken with the limitations of a Cyclops", as observed by *The Guardian's* David Lacey . Seeing such misdemeanours go unpunished, Spurs responded by giving almost as good as they got. Coupled with some excellent and purposeful attacking play, it made for an all-round entertaining match. The scoring started after 12 minutes when Chivers held off Vasilis Siokos's challenge to lay the ball off for Jimmy Pearce who registered the first of his brace. Thirteen minutes later, Chivers helped himself to Tottenham's second from a Coates cross and returned the favour four minutes after the break. Pearce wrapped the scoring up on the hour.

Jennings, Evans, Knowles, **Pearce 2,** *England, Beal (Naylor), Gilzean (Neighbour), Perryman,* **Chivers,** *Peters,* **Coates**

8 November 1972, second round, second leg

OLYMPIAKOS PIRAEUS 1 (1)
TOTTENHAM HOTSPUR 0 (4)

Karaiskakis Stadium, Piraeus, Greece
Att: 35,000

With the tie already won, in the grand scheme of matters the reverse in Piraeus was not a serious blow. Indeed, Spurs could take credit for their performance in a testing match and atmosphere. As the *Daily Express's* Norman Giller noted, this was Spurs' sixth match in 14 days, and it showed. Martin Peters was absent with a stomach upset, while Mike Dillon and Terry Naylor were drafted in to provide fresh legs. Led by stand-in skipper Steve Perryman, a tired but determined Spurs withstood the first-half pressure only to concede just before half-time when Pat Jennings spilled a shot, allowing Argiroudis to give Olympiakos the lead and hope. It was to prove fleeting. The Greeks could not breach the opposition again and the frustrated home fans turned their ire on Bill Nicholson and assistant Eddie Baily. The pair were pelted with rubbish until police intervened.

Jennings, Evans, Knowles, Pearce, England, Dillon, Gilzean, Perryman, Chivers, Naylor, Pratt

LOOKING BACK WITH
STEVE PERRYMAN

"Bill Nicholson walked into the White Hart Lane dressing room at 6.30pm to announce that Martin Peters had failed a fitness test and that I would be captain for the night and vice-captain of the club."

Steve Perryman, at the age of 21, was "shocked". He had become the youngest player to skipper Spurs, when he led the team in Europe against Lyn. He played in more European campaigns than any other Spurs player and served the club for 11 years as skipper when he got the job on a permanent basis. Perryman made a fine start as Peters's understudy.

"There were many experienced internationals in that dressing room when Bill Nick walked in an hour before kick-off. I'm sure Bill was looking to the future. I can remember wondering if there would be any resentment, but I am not sure whether I recall it or read it somewhere, that the players showed their delight by cheering.

"Certainly, I didn't know what captaincy was all about in those days, but it was a nice introduction. Martin Peters was soon back and the following season played 35 games, including captaining the team in the UEFA Cup Final against Feyenoord.

"Bill Nick started the next season but didn't stay for very long. I don't think Terry Neill realised that I was vice-captain when he made me skipper in succession to Martin."

Spurs had a knack of adjusting to a variety of styles. No matter how poor the club's league form, they came to life in Europe.

"Foreign coaches would come to watch us play in a league game just before our European ties and we'd play badly and probably lose. They would go away thinking they've got nothing to beat. They would be shocked to think that our team could possibly have won the UEFA Cup.

"But European nights always brought the best out in our team. Somehow we produced something special. There was only one night I didn't think we deserved to go through. That was against Nantes, when Bill Nick had a furious row with Martin Chivers.

"We had an expertise of playing away. We'd go on our travels talking about concentrating on defence, getting behind the ball, and making sure we're safe… and score ourselves inside 10 minutes! Away goals are so vital. And scoring in Eastern bloc countries early on considerably eased the pressure.

"Sometimes, it seemed strange playing the away leg in the afternoons. It was also difficult to get used to some of the places, particularly behind the Iron Curtain. It made us appreciative of our own country and facilities. We'd take our own food, even our own chef! Steak and cornflakes always went with us, plus, of course, tomato sauce."

Perryman praised the organisation of Nicholson and his assistant Eddie Baily on these trips.

"Eddie would come back with photos of the players we'd be up against. He'd always give a glowing report of the opposition, no doubt to keep us on our toes.

"Once, he returned from watching Tbilisi and was adamant that we would not beat them. He went into raptures about their skills, their movement off the ball, everything he would like to see from his own team. I'm convinced he was using a bit of kidology. Well, it worked. It motivated us. But Eddie was right in one respect: they were an outstanding team. We rose to the challenge and got through."

Steve Perryman, captain of Spurs aged just 21, v Olympiakos in 1972

IN THE
PROGRAMMES

Welcome Tottenham!

On behalf of the Ski and Football-club LYN — this evenings crowd of spectators — and we might add the whole football-loving Norway — we want to welcome Tottenham Hotspurs to the European cup match here at Ullevål stadium.

We have to admit that it is not often we have the honour of seeing such celebreties here in Oslo. In fact — this is the first time that this London club — world known and rich in tradition — is visiting Ullevål stadium. We want you to know — however — that English football is — and has always been — greatly admired and hailed by all Norwegians. We Norwegians were taught Football by you britons — and still today — or we might put it this way: more than ever Norwegians are jubilant fans of British top football and its star players.

We also want you to know that Norwegian supporters and there are tens of thousands of them — possess a wide knowledge of English football. A wide newspaper coverage and of course the popular pools has made the Norwegian fan an expert on what is going on in English football. That's why we all know and appreciate what Tottenham and its famous players stand for.

We know for sure that you all will experience a warm and genuine enthusiasm coming from the stands tonight.

We want you to know that it is an honour — and that we greatly appreciate — to watch the white players here at Ullevål tonight. You are surely welcome.

ABERDEEN
Referee: C. LO BELLOE (Italy)

1 BOBBY CLARK
2 IAN HAIR
3 JIM HERMISTON
4 EDDIE THOMSON
5 WILLIE YOUNG
6 WILLIE MILLER
7 ALEX WILLOUGHBY
8 DAVE ROBB
9 ARTHUR GRAHAM
SUBSTITUTES
10 DREW JARVIE
11 BERTIE MILLER

Contrasting styles of welcome in the programmes of Lyn Oslo (left) and Red Star Belgrade (bottom right). The Aberdeen line-up (right), featuring future Spurs player Willie Young and the Liverpool side (below) including Ray Clemence, another future Spurs player

TEAMS FOR TONIGHT'S MATCH

LIVERPOOL (Red Shirts)		TOTTENHAM H. (White Shirts)
1 Ray CLEMENCE	Referee: Mr. B. Loow Sweden	1 Pat JENNINGS
2 Chris LAWLER		2 Joe KINNEAR
3 Alec LINDSAY		3 Cyril KNOWLES
4 Tommy SMITH (Capt.)	JACK SHARP SPORTS LIVERPOOL	4 Ralph COATES
5 Larry LLOYD		5 Mike ENGLAND
6 Emlyn HUGHES		6 Philip BEAL
7 Kevin KEEGAN		7 Alan GILZEAN
8 Peter CORMACK	Linesmen:	8 Steve PERRYMAN
9 Brian HALL	Mr. G. Carlstrand (Orange Flag)	9 Martin CHIVERS
10 Steve HEIGHWAY	Mr. C.A. Johansson (Red Flag)	10 Martin PETERS (Capt.)
11 Ian CALLAGHAN		11 Jimmy PEARCE
Substitute:		Substitute:

FINAL SPUR—AT THE DOUBLE!

AS Liverpool begin their bid tonight for a place in the final of the E.U.F.A. Cup—180 minutes of football away—we offer our congratulations to the Reds' reserves, who have already reached the final of a Cup competition . . . the Lancashire County Cup.

Liverpool's senior and Central League sides, in fact, are both battling to achieve a championship-Cup double, for the reserves are bidding for the Central League title, and their semi-final victory over Preston in the Lancashire County Cup, at Deepdale, takes them on to a final against Bury at Gigg Lane.

The date for this final has now been fixed for Tuesday, May 1st, 6 days before our Central League game at Bury, and if the seniors reach the final of the E.U.F.A. Cup, it's going to be all systems go right to the end, with the championship at stake, as well.

Incidentally, tonight's game against Tottenham should take the Anfield attendance aggregate for E.U.F.A. Cup matches to well over the 150,000 mark, for already our ties against Eintracht Frankfurt, A.E.K. Athens, Dynamo Berlin and Dynamo Dresden have given us a total figure of just under 133,000.

Tonight's gate, all being well, could push the aggregate up to around 175,000—which would be a magnificent achievement, and a very real testimony to the support from our fans, considering how many matches Liverpool have played this season.

TOTTENHAM HOTSPUR, WELCOME TO BEOGRAD!

WE ARE VERY HAPPY TO HAVE THE OPPORTUNITY TO REGARD ONE OF THE BEST ENGLISH TEAMS

THE FIRST U.E.F.A. CUP'S MATCH TOTTENHAM — CRVENA ZVEZDA WAS AN EXTRAORDINARY PLEASURE FOR ALL FANS OF SOCCER IN ENGLAND AND YUGOSLAVIA.

WE ARE SURE THAT THE RETURN MATCH IN BEOGRAD WILL BE AT THE SAME LEVEL IN SPORTS AND FRIENDLY SENSE.

IT IS THE REASON THAT WE WISH TO SAY, ON BEHALF OF ALL MEMBERS OF THE FOOTBALL CLUB CRVENA ZVEZDA:

WELCOME TO BEOGRAD, DEAR FRIENDS OF TOTTENHAM HOTSPUR!

RED-HOT SPURS KNOCK THEM COLD

Alan Gilzean gets on the end of a Martin Peters' cross to score Spurs' second goal on the night against Red Star Belgrade

29 November 1972, third round, first leg

TOTTENHAM HOTSPUR 2
RED STAR BELGRADE 0

White Hart Lane *Att*: 23,958

As the later rounds loomed, so the quality of opposition increased. Red Star provided a considerable test; their 5-2-3 formation suggested a defensive mindset but the strength of their all-round play showed otherwise. Led by Yugoslavian star Dragan Dzajic they had enough chances to score the invaluable away goal. As it was, Tottenham's all-round excellence and the reliability of their leading marksmen engineered a vital home victory. Chivers struck first. With 26 minutes gone, he interchanged with Martin Peters and Alan Gilzean before using his strength to hold off his marker and score with a low left-foot shot. Twenty minutes into the second half, Gilzean displayed his unerring knack for sniffing out a chance when he scored from Peters's cross. It was far from a comfortable win – Red Star missed four good chances – but Spurs had done enough and crucially without conceding that precious away goal.

Jennings, Evans, Knowles, Pratt, England, Naylor, **Gilzean***, Perryman,* **Chivers***, Peters, Pearce*

13 December 1972, third round, second leg

RED STAR BELGRADE 1 (1)
TOTTENHAM HOTSPUR 0 (2)

Red Star Stadium, Belgrade, Yugoslavia *Att*: 70,000

Norman Giller, a shrewd judge of trips to hostile foreign territory, considered this performance "one of the greatest defensive displays I have seen from a British team in Europe". His report for the *Daily Express* praised the nous and experience Spurs had employed in seeing out the tie. As in Greece, Tottenham returned home with a defeat but were victorious overall. Bill Nicholson picked three full-backs in a makeshift defence, with Joe Kinnear in a sweeper role alongside Mike England. Kinnear was reportedly looking for a move away from the Lane, but performed like he was a permanent part of the set-up. Throughout, Spurs were resolute. Martin Chivers played despite having the 'flu. John Pratt had a goal disallowed in one of the visitors' rare sallies forward, but Red Star had only a single goal from Lazarevic to count for their pressure.

Jennings, Evans, Knowles, Pratt, England, Kinnear, Coates, Perryman, Chivers, Peters, Pearce

SPURS SAVED BY ANOTHER SUB!

Thank Evans for winner

OFFICIAL PROGRAMME
price 5p

U.E.F.A. Cup. Quarter-Final
1st Leg

TOTTENHAM HOTSPUR

v

VITÓRIA, SETUBAL
(PORTUGAL)

SEASON 1972-73
Vol. 65 No. 45

7 March 1973, fourth round, first leg

TOTTENHAM HOTSPUR 1
VITORIA SETUBAL 0

White Hart Lane *Att*: 30,469

Four days before the meeting with the Portuguese side, Spurs had beaten Norwich City in the League Cup Final to ensure that, whatever happened in the 1972/73 UEFA Cup, Spurs would be playing in the competition the next season. One man whose celebrations had been less joyous, however, was Ray Evans. His omission from the Norwich game had led to talk that he wanted away. But Evans was soon to be the toast of Tottenham. His goal-scoring appearance as a substitute was pivotal to a tight game. The Edmonton-born Evans had come on for Alan Gilzean with just 14 minutes remaining, as Spurs laboured to overcome a "Setubal defensive wall that looked more impregnable the longer the game wore on", as observed by the *Daily Mirror*'s Harry Miller. Four minutes after Evans's introduction, he took his chance. Martin Chivers arrowed in a long throw, Martin Peters nodded on, and Evans headed in from close range.

Jennings, Kinnear, Knowles, Coates, England, Beal, Gilzean (Evans), Perryman, Chivers, Peters, Pearce

21 March 1973, fourth round, second leg

VITORIA SETUBAL 2 (2)
TOTTENHAM HOTSPUR 1 (2)

Spurs won on away goals
Estádio do Bonfim, Setubal, Portugal
Att: 30,000

Martin Chivers would become Spurs' most prolific goalscorer in European competition, but few of his goals were as cherished as his tie-winning effort in Portugal. With Spurs having surrendered the slender-advantage they had won in north London, the holders were heading out, until Chivers's magnificent long-range strike in the second half. The 1-0 lead had been wiped out after just 20 minutes when a defensive mix-up led to a free-kick for Setubal, from which Campora scored. The hosts pressed forward and Spurs defended desperately, but on 65 minutes Cardoso's free-kick left Jennings stranded and Torres gave Setubal the aggregate lead. Four minutes later, enter Chivers. "With one crushing blow from the right foot," reported Jeff Powell in the *Daily Mail*, he propelled Spurs into yet another European semi.

Jennings, Kinnear, Knowles, Coates, England, Beal, Gilzean (Naylor), Perryman, Chivers, Peters, Pearce

Substitute Ray Evans scores the only goal of the home leg against Vitoria Setubal at White Hart Lane

CUP ODDS ON SPURS NOW

Liverpool held to one goal in fight for final place

10 April 1973, semi-final, first leg

LIVERPOOL 1
TOTTENHAM HOTSPUR 0

Anfield, Liverpool, England *Att:* 42,174

With the UEFA Cup Final a potential 180 minutes away, once again, Spurs faced a "Battle of Britain"-style encounter amid the exacting trials of the European game. Once again Spurs came away from a ground synonymous with defeat for the north Londoners, prolonging a miserable run of form dating back to the sinking of the *Titanic* in 1912 and their last win in Liverpool L4; but once again, Pat Jennings showed why he was the best goalkeeper in Britain and probably the world.

Big Pat had pulled off a series of miracle saves in the league fixture between the teams 10 days earlier. Now he repeated the feat to further frustrate Bill Shankly's men. After the home side had taken the lead through a fortuitous rebound off Alec Lindsay in the confusing midst of a frenzied 27th-minute goalmouth scramble, Jennings made three superb saves to keep Spurs in contention.

At the other end, chances were few and far between, with both Martin Chivers and Ralph

Coates going close but not close enough. Shankly grumbled about a penalty that never was for Liverpool at the death, and with some justification, but the 1-0 advantage for the Reds seemed just about right after a night of often frantic activity. Mike England and John Pratt in particular emerged with great credit, throwing themselves into last-gasp challenges and blocks to keep Liverpool at bay.

On the final whistle, Spurs fans left to make the trip home happy with their team's work on the night, but the *Daily Mail*'s Jeff Powell advised caution. "The trainload of Londoners who cavorted away from Anfield last night would do well to remember that Spurs are no longer an irresistible force at White Hart Lane." Powell's words were to prove prophetic.

Jennings, Kinnear, Knowles, Coates (Pearce), England, Beal, Gilzean, Perryman, Chivers (Evans), Peters, Pratt

Martin Chivers acrobatically shoots at Anfield where a narrow defeat left the tie wide open for the second leg

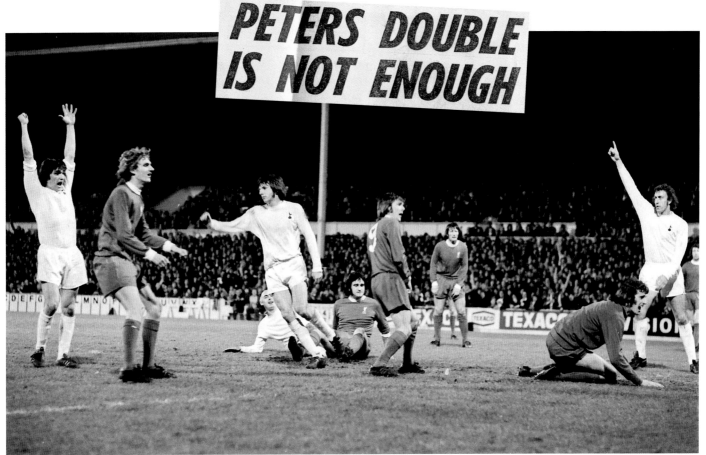

PETERS DOUBLE IS NOT ENOUGH

25 April 1973, semi-final, second leg

TOTTENHAM HOTSPUR 2 (2)
LIVERPOOL 1 (2) *Spurs lost on away goals*

White Hart Lane *Att:* 46,919

Looking back 40 years on, it can be argued that this epic and memorable match was pivotal for the futures of both clubs. Liverpool went on to win the competition and never looked back, becoming an irresistible force that dominated at home and in Europe. Spurs were not to hit quite the same heights for nearly a decade, and while they enjoyed one last if fruitless hurrah in the following season's UEFA Cup, this narrow and heartbreaking defeat to the team that would rule the English league for a generation seemed to land a terminal blow to Bill Nicholson's Spurs. The night had the tangible sense of the end of an era.

It was not for want of trying. White Hart Lane reverberated to the sounds of the Sixties, summoning up the spirit of previous heady nights to show Liverpool that the special atmosphere of European evening games under the lights had a long and proud Tottenham lineage that preceded that of Anfield.

The support earned its reward three minutes after half-time when Martin Peters capitalised after a Chivers throw-in was flicked on by Alan Gilzean. Throwing men forward, Spurs were exposed at the back and when an Emlyn Hughes clearance found the feet of Kevin Keegan, who striker sped into the Spurs area and delivered a cross which Steve Heighway converted.

Back came Tottenham with attack after attack. Peters eventually found a way through for his second, but it was too little and way too late. On the final whistle, Spurs fans sportingly applauded Liverpool's players off the pitch and they responded in kind. They knew they had been in an almighty contest, but the result was further evidence that the balance of English football power was shifting remorselessly to Merseyside.

Jennings, Kinnear (Evans), Knowles (Pearce), Coates, England, Beal, Gilzean, Perryman, Chivers, **Peters 2**, *Pratt*

Frustration for Spurs as chances go begging and they go out of Europe on away goals. Liverpool went on to win the UEFA Cup beating Borussia Mönchengladbach of West Germany 3-2 on aggregate in the final

THE ROAD TO EUROPE
1973

Spurs made up for the huge disappointment of losing to Liverpool in the UEFA Cup semi-final by beating Norwich City to lift the League Cup for the second time in three years and make it nine finals won out of nine played. The return to Europe was a relief, especially as league form was patchy. Relief was the emotion also felt by Brian Glanville of *The Sunday Times*, who welcomed the Football League's decision not to allow extra-time at Wembley on the basis that the final was "so abysmally mediocre that it was hard enough to bear the 90 minutes, let alone an additional half an hour". Victory came through a 73rd-minute goal from Ralph Coates, who had come on for the injured John Pratt. It was probably the least memorable of any of the finals Tottenham Hotspur have played in, and the headline writer for Glanville's piece observed that the League Cup was "just another trophy to Spurs". It was, but it was savoured nonetheless for returning the team to where Bill Nicholson said it had to be. This campaign, though, would be the end of an era.

Martin Peters and Ralph Coates parade the League Cup in March 1973 after Spurs won the trophy for the second time in three years

SPURS RIDE ON

19 September 1973, first round, first leg

GRASSHOPPERS 1
TOTTENHAM HOTSPUR 5

Hardturm Stadium, Zurich, Switzerland
Att: 11,200

Spurs opened the campaign and experienced something new. "It was the first time we had been given the opportunity to warm up before a game," remembers Martin Chivers. Most of the team took advantage, but Phil Beal stuck to his routine. Although Grasshoppers were a semi-professional side, they gave Spurs a fright, with Pat Jennings turning in a superb display. In the *Daily Express*, Norman Giller said: "Jennings made a dozen superb saves as the Tottenham defence was continually driven to disorder during a rush-hour of attacks by the fast, skilful Grasshoppers forwards." This was despite Chivers firing Spurs into the lead on five minutes and Ray Evans grabbing one against the run of play in the 31st. The introduction of Alan Gilzean in the 62nd minute was key. He bagged two, Chivers one more, and Spurs looked safe.

*Jennings, **Evans**, Knowles, Coates (Holder), England, Beal, Pratt, Perryman, **Chivers 2**, Peters, Neighbour (**Gilzean 2**)*

3 October 1973, first round, second leg

TOTTENHAM HOTSPUR 4 (9)
GRASSHOPPERS 1 (2)

White Hart Lane *Att:* 18,105

There was another fright in the return. On 24 minutes, Grasshoppers went ahead, keeping the lead for long enough to raise fears that the unbeaten home record in Europe was in danger. It wasn't until the 74th minute that Spurs pulled level, after which the Swiss rolled over, tiredness sapping their strength and their admirable spirit. Ray Evans set up the equaliser with a low centre from the right which bamboozled Robert Lador into turning the ball into his own net. Evans went on to provide a hat-trick of assists, setting up first Martin Peters and then Mike England, with Peters heading home a minute from time to make it 4-1. In the *Daily Telegraph* Robert Oxby commented that the scoreline was "another flattering result" for Spurs. They had only won three of the nine league games played and seemed far from the force of days gone by. But they were in the second round.

*Daines, Evans, Knowles, Pratt, **England**, Beal, Gilzean, Perryman, Chivers, **Peters 2**, Coates [Lador og]*

Spurs salute the home crowd prior to their match with Grasshoppers. It was the start of the club's third consecutive season in the UEFA Cup

SO-COOL SPURS HIT BY A LATE PENALTY

24 October 1973, second round, first leg

ABERDEEN 1
TOTTENHAM HOTSPUR 1

Pittodrie Stadium, Aberdeen, Scotland
Att: 30,000

Another stumble in the far north of Scotland looked likely. Spurs were missing three internationals – Pat Jennings, Cyril Knowles and Martin Chivers – but took the lead through a Ralph Coates goal in the 15th minute. Steve Curry, covering the game for the *Daily Express*, said: "There were times during this lively game when Spurs' authority seemed beyond challenge." Coates, along with Joe Kinnear, succumbed to injury during the game, meaning Spurs were now five internationals down. But still Aberdeen could not find a way through. Then, on 88 minutes, Dons' substitute Berty Miller powered into the box. Ray Evans moved to challenge and nudged him over. The referee pointed to the spot. Jim Hermiston stepped up to slam the spot kick past Barry Daines in the Spurs goal and put the tie on a knife edge.

Daines, Evans, Kinnear (Naylor), Pratt, England, Beal, Gilzean, Perryman, McGrath, Peters, Coates (Neighbour)

7 November 1973, second round, second leg

TOTTENHAM HOTSPUR 4 (5)
ABERDEEN 1 (2)

White Hart Lane *Att:* 21,785

It took a young Irish striker to settle this England v Scotland clash on a night when, according to the *Daily Mirror*'s Nigel Clarke, "Spurs showed none of the sophistication that has been a feature of their European campaigns". Chris McGrath scored two goals in nine minutes after replacing the injured Jimmy Neighbour in the 71st minute. Spurs led through a Martin Peters volley on 14 minutes, but Aberdeen's swift breaks kept them on the back foot. The visitors were unlucky to have a penalty appeal turned down, and Alex Willoughby went close with a curling shot on the half hour. Neighbour grabbed a second for Spurs, but the Dons dragged themselves back with a goal just after half-time. Cue McGrath, 18. He first turned a Cyril Knowles flick into the net, then danced through the defence to finish low under Aberdeen keeper Bobby Clark a minute from time.

Jennings, Evans, Knowles, Pratt, England, Beal, Gilzean, Perryman, Chivers, Peters, Neighbour (McGrath 2)

Ralph Coates slides in to grab the lead for Spurs at Pittodrie, but they were deprived of a win by a last-minute Aberdeen penalty

CROCK' PETERS KILLS RUSSIANS

Martin Chivers challenges for a high ball v Dinamo Tbilisi on a night when he scored a fine brace to add to his growing European tally

28 November 1973, third round, first leg

DINAMO TBILISI 1
TOTTENHAM HOTSPUR 1

Locomotiv Stadium, Tbilisi, Soviet Union
Att: 45,000

Tottenham's under-pressure band of comrades rediscovered their European mojo on this trip to what was then the Soviet Union. For John Pratt, in particular, it was a triumph as he turned in an exceptional performance to bounce back from a shocker at Wolves in the league three days earlier when he had been heckled by Spurs fans. "Terry Naylor and Steve Perryman also stood out," said the *Daily Mirror*'s Harry Miller, as Spurs delivered "on a rubble heap of a pitch deep in the heart of Georgia". Spurs went ahead on 25 minutes thanks to a 25-yard screamer from Ralph Coates's left foot. "It was the best goal I've ever scored," he told the press. Pat Jennings pulled off a string of superb saves as Tbilisi tried to hit back, and was beaten just once, 17 minutes from time. Spurs also had the vital away goal, as security.

Jennings, Evans, Knowles, Pratt, England, Beal, Naylor, Perryman, Chivers, Peters, **Coates**

12 December 1973, third round, second leg

TOTTENHAM HOTSPUR 5 (6)
DINAMO TBILISI 1 (2)

White Hart Lane *Att:* 18,602

In the event, the away goal was not needed. Instead, said *The Guardian*'s Frank Keating, "Old memories were summoned up in a glorious evening… when Tottenham Hotspur found inspiration in the clean, fair, open talents of Dinamo Tbilisi and beat them at their own attacking game". It was Chris McGrath who opened the home account, heading in after 30 minutes. Then Martin Chivers headed a second, rising perfectly to meet a high ball from Ralph Coates after another of Coates's determined runs down the wing. But Tbilisi continued to fight and pulled one back after coming close three times. In the end, it was Spurs' crossing that proved decisive. Martin Peters headed home a flick on from Mike England, then crossed for Chivers to head home. Peters then got his head to a centre from John Pratt to leave Tbilisi well beaten.

Jennings, Evans, Naylor, Pratt, England, Beal, **McGrath***, Perryman,* **Chivers 2***,* **Peters 2***, Coates*

McGRATH STUNNER
Young Chris makes it a night of glory for Spurs

19-year-old Chris McGrath makes a name for himself by opening the scoring for Spurs in Cologne, helping to secure an impressive away victory

6 March 1974, fourth round, first leg
FC COLOGNE 1
TOTTENHAM HOTSPUR 2

Müngersdorfer Stadion, Cologne, West Germany *Att:* 28,000

Spurs turned in a magnificent performance which inflicted only the second defeat in 31 European games on the home side, preserving the Londoners' own unbeaten record in that season's competition. In *The Times*, Geoffrey Green described it as "a magnificent performance of shadow boxing; of a rearguard action; and of breakaways that turned the match against the odds and the ceaseless pressure of the Germans, Tottenham's way". Chris McGrath put Spurs in front on 18 minutes, turning a Martin Chivers strike across the box in at the far post. Cologne, orchestrated by Wolfgang Overath, laid siege to the Spurs goal. Ten minutes after the break, they levelled. But Spurs stayed resolute and, with 15 minutes left, regained the lead. Terry Naylor overlapped on the right, got a pass from Ray Evans, hit the byline and centred for Martin Peters to head home.

Jennings, Evans, Naylor, Pratt, England, Beal,
***McGrath**, Perryman, Chivers, **Peters**, Dillon*

20 March 1974, fourth round, second leg
TOTTENHAM HOTSPUR 3 (5)
FC COLOGNE 0 (1)

White Hart Lane *Att:* 40,968

"These pale players of League football are inspired when they turn to the UEFA Cup," said Peter Moss in the *Daily Mail*. With over 40,000 turning up for this game, the fans knew where the magic was, but in truth it did not take much for Spurs to advance. The tie was over within the first quarter of an hour. Terry Naylor went on another of his overlapping runs and centred to Martin Chivers as the defence stood off. Big Chiv flicked the ball to a defender who, said Moss, "obligingly returned it". So Chivers slammed it home. He turned provider four minutes later, heading over for Ralph Coates to nod home. And Chivers once again put his head to good use when he set up England colleague Martin Peters for a third just after the break as Cologne's defence again played statues. With Ipswich going out, Spurs were the sole English club left in a competition English clubs had previously dominated.

Jennings, Evans, Naylor, Pratt, England, Beal,
*McGrath, Perryman, **Chivers**, **Peters**, **Coates***

Peters stars in semi-final thriller
ELEGANT SPURS SILENCE GERMANS

10 April 1974, semi-final, first leg

LOCOMOTIVE LEIPZIG 1
TOTTENHAM HOTSPUR 2

Zentralstadion, Leipzig, East Germany *Att:* 74,000

East German side Locomotive Leipzig had a reputation as a very defensive side. They had eliminated Ipswich Town on penalties in the previous round, and reached the semi-final after also putting paid to Wolverhampton Wanderers' hopes. Trips to the Eastern Bloc were always testing, and the game would be played in suffocating heat. In the circumstances, reasoned Bill Nicholson, Spurs could do only one thing – attack. Nicholson gambled on surprising the Germans by taking the play to them on their own pitch. And, as Jeff Powell reported in the *Daily Mail*: "Two goals inside half an hour were a glorious vindication of manager Bill Nicholson's plan to gamble Tottenham's UEFA Cup lives on attack." The great manager was drawing on every last ounce of his experience, this time unleashing a masterclass of offensive play after surprising in the previous visit to Germany with a tight 4-4-2 formation that closed the game down.

On 15 minutes, with a passionate crowd in full banner-waving, klaxon-blowing flow, Mike England drove forward from halfway, flighting the ball to Jimmy Neighbour who chested it down just too far away from himself to take the shot. Martin Peters stepped across him to lash a half-volley high into the net with his left foot. Ten minutes later, Ray Evans ran to the byline and crossed. Martin Chivers leapt but could not connect, leaving the ball to hit the crossbar, and there was Ralph Coates to slam home the rebound. Chivers should have had another, but the ball bounced freakishly off the post, onto the German keeper's head, and back into play. In the second half Leipzig threw themselves forward and Wolfram Lowe pulled a goal back in the 58th minute. But Spurs survived to take a healthy lead back to London.

Jennings, Evans, Naylor, Pratt, England, Beal, Neighbour, Perryman, Chivers, **Peters**, **Coates** *(Holder)*

Ralph Coates runs away in delight after securing a win on the night in Leipzig. In the background the two Martins, Chivers and Peters, are in similar celebratory mood

24 April 1974, semi-final, second leg

TOTTENHAM HOTSPUR 2 (4)
LOCOMOTIVE LEIPZIG 0 (1)

White Hart Lane *Att:* 41,280

SUPER EUFA SPURS BACK ON THE TRAIL

"Tottenham last night walked away from a season of domestic mediocrity and towards a glorious European finale," wrote Harry Miller in the *Daily Mirror*. In truth, the scale of the achievement outweighed the quality of the performance. But it did not matter. Of the 10 games played, Spurs had won eight and drawn two. They had scored 29 goals and conceded only seven. The club had travelled a road which, said Miller, "they now know better than any other side in Europe", and could look forward to a second European final in three years. If the performance "made the old Glory Glory anthem the most muted of sounds around north London", observed Miller, "the facts speak for themselves".

Tottenham opted to stay solid, with Phil Beal and Mike England the rocks at the back. Their tackling, Miller thought, "was uncharacteristically crude" but the tactic was clear – hold the line and force the Germans to push forward, at which point the space they

left could be exploited. As Leipzig's efforts to grab the goal that would get them back into the game got more frantic, those gaps began to open up. Phil Beal nearly scored with a 35-yard drive. Martin Chivers had a penalty appeal turned down, blazed over after rounding the keeper, then saw a header cleared off the line.

East German World Cup star Wolfram Lowe then spurned a great chance, opting to run round Pat Jennings instead of applying the finish. Jennings swiped the ball and the chance was gone. On 55 minutes, Chris McGrath headed home a Ralph Coates cross to net his fifth goal in five UEFA Cup games. Then, four minutes from the end, Steve Perryman ran forward and passed to Chivers, who scored with a low left-footed shot to seal the win.

Jennings, Kinnear, Naylor, Pratt (Holder), England, Beal, **McGrath***, Perryman,* **Chivers***, Peters, Coates*

Martin Chivers is on target again against Locomotive Leipzig, helping secure Spurs a place in the UEFA Cup Final for the second time in three years

21 May 1974, Final, first leg

TOTTENHAM HOTSPUR 2
FEYENOORD 2

White Hart Lane *Att*: 46,281

Spurs had got through the campaign, only coming really good in the latter stages. Between them and success stood Feyenoord. The Rotterdam club's success has often been overlooked in the light of the exploits of the Ajax total-football side, but Feyenoord had been the first Dutch club to win a major European trophy – the European Cup in 1970 – and the first to lift the world club crown, in 1971. Reigning Dutch champions, they boasted eight of the Dutch internationals who would light up the World Cup finals just months later, including the legendary Wim van Hanegem. Sure enough, the first leg at a packed and expectant White Hart Lane was a thriller and, in the *Daily Mirror*, Harry Miller observed the Dutch masters "made the teams Tottenham have beaten in previous rounds look positively pedestrian". And, he said: "they always gave the impression that anything Tottenham did, they could do better."

Below: Feyenoord forward Theo de Jong, who scored the visitors' second equaliser on the night, leaps through the Tottenham Hotspur defence

But at the start, it was all Spurs, as Nicholson's team piled on the pressure. Goalkeeper Pat Jennings did not even touch the ball for the first 20 minutes, and even then only to collect a Phil Beal backpass. On 39 minutes Spurs won a free-kick and Ray Evans shaped to take it. But Feyenoord's Danish star Jorgen Kristensen obstructed him. Evans set the ball again, only for Kristensen to obstruct again – earning himself a booking. At the third attempt, Evans managed to flight the ball across the box and in charged Mike England to head the ball down into the net. Spurs were in front.

Just four minutes later the Dutchmen were level, van Hanegem curling a beauty of a free-kick around the wall with his left foot. The gauntlet had been thrown down and Spurs grabbed it, upping the tempo still further in the second half. On the 63rd minute they regained the lead from another Evans free-kick. He chipped the ball forward and Feyenoord keeper Eddy Treytel missed it, prompting a scramble which ended with Dutch defender Joop van Daele touching the ball over the line.

The Dutch side had begun to control the game and the Spurs goal came as a real blow. But instead of seeking to press home their advantage, Spurs appeared to be settling for taking a one-goal lead to Rotterdam. Nine minutes from time Beal limped off, with Mike Dillon coming on to replace him. Three minutes later Kristensen split the Spurs defence with a superb through ball which Theo de Jong ran on to and slammed home low past Jennings.

Centre-half Mike England felt the pain more than most. He had suffered injury

Above: Mike England wheels away in celebration after opening the scoring with a header from a free-kick – but it was a night of mixed emotions for England and Spurs

Van Hanegem wipes out England lead
DUTCH MASTERS TANGLE UP SPURS

after injury in silence throughout the run, had scored one goal and been heavily involved in the second. He was utterly dejected at the final whistle.

The goal changed the complexion of the tie. Wrote Miller in the *Daily Mirror*: "Tottenham are on the brink of being pulled from the top of the European mountain they have climbed so successfully this season." To achieve victory, he said, would take "a performance pulled from their triumphant past" because Feyenoord "really are something special".

But Bill Nicholson, so often ready, according to Chivers, to see "the best teams ever in Europe when he analysed our opponents", was quick to say: "This tie is not over yet. Feyenoord are a really fine side. But they would be foolish to take anything for granted. We shall fight all the way for victory in Rotterdam next Wednesday." Events off the pitch, however, would overshadow the return.

Jennings, Evans, Naylor, Pratt, **England**, *Beal (Dillon), McGrath, Perryman, Chivers, Peters, Coates* [van Deele og]

29 May 1974, Final, second leg

FEYENOORD 2 (4)
TOTTENHAM HOTSPUR 0 (2)

Feyenoord Stadium, Rotterdam, Netherlands
Att: 62,988

There was some excellent football played by both sides in the second leg. Unfortunately, this game will not be remembered for that, but for one of the worst nights of violence ever witnessed in a European football stadium. The *Daily Mail*'s Brian Scovell said: "In 14 years of reporting football in Europe, I have never seen anything like it. Hundreds of Dutch fans were bombarded by bottles, banners and broken chairs." In the *Daily Mirror*, Harry Miller said: "The huge gaps on the terraces bear testimony to the carnage caused by Tottenham's rioting supporters."

And yet before the game, remembers Martin Chivers, "there was not a hint of what was to come". Despite their worries – Phil Beal played with his left ankle heavily strapped, Ray Evans had a bruised instep, while Ralph Coates's thoughts were with his five-year-old daughter who was in hospital with a ruptured appendix – Spurs started brightly. Martin Peters worked a free-kick routine to send the ball over the Dutch wall. Steve Perryman peeled off the end of the wall and sent a right-footed shot scudding just wide of the post. Spurs pushed on and Chris McGrath scored – only for the goal to be disallowed. "To this day I don't know why the ref didn't give it," says Chivers. The tension was rising. Then Feyenoord scored, just three minutes before the break. Peter Ressel set up Wim Rijsbergen, who powered a shot through the ranks of Spurs defenders and into the goal.

Before Spurs had time to regroup, the players noticed trouble on the terraces.

Right: Spurs' Mike England in an aerial duel during the ill-fated UEFA Cup Final second leg in Rotterdam

Below: The team line-ups as printed in the match programme

Far right: Wearing a swapped Spurs shirt is Feyenoord's Mladen Ramljek, with the trophy Spurs had so wanted to reclaim

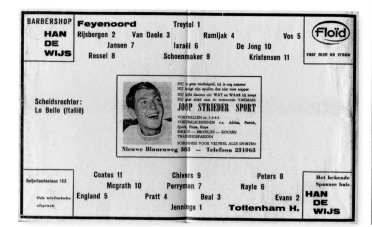

Smoke and flames could be seen from one part of the ground. "I looked up," says Chivers, "and saw one person hanging off the stand and behind him seats being thrown into the air like missiles, some of them on fire."

Spurs had created more chances in the first half than their opponents. Peters had headed just wide twice. Half-time was the chance to regroup and for Bill Nicholson to provide that last talk urging his players on.

But Nicholson was out on the pitch with a megaphone trying to calm the fans. The radio commentary described him standing there amid the carnage, pleading "Stop the violence, please stop the violence." But to no avail. The rioting continued. Nicholson could not give his team talk. His players were worried about their families in the stands. It was no way to take the field for the climax of a major final.

As Spurs came back out for the second half, the crowd booed them. Chants of "British go home" were heard. Peters, the skipper for the night, tried to placate the crowd. They shouted him down. The mood was ugly, the sound of screams and breaking glass swirled across the pitch, the smoke from the fires in the stands drifted across the pitch. Despite all this, the team managed what Scovell described as "a gallant performance" amid the mayhem of the second half. But to no avail. Seven minutes from the end Reseel scored the goal that secured the cup for Feyenoord. The six-year dominance of English clubs in the

UEFA Cup, and its predecessor the Fairs Cup, had been broken.

Spurs had lost the first major final in their history. But the club lost more than just a competition. Their reputation was tarnished, and their manager – a true legend of the game – had lost his love of football. "I remember him looking sadly out of the window of the coach back to our hotel and saying, 'What have they done to my game?'" says Chivers.

Jennings, Evans, Naylor, Pratt (Holder), England, Beal, McGrath, Perryman, Chivers, Peters, Coates

Spurs fans battle with police

POST-MATCH **REACTION**

Unfortunately all the headlines were dominated by the repercussions of the riots in Rotterdam. Spurs received a European ban but it never came into effect. Bill Nicholson retired a few games into the 1974/75 season, the team declined under his successor Terry Neill and Keith Burkinshaw was unable to prevent the club from being relegated to Division Two in 1977. European football seemed a world away and another decade had begun before the glory nights would return.

LOOKING BACK WITH
BILL NICHOLSON

Bill Nicholson's love of European football was crushed that night in Rotterdam's Feyenoord Stadion. The arena was all-but wrecked by hooligans as Tottenham slumped to their UEFA Cup Final defeat. A man who had put so much effort into the game was sickened by the sights that were to be repeated all too often during the next 10 years. Nicholson's daughter was in the near-63,000 crowd that night. It was a night he never forgot.

He stood in the police room under the Feyenoord stadium making appeal after appeal for the crowd to behave. Each appeal was ignored. His team were sitting stunned throughout half-time in the nearby visitors' dressing room.

Nicholson later recalled: "We had such a good relationship with the Feyenoord club. The stadium, such a lovely place, was just smashed to pieces. It proved to football that there is a certain section who, if hell bent on trouble, will cause trouble. It is something that has been proved all too regularly since those days.

"I cannot understand why people should do such things. I don't know why they don't respect law and order. In the old days we had a respect for that sort of thing. But that night in Rotterdam was so bad. I don't think I have ever seen anything like it. I remember the days of battles during the depression but this was much worse.

"My daughter went over on the boat and coach and said that the fans were so drunk they had to lock themselves in the cabin. There was so much drinking going on and there was so much trouble.

"We knew nothing of what might happen while we were preparing for the match. It was never an excuse for our defeat, but they were not ideal conditions in which to play a match.

"It showed the controls that were needed for fans travelling away and what could happen if things went wrong. You have to be aware of what might happen. I still cannot forget the scenes of the seats spinning down the stands. It was fortunate a lot more people did not get hurt."

A devastated Bill Nicholson and his wife, Darkie, arrive back in the UK after the club's ill-fated trip to the Netherlands in May 1974

LOOKING BACK WITH
JOHN PRATT

John Pratt remembered Bill Nicholson walking into the Spurs dressing room in the bowels of Feyenoord Stadium, screwing up his coat and hurling it in the corner.

"He just said: 'They are tearing the place to pieces'," said Pratt. "He stormed out and we never saw him again.

"The immediate reaction of the players was to worry if their families were alright. I had my mother, father, mother-in-law and wife out there for the match. We wondered where they were in the ground and if the trouble was near them.

"When we left the dressing room for the second half we spent most of our time looking around the stands to try and catch a glimpse of our families.

"It was no way to play a football match – not one as important as a European final. We could see the seats coming down the stands. No one could concentrate."

Pratt was convinced that without the intervention of the Tottenham hordes Spurs could have won the match and the UEFA Cup.

"We were only a goal down at half-time,

we had created some clear-cut chances and Chris McGrath had even had a goal disallowed. We were confident that we could come back and tie the game up. We just needed a good talking to and some new thoughts and you never know."

The team never got those words of encouragement and inspiration from Nicholson that they needed. "Instead there were a stream of police and stadium officials coming to the dressing room," continued Pratt, "and Bill was dragged away to make his appeal. It was terrible."

Spurs went on to lose the game and the cup. Next day Pratt recalled: "It was a day off. We were supposed to be with our families and take a stroll through Rotterdam. You just couldn't open your mouth. You were ashamed to be English. We just wanted to keep our heads down and get out as quickly as possible. I just wanted to crawl into a hole and die."

Bill Nicholson consoles John Pratt after the match in Rotterdam. Martin Peters (right) also reflects on a terrible night for the club

IN CONVERSATION WITH
MARTIN CHIVERS & PHIL BEAL

Bill Nicholson's third trophy-winning side was one that re-established the club's reputation in Europe. In a remarkable period between 1972 and 1974, Spurs reached two European finals and a semi-final – rekindling the glory nights flame in the hotly contested environment of the UEFA Cup.

Two of the key protagonists of that era made their mark with outstanding displays and each with 30 appearances or more: Phil Beal, a reliable defensive rock, and Martin Chivers, who set a record as Tottenham's top European goalscorer.

Spurs had a superb level of consistency over those three seasons. What lay behind that success?

Martin Chivers When you look round that team it was as good as anything. It was a strong unit. Almost everyone was an international. Skill-wise we could match most teams. We had two great full-backs in Cyril Knowles and Joe Kinnear. People talk about overlapping full-backs – I think they were two of the first. In Mike England we had one of the best centre-halves who was powerful in the air and very skilful for a centre-half; Phil Beal read the game as well as anybody and would have played for England if Bobby Moore hadn't been in the way.

Phil Beal A lot of people have said that to me. That's just one of those things. No one can take away how good Bobby was. I just got on with what I had to do for Tottenham.

MC Pat Jennings was worth a goal every game; we relied on him and he never failed. Then we had the midfield of Stevie Perryman, Alan Mullery and Martin Peters – I think there's enough skill amongst those three to match anybody – and up front unbelievably skilful Alan Gilzean, who was the perfect foil for me, and Ralphie [Coates] who never stopped running and scored some important goals.

What about Chiv, Phil?

PB Chivvo was a top, top goalscorer. He wasn't hard as such but strong. There were times we had to keep on at him. And it would work! But we had a good team spirit. Bill Nick expected that. I was brought up in the Dave Mackay era. He would train with the youngsters when the first team had finished training. Well, it didn't matter if you were 15 years old or 30: if you were on Dave Mackay's side in a five-a-side game you had to win [laughs]. It was part of the Spurs team spirit and why we got on so well.

MC The camaraderie of the players was second to none. That's why we became such a good family. Most of the players played eight years at the club, many had testimonials. There was loyalty at the club. We stuck together and were as a good as any team partly because we were so close.

PB We had a great side together for a long time, between eight and 10 years, as Chiv said. We just knew everybody completely and were organised, and knew what to do. Bill Nicholson had us off to a fine art. Everyone knew where to go for corners, free-kicks, even Pat – he was told to kick the ball out to a certain area.

MC We practised free-kicks till we were blue in the face at Cheshunt.

Europe and Spurs were a good fit?

MC I loved European football, not because I was strong. It was because we had a go at teams when we played away, and I was in a very strong team. I was the fortunate one to get the accolades by scoring goals.

You're being modest.

MC It suited me. I wasn't an out-and-out physical player, I was very strong but I wasn't a typical English centre-forward who used to put his weight about and knock people about, I feel I had a better touch than [that type of]

player and we literally played good football right the way through.

Europe suited us down to a tee. Don't forget we were a very successful cup team in domestic competition. I just think we were better suited to cup rather than league football, which was a disappointment as we were good enough to beat anyone on our day. We played 60 games and more a season, and as a result the league tended to take second place because we just couldn't turn it on every week. We won the UEFA Cup with 16 players – teams these days have a squad of 16 for just one game. If you look at the appearances, over three years a good half a dozen of us played in 30-odd games in Europe.

How meticulous was Bill in his preparation?

MC He and Eddie Baily did the homework like nobody else could; they were so thorough to the point that Eddie would be sent away on his own on occasion to far-flung locations. He came back with all the info, and would often say, "I've seen the best team in Europe." That happened three or four times and I thought, "Well, who the hell have we got to beat, then?" It was their way to keep us on our toes to ensure we weren't going to relax.

"WE ALWAYS FELT IT WAS SPECIAL TO PLAY IN EUROPEAN GAMES. WE ALL LOVED PLAYING IN WHITE, IT WAS A BIG THING. IT DID MAKE IT SPECIAL – IT JUST SEEMED TO MAKE IT DIFFERENT PLAYING IN EUROPE THAN IN DIVISION ONE"
PHIL BEAL

MARTIN CHIVERS
Spurs career:
367 apps 174 goals
Europe:
32 apps 22 goals
European honours:
UEFA Cup
Winner 1972

PHIL BEAL
Spurs career:
420 apps 1 goal
Europe:
30 apps 0 goals
European honours:
UEFA Cup
Winner 1972

PB You could never be too complacent because you thought you were playing the European champions every game. Bill was so thorough. Teams would be watched three times, Bill would then do a dossier on the opposition, from goalkeeper down to the subs, on what they could do – whether they had a good left foot or not, if they liked to come inside. Bill would give you a sheet a couple of days before and list the strengths and weaknesses of every single player. We used to have a little giggle about it, but I would read it and it did help. And I know the other players did as well.

It's a common assumption that players don't like too much information, though?

PB Bill made us understand. I think it was a way of thinking that no matter who you play, take nothing for granted. It's still relevant today. Bill didn't want us to go out and think it was going to be easy. It would be the same for every game, whether we were playing Keflavik or AC Milan.

MC We had comprehensive team meetings. They didn't put pressure on us right before the game or on the day, but we certainly had a lot of info to take in. He'd have lots of photos. They would tell us specifics – for me for example they would say one centre-half would play tight, the other would sweep and lay-off, whether they came up for corners, were physical, were one-footed or not, good in the air, slow etc.

So foreign opposition presented different challenges and you adapted how you played?

MC There was a team over here that played a sweeper and that was Carlisle, believe it or not. Stan Ternent played it; Bill would tell me to go and press on the sweeper. It was something we could deal with. I had to occupy two in the middle because we would have Gilly

on the right-hand side and Ralph on the left, and rather than have one sweeping behind you – which is hard to break down – I would push on to the deepest man – and it did upset them a bit.

PB Foreign teams very rarely hit the long ball, it was all short passing. A lot of sides had their own nationals. You played Cologne and AC Milan and most were German, most were Italian. I thought even then their control was perfect. They kicked a ball to feet and it stayed, none of this two touches to get the ball under control. It was all one touch and that stands true today, it's how they've been brought up.

Phil, did your role change – you became almost a sweeper?

PB My position, especially away from home, was that I covered the two full-backs and Mike England, and anything that went beyond the midfield player coming deep in our half, I would pick up because I was the spare man. We just made sure that I covered Mike, Cyril and Joe. Depending on the game, when we had a lone striker up front, Bill would tell Chiv to close them down.

MC All the continental teams used to drop back and let you play in your own half. We would have long team talks about how far up the field we were going to try and win the ball back from them. They would expect us to do what other continental teams did and drop back to the halfway line when they had the ball. Instead we concentrated on how to win the ball back as soon as possible.

That might seem like a small thing, but it was successful. Alan Gilzean, myself and Ralph pressed them in their own half. We actually frightened teams by trying to win the ball the ball back in their half and very often scored important away goals. We all know how important that is. I don't think there

were many games where we went away and didn't score goals.

What was it like to travel abroad in those days?

MC I hate flying! I think I've cracked it now, I've got to the grand age when you don't worry about things so much. But then I wasn't a good flyer and neither was Ralph. For one game Bill took us on a Tuesday by turboprop, a Vanguard or something. It wasn't a calm day, a bumpy flight. I was scared stiff. When we got there I was absolutely shattered; I spoke to Bill and from then on we travelled on a Monday.

The travelling was very well organised by the club. The press would fly with us and they were good as gold. You could talk to the press in those days without them being under pressure to write something stupid about you. They were the old brigade, you could confide in one another, but they wouldn't write anything without permission.

We were fortunate to have wonderful fans travelling with us. We had some of the best fans in the country and still do now. Fans would be in the hotel in advance of us and I don't know how they got to some of these places; they made us feel we were with a travelling army. It made a real difference, knowing that people had made such an effort, were so dedicated and wanted to follow you, it was brilliant.

What effect did travelling abroad have on the team?

MC You build up relationships with people knowing what you want on the football field. Martin Peters didn't have to look up for me running into the near post for a free-kick, he *knew* I was going there. And I knew when he was going to kick the ball. I roomed with Ralph Coates at Spurs. I tried rooming with various people but no one could suffer my snoring;

IN CONVERSATION WITH
MARTIN CHIVERS & PHIL BEAL

only Ralph could and he put up with it for four years. He must have been a bit deaf. [laughter]

What's the dynamic to that? How do pairings work out?
MC I met Ralphie when he came down from Burnley. He was in the England squad, he moved to a house near me, and we became very good friends. Everyone tended to link up with someone they got on well with, but one of the strangest arrangements was for young Stevie [Perryman]. Bill put him in with Alan Gilzean. We all thought, "Blimey, what are you doing, condemning him to room with Gilly!" [laughs] But it worked. It was wonderful.
PB I was with Mike England more or less all the time. We just hit it off and became friends.

There were some real characters in that team, and a few pranks played?
PB I used to do a lot. We played Vitoria Setubal and were having lunch the day before the game. I chose Dover Sole on the bone. There was a telephone call for me; when I came back Cyril and Pat said, "It's OK Phil, they've kept your meal warm by putting one of those hot plates over it." I lifted the lid and all that was left was the bones, head and tail. [laughs]

I'm not one for letting that slip. I had to get my own back. So, that afternoon I went down to the harbour for a walk with Chiv, Martin and Stevie. There was a bloke selling fish, including heads for stock. So I bought four fish heads. We went back to the hotel, and I got the key to Cyril and Pat's room. I crept in and put the heads under Cyril's pillow. The next morning Pat came down and said, "Cor, there's a horrible stink in our room." I'd got my own back. [laughs]

Any new player, didn't matter who it was, when we went away we'd get all the players in a room apart from the new man who would get a phone call in his room from me pretending to be from the press. I kept a straight voice and tried not to laugh while the others would be putting pillows over their mouths to stifle their laughs. I'd ask the new

player what it was like at Spurs, who'd been supportive, this and that. I got Martin Peters, Chivvo, Ralphie, all the new ones!

I would buy stuff from joke shops. I got Pat once with a fake mustard jar on the table at a pre-match meal. Pat asked someone to pass the mustard and of course when he opened it a great big snake springs out. Stupid games, it was like being at school, but we knew when to have a laugh and when to be serious. It was good for camaraderie.

We haven't seen Alan Gilzean for years, since he left. At [a] Fulham game recently, Pat was on the phone and said, "It's Alan Gilzean." I spoke to him and he said, "Are you still taking the mick?" [laughter]

It was serious stuff when the campaign started in 1971, though. You had a convincing win against Keflavik and then a very tight tie with Nantes?
MC In the dressing room afterwards there was a very heated argument between Bill and Eddie, myself, Cyril, and others. We can talk about it now, but at the time those things never came out of the dressing room; thankfully we kept it in-house. But we felt very

passionate about our game and Bill was saying we didn't try hard enough, we were pathetic. We said, "Wait a minute, you said Nantes were a bad team" – and they weren't, they were very useful.
PB I think it was a time when Bill wanted the players to give their view and be constructive as to what players weren't doing and should be doing. A few points were picked out, people gave their opinion and pointed the finger. It did work – it made us better for it.
MC It probably did us the world of good to have that kind of game and clear the air, it's always best. If things are annoying people and you're not playing well together it sharpens you up and maybe that was the wake-up call we needed to go into the next round.

There were the two ties in Romania – how contrasting an experience was that?
MC [laughs] It was chalk and cheese to go from Nantes to Bucharest. The first match [against Rapid] was the most physical game I think I ever played in, to the point that eight of us finished up on the treatment table at the end of game. A very volatile crowd – thankfully they had a running track so they weren't close to us. We won and Bill got on the coach and said, "I'd like to congratulate all you players for keeping your cool and not getting into big trouble because you were intimidated like I've never seen a team intimidated." Alan [Gilzean] was literally kicked off the field by half-time, I was set upon – we all were.
PB Rapid was terrible. The game was horrendous. We kicked off about 4pm and got kicked all over the place. Jimmy Pearce came on as sub and was sent off after five minutes; Martin Peters took a penalty and the keeper was three or four yards away from him. The ref had no control; it was the dirtiest game I've ever played in. It showed we were no pushovers though.
MC Sods law, the next round we get a Romanian team again in Arad.

Fortunately they weren't as strong and physical as Rapid.

Playing in the Eastern Bloc must have been different?

MC I think the only place to go was the cinema, which I think a few of us did – though we couldn't understand a word of it. Bucharest was one of those places where you never went out at night.

PB When we played Dinamo Tibilisi [in 1973], to go there in those days, no one dreamed of it. We had about 10,000 watching us train, we couldn't believe it. We played well out there. But it was so, so cold – it was the first time Bill Nick said, "Does anybody want to wear mittens?" I know Chiv did [laughs]. It was a long old trip as well, to Moscow, then down to Tibilisi. Whenever we stepped out of the hotel for a walk you had people following you. When you went to your room you had to give your key to a woman who sat by the lift. It was like being in a spy movie. It was strange, not what we were used to, but a great experience.

In 1972 you met AC Milan in an epic semi-final.

MC We thought it would be sod's law and we'd get Wolves but no, we got AC Milan, Wolves get Ferencvaros. To go 1-0 down in the first leg against Milan with Benetti scoring after half an hour was a hammer blow. Pat Jennings had no chance with the shot. We thought hello, the writing's on the wall, but then of all the people to turn up with two very important goals it was Stevie Perryman. He didn't score often but they were vital. It was wonderful, absolutely fantastic.

The meeting out there was quite something, in front of a very hostile crowd?

MC We went out to inspect the pitch. We walked out near the halfway line and then all of a sudden these firecrackers started falling all around us. They were literally bombarding us.

PB An iron bar was chucked onto the pitch.

Martin Chivers in action v AC Milan, 1972

"THE SAN SIRO WAS THE MOST VOLATILE PLACE I'D EVER PLAYED AT. WE GOT THAT ALL-IMPORTANT AWAY GOAL WHEN ALAN MULLERY SMACKED IT INTO THE TOP CORNER. I'VE NEVER KNOWN 69,000 FANS SO QUIET"
MARTIN CHIVERS

But the stadium and atmosphere was brilliant.
MC It was probably the most volatile place I'd ever played at. We got that all-important away goal when Alan Mullery smacked it into the top corner. I've never known 69,000 fans so quiet. What a start. Alan had come back from loan at Fulham. We were short and we needed him back, and what a goal.

We held out for the rest of game; there were punch-ups, Alan Gilzean was injured I was meant to play up front with Martin Peters but from the first two minutes he was in our half and not in theirs. I was the Lone Ranger up front. I could have scored one, I missed just past the post which, if it had gone in, would have put it to bed before they scored a penalty. It was like the battle of the Alamo for the last 10 minutes.

Did their style present a different challenge – the infamous catenaccio system?

MC Italian football in those days was different. They used to gouge you, spit, pinch, pull your shirt – everything went on. It was just something we weren't used to. You only had to retaliate and you'd be off. They tried every trick in the book. Phil went down with one of their players and was nearly sent off.

PB I got into trouble with Benetti. We went into a tackle and went on to the floor. As we got up he spat in my face from a yard. Out of instinct I threw a punch. It was just a touch on the face really, but you can't condone it. His lip went into his tooth and there was a little bit of blood and he went on the floor. Mike said, "You better stay on the floor as well, Bealey, hold your ankle". The play was going on up the other end, but the ref saw there were two players down, stopped the game, came up to me and Benetti and booked both of us. But he booked the two wrong players – No.6 of AC and No.8 of Spurs, Stevie P. Nowadays with TV I'd have been banned for four months!

We won through, but the Italians could not accept it and after the game were rocking our coach outside the ground with us in it. A brick was thrown at the window and smashed it. Bill got off and told the police to give us an escort straight away.

The final was against Wolves. How did it feel to be playing an English side in a European competition?

PB It was a little bit strange because you expect to play a continental team.

MC The club had promised our so-called WAGs – who were usually lucky to get a cup of tea in the car park standing in the pouring rain – an all-expenses paid away trip if we reached the final. So they start thinking of Paris, Madrid, Rome and who do we get? Wolverhampton Wanderers! [laughs] They couldn't believe it; I think only half of them took up the offer.

PB The first leg was when Chivvo really showed the power in his shooting. He had a

IN CONVERSATION WITH
MARTIN CHIVERS & PHIL BEAL

tremendous shot on him. Alan Mullery and Chiv watched the game on DVD the other month and Mullers said I was man of the match! Well, I don't remember that [laughs]. But Chiv's goals got us the cup.

MC I speak to so many people even to this day who talk about the winning goal. It was the hardest shot I ever hit. Fans tell me they were behind the goal that night. I have to shake their hand because I've shaken about 3,000 people's hands – everybody was there [laughs]. I just feel they are part of me.

Mullery made an overlap to receive the ball and was just about to give me a rollocking for not passing when I let fly, and then he jumped all over me. It was a shot out of the blue. There were only a couple of minutes to go, I thought, "I've got nothing to lose". It met my instep and when you hit the ball like that you know where it's going.

Where does winning the trophy rank?

MC At the top. For the home leg, thankfully Mullers scored that all important goal, knocking himself out in the process and we relaxed a bit. We struggled badly in the second half to the point that we were looking round the dressing room with the cup and champagne in our hands and Bill wasn't there. We were wondering where he was when he came in and said, "I'd just like to let you lot know that I've been in the Wolves dressing room telling them that the best team lost." How honest can you get?

PB Typical of Bill.

MC You can imagine what we said to him! "Have a drink of this, Bill." And he did, and then relaxed.

PB It was brilliant. I still think the semi-final was the best game. They had a top team.

How tough was the UEFA Cup as a competition?

MC Bill would say, "Don't forget you fellas, these teams that are in the UEFA Cup are the top teams" – only one went into the European Cup so the teams in UEFA were those that

finished second, third, fourth in their leagues, or won the [domestic] cup. Generally they were the sides who would win or have the chance to win their league the following year. Therefore every game was a strong game. There were 64 teams and it was a knockout, not a league like now, so you couldn't afford to make a mistake in one game, you had to be on your mettle right from the off.

PB The UEFA Cup was strong – you played some really top sides. I don't agree with it now with the Europa League and teams dropping down into it from Champions League. But back then there were some very good teams.

You were a good side also, to the point that Spurs almost retained the trophy the next season. There were some tough games in that run as well, Setubal for example?

MC We were 2-1 down on aggregate, with Torres running us ragged. There was a free-kick about 10 minutes from time. I would take them from outside the box; I hadn't had a very good game, they had been attacking all the time. I just smacked the ball and, well, it was like Moses and the parting of the waves. The wall just separated and it went right through into the top corner of the net.

On the coach back to the airport, Joe Kinnear was winding Bill up. Bill was sitting just in front of me. Joe, being the joker he is, was saying, "Well Chiv, I suppose you'll make the headlines again: 'Chivers Saves Spurs Again'". You could see steam coming

> **"FANS TELL ME THEY WERE BEHIND THE GOAL THAT NIGHT AT MOLINEUX. I'VE SHAKEN ABOUT 3,000 PEOPLE'S HANDS – EVERYBODY WAS THERE. I JUST FEEL THEY ARE PART OF ME"**
> MARTIN CHIVERS

out of Bill's ears. Suddenly Bill took the bait and flipped. He stood up, turned round to everybody and said, "That won't be the bloody headline if I've got anything to do with it!" I'm sat just behind him and I thought, "Oh, thanks Bill!' [laughs]. They wound him up so much.

How close did you come to beating Liverpool in the semi-final?

PB We should have gone through, we played that well.

MC It was always a torrid affair playing against them in the Seventies, they were such a strong team. We had chances we didn't convert and they got that vital away goal which got them through.

The next season of course, you came very close again. Did it feel like it was the last hurrah for that side?

MC We still felt strong. Legs were getting a bit tired, Gilly, perhaps, Mike England as well dare I say, was struggling with his legs. Ten years of football at Tottenham had incurred wear and tear. One or two others were struggling. We'd lost Alan Mullery who was hard to replace. Thankfully we had Pat, Mike, Phil, the two full-backs, but it wasn't quite the same team, we were tailing off a bit. But in Europe we did fine and reached the final again. We played some tough teams that campaign.

PB Tbilisi were a good side, so were Cologne and Leipzig. In the home leg of the final, Feyenoord had a free-kick just outside the penalty box and van Hanegem took it and curled it round the wall into the top corner. I still think Pat was lining up the wall and not ready. The game was evenly balanced 2-2 at home. We scored a disallowed goal on 20 minutes and that's when the trouble started.

As a pro trying to concentrate on your game that must have been hard seeing what was going on in the crowd?

MC It was impossible. You don't hear the fans normally – as soon as that whistle goes you switch off. But when you've got fires,

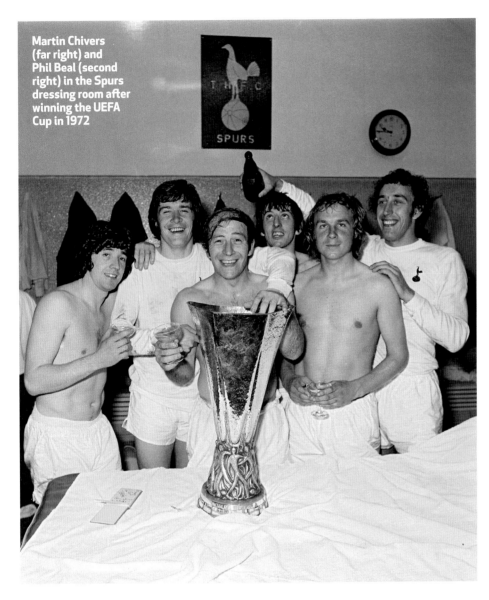

Martin Chivers (far right) and Phil Beal (second right) in the Spurs dressing room after winning the UEFA Cup in 1972

people hanging off the stands, seats flying around everywhere and you know there's a disturbance going on, it's very difficult not to look up and see what's going on.

Did you have family and friends in the ground?

MC My wife was in the hospitality area with the other wives. She was lucky to be undercover. Glasses were being thrown down from above. The glass was breaking on the ceiling and shattering in front of her. She was one of the few wives who stayed outside, the others went indoors. She said it was horrific at half-time.

PB We could see what was happening, with a great big gap opening up. There was no

team meeting at half-time, Bill went on the PA to ask fans to calm down. A lot of players lost concentration after that – it ruined the final. You don't know what's gone on, if there are injuries, even fatalities. It wouldn't have surprised me if they had called the game off.

MC I can always remember the words of Bill Nick. "What have they done to my game?" He couldn't get over it, he really couldn't. I've been away with Spurs for many years now. I can't say our fans caused that trouble, I didn't know what happened. I only know that on occasion, if you treat people like animals they are going to act like animals. I'm not sure whether our boys instigated it or the security. But it was the beginning of the hooligan element in football, and that contributed to Bill resigning.

What was the atmosphere like at the club the season after?

MC Deadly. Some think I instigated Bill leaving. That was a lot of rubbish. It just happened to be at a time when my contract was being renewed. But Bill thought they had killed his game to a point.

The three-year spell in the UEFA ended on a low, but it was a magnificent period for the club as a whole.

PB You played different players, people you didn't really know. It showed you how good you were. A real test against the best players in Europe and I enjoyed every single minute of it – we all did, because that's what you played for. We always felt it was special to play in European games. We all loved playing in white, it was a big thing. It did make it special – it just seemed to make it completely different playing in Europe than in Division One.

MC To go out under lights wearing it was something special. It contributed to the best atmosphere we had at the club.

Martin, how proud does it make you to be the club's top scorer in Europe?

MC I've got a wonderful record in Europe and I will treasure it for the rest of my life.

And what of the modern generation and their exploits?

PB They did really well in the Champions League and played some very good sides. It was a great experience – everybody wants to play in Europe.

MC That campaign was very exciting. We've had a sample of it and we want it back again. I loved it. It just showed you that we can match teams at the highest level. At one time [in the 2010/11 season] all the old players who work at the club – Cliff Jones, Alan Mullery, Martin Peters, myself, Pat, Phil – we all said, "We're playing the best football we've ever seen at this club." Up until Christmas that was the best run of football that I've seen at Spurs.

1970s AWAY DAYS
IN PICTURES

Local agency Carleton Photographic were Spurs' official club photographers from 1971 to 1979. It was their job to shoot match action for the club programme, the annual team photos, new signing portraits and club functions. Spurs went on 17 European away trips during their three UEFA Cup campaigns between 1971 and 1974. Carleton travelled with the team, capturing the unique flavour of European travel and spending time with the players as they relaxed before and after games.

One of the highlights of the 1970s was the visit to Milan in April 1972. Cyril Knowles (above) is the Spurs player in the cockpit of the plane to Italy – a photo set-up that was a particular favourite of the club programme at the time. In the San Siro, Spurs were greeted by a hostile crowd of 68,000 (left). Carleton also had unique access to the team's hotels, pre-match preparations, tourist outings and occasionally to football's inner sanctum, the changing room itself.

After Carleton ceased working for the club many of these photos went into storage and have been unearthed and printed here for first time in 40 years. They provide a rare and illuminating insight into the club during a fascinating period, when travelling abroad was no small undertaking and opponents' stadiums and pitches could be virtually unknown before arrival. So, follow Spurs into Europe in the Seventies, once again.

1970s AWAY DAYS
IN PICTURES

This page: Spurs players unwind in the dressing room in Leipzig after the match in April 1974, Terry Naylor is the player receiving a debrief from coach Eddie Baily; Spurs players Phil Holder, Alan Gilzean, Cyril Knowles, Mike Dillon and Steve Perryman pose for a photo in front of the Acropolis in Athens, November 1972. Facing page: Alan Mullery and the squad enjoy a game of golf in Italy prior to the AC Milan game in 1972; a team photo outside the Grasshoppers' stadium in Zurich in September 1973; Mike England is the moustachioed Spurs player surveying the scene in the imposing Red Star Stadium in Belgrade where a crowd of 70,000 attended the match in December 1972.

1970s AWAY DAYS
IN PICTURES

This page: Cyril Knowles, sitting far right, and his team-mates at the dinner table in Tblisi, then part of the Soviet Union, in November 1973; Pat Jennings strolls out with the Spurs team as they inspect the pitch and sample the atmosphere prior to the game v UT Arad in Romania, March 1972.

Facing page: Martin Peters leads the team out through the ornamental pots at Rapid Bucharest's stadium in December 1971; Mike England holds up a fresh catch at a fish market in Setubal, Portugal, in March 1973 – it wasn't the last time fish were to rear their heads on the trip (see p110); the Spurs squad board the plane to Leipzig for what turned out to be Spurs' penultimate European trip of the decade in April 1974.

The 1980s

It had only been seven years since Spurs had last qualified for European competition, but it felt like another age. Much had changed, and not just for Tottenham Hotspur.

In the interim Spurs had succumbed to the heartbreaking disappointment of relegation as the Nicholson era receded into history. Following such a legend proved difficult for his successors as the club struggled to revive fortunes, and after a succession of near misses Spurs finally dropped down in 1977. In time relegation came to be viewed as a necessary chance to regroup and rebuild. The board admirably persisted with former coach Keith Burkinshaw, and after immediate promotion and three seasons of development the new Spurs were back in the big time, winning trophies and returning to the European stage.

Only Steve Perryman survived from the line-up who played in Tottenham's last foreign forays. Indeed the man who would forever be known by his team-mates as "Skip" had become permanent captain – the on-field deputy for Burkinshaw as the Yorkshireman assembled one of the club's best-ever sides.

Glenn Hoddle was the new superstar, the most gifted Englishman of his generation. A lethal strike pairing of Steve Archibald and Garth Crooks had given Spurs a potent goalscoring edge they had not enjoyed since Greaves and Gilzean. Home-grown talents like Paul Miller and Chris Hughton were complemented by the likes of Tony Galvin and Graham Roberts, plucked from non-league football and with a clear hunger to succeed.

Most eye-catching of all was the addition of exotic South American flair. When Burkinshaw signed the Argentinian World Cup-winning duo of Osvaldo Ardiles and Ricardo Villa in the summer of 1978, it was a landmark in not just Tottenham's history but that of the English game. "Spurs Scoop The World" ran the famous *Daily Express* headline. Domestic football would never be quite the same, as the signings tackled English isolationism head on. England was now part of the international football market, and Ardiles and Villa's arrival was a precursor to the modern age of the Premier League.

Back in the early 1980s, Tottenham's blend of traditional and innovative was a delight to watch. The team won the 1981 FA Cup Final in glorious Tottenham style. Ricky Villa's epic winning goal became one of the competition's most cherished moments and at the time embodied the new swaggering Spurs: daring, ambitious, entertaining and distinct.

Off the pitch, things were different, too. Spurs were poised to become a PLC. A harder, more commercial approach was taking hold as a number of clubs sought to become leisure enterprises, partly in response to the continuing menace of hooliganism that was having a terrible drain on attendances.

Spurs embarked on new European adventures at a time when British sides were utterly dominant, with Liverpool, Nottingham Forest and Aston Villa monopolising the European cup for six years in succession. In comparison with Spurs teams of the past and their home rivals, the new Tottenham had a lot to live up to, but they entered the fray with an exciting and confident young side that would provide some of the finest moments in the club's history.

Left to right: Mark Falco celebrates scoring on his home European debut v Ajax in 1981; Graham Roberts lifts the UEFA Cup on an emotional night at White Hart Lane in 1984; Glenn Hoddle turns on the style v Feyenoord in 1983

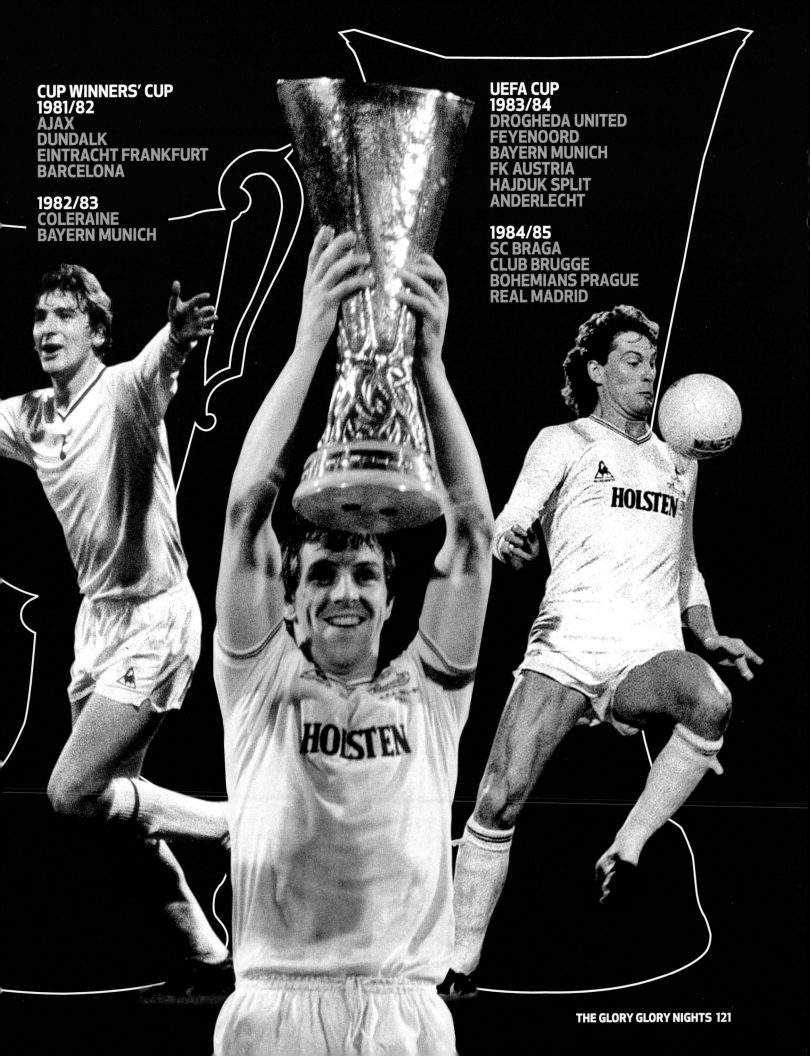

CUP WINNERS' CUP
1981/82
AJAX
DUNDALK
EINTRACHT FRANKFURT
BARCELONA

1982/83
COLERAINE
BAYERN MUNICH

UEFA CUP
1983/84
DROGHEDA UNITED
FEYENOORD
BAYERN MUNICH
FK AUSTRIA
HAJDUK SPLIT
ANDERLECHT

1984/85
SC BRAGA
CLUB BRUGGE
BOHEMIANS PRAGUE
REAL MADRID

F.A. CUP FINAL
WEMBLEY 1981

THE ROAD TO EUROPE

1981

Tottenham's passport back into Europe came courtesy of one of the most famous matches in the club's history. League form had been modest since Spurs were promoted to Division One in 1978, with finishes of 11th, 14th and 10th, but the momentum to challenge for honours was building thanks to strong cup runs. The potential was finally realised at Wembley for the 100th FA Cup Final. Tottenham's name appeared to be on the trophy – they had won a semi-final replay at Highbury of all places – and they went into the meeting with Manchester City as clear favourites. City's negative tactics almost spoilt the script, but a late equalising own goal for Spurs sent the final to a replay.

Floodlit games on balmy nights always had an appeal for the north Londoners and the team were inspired by the occasion, winning one of the best FA Cup Finals ever with the kind of football that was garnering widespread praise. City's second-half penalty appeared to have shattered "Ossie's dream", the phrase that had embodied the contest once Ardiles had made plain his desire to earn an FA Cup winners' medal. But an equaliser from Crooks and then Villa's mazy, mesmerising run won the cup and entry back into Europe.

Glenn Hoddle and
Ricky Villa parade
the trophy after
the famous FA Cup
Final replay win
over Manchester
City at Wembley

SUPER SPURS TWO AHEAD–THANKS TO MARK FALCO

16 September 1981, first round, first leg

AJAX 1
TOTTENHAM HOTSPUR 3

Olympic Stadium, Amsterdam, Netherlands *Att:* 35,000

Tottenham's return to continental competition had a sense of squaring a circle. The last outing had been a night of shame in the Netherlands. Now, Spurs faced a Dutch side again, this time Feyenoord's rivals, Ajax. As an exercise in redemption, it worked out almost perfectly.

The fans, by and large, behaved well as Spurs went some way to atoning for the misery of the 1974 UEFA Cup Final. On the pitch, the players performed far better. The 3-1 victory represented a tactical success that Bill Nicholson would have been proud of. Burkinshaw had been forced into fielding home-grown striker Mark Falco due to injury to Garth Crooks, but the 20-year-old repaid his manager's trust with interest.

Falco scored twice, after Tottenham's defence weathered an early Ajax storm. Ossie Ardiles found him for the first after 19 minutes, before the man they nicknamed "Bilko" added his second seven minutes later with a far-post finish after Graham Roberts had flicked on Tony Galvin's corner.

Spurs asserted their superiority 21 minutes into the second half with Ardiles again the provider. This time he burst into the Ajax half and slipped a fine pass to Ricky Villa, who rounded goalkeeper Pete Schrijvers to make it 3-0. Danish international Soren Lerby pulled one back a minute later, but Tottenham had the game won, and with some degree of comfort. This was not the mighty Ajax that had ruled Europe with Johan Cruyff-inspired Total Football, but Tottenham's impressive victory showed the club were back into the European groove at the first time of asking

"Burkinshaw faces a genuine problem," observed the *Daily Mirror*'s Harry Miller, drawing comparisons between Tottenham's attacking riches and the paucity of similar talent at Arsenal. "It is the sort of problem they wouldn't mind across north London."

Clemence, Hughton, Miller, Roberts,
***Villa**, Perryman, Ardiles, Archibald,*
*Galvin, Hoddle, **Falco 2***

Left: Double goalscorer Mark Falco wheels away in delight after one of his strikes

Right: Ricky Villa bursts through the Ajax defence – he added Spurs' third goal on the night

GLORY, GLORY SPURS!

Ajax taken to the cleaners by three-goal blitz

29 September 1981, first round, second leg

TOTTENHAM HOTSPUR 3 (6)
AJAX 0 (1)

White Hart Lane *Att:* 34,606

Tottenham secured a 6-1 aggregate win thanks to "12 thunderous minutes of striking power", according to the *Daily Star*'s Bob Driscoll. The real damage had been done in the Netherlands, but three late goals emphasised the home side's superiority over the whole tie.

The night provided further evidence of Tottenham's European renaissance and Ajax's sad decline. The Dutch side were never really in contention, and the only real surprise was that it took until the 70th minute before Spurs opened the scoring.

With the new West Stand nearing completion, the home fans were treated to a Glenn Hoddle and Ricky Villa first-half show as the pair dominated midfield and nullified the hosts' attacking impetus. Twice Villa fed Hoddle, and twice Hoddle went close – first with a shot just over the bar and then he was denied by a fine save from keeper Hans Galje.

Frustrated in his own attempts to score, Hoddle turned provider in the second half.

First, on 70 minutes, he launched a typical precision pass from deep inside his own half to Mark Falco, 40 yards away on the right. The striker checked, played a short pass inside, and Tony Galvin clipped a fine shot home from the edge of the area. Six minutes later, another Hoddle through ball to the unmarked Steve Archibald sent the Scotsman clear, and after evading Galje, who had raced off his line, Archibald squared for Falco to score from close range as the hapless Ajax defenders floundered.

Ossie Ardiles wrapped the scoring up eight minutes from time with arguably the best goal of the tie. Galvin bisected the Ajax midfield with an incisive square pass for the arriving Ardiles. He had to stretch to make a connection but, as he fell, launched a 20-yard shot that flew into the top right-hand corner.

*Clemence, Hughton, Miller, Roberts (Lacy), Villa, Perryman, **Ardiles**, Archibald, **Galvin**, Hoddle, **Falco***

Ossie Ardiles nips past an Ajax opponent in typical style – he went on to add the final goal in a convincing win

LOOKING BACK WITH **KEITH BURKINSHAW**

Tottenham's return to Europe in 1981 had been a sad reminder of their last disastrous experience, but this occasion was one of celebration.

The South American flair of Ossie Ardiles and Ricky Villa that manager Keith Burkinshaw had brought to British football was on full display that night in Amsterdam.

Villa's goal in the 3-1 win over Ajax and Ardiles's ability to dictate play from midfield re-confirmed what an astute piece of business it had been to sign the pair – and how vital their presence was to meet the tests of European competition and aid the side's development. Burkinshaw said afterwards: "That reappearance in Europe lifted the side into a different bracket. Now we were one of the big teams. In England there are only a handful of teams who regularly qualify for the European competitions. To reach Europe, as we were about to do, for four consecutive seasons made us into a Liverpool-class team.

"The team gains more experience and more confidence from the exposure to European tactics and styles. They get the knowledge of how to handle different systems. That is something that you cannot learn from the domestic game because you don't come up against that many differing approaches. It helps them as young players and rounds them into more mature and commanding players.

Europe is the great schooling ground.

"The young fellas started to find their feet and blossom. People like Micky Hazard developed splendidly in European competition. Tony Parks came through and thrived in the extra responsibility. It all gave them added confidence.

"If the young players are developing then the club benefits too. If you get into Europe you seem to find that your league position improves and that the general professionalism of the club develops.

"It helps add interest and impetus to seasons, and the city benefits from the exciting prospect of the visit of top continental glamour sides."

Certainly there were not many more glamorous sides in Europe than Ajax of Amsterdam. In the early 1970s Ajax were the pioneers of "Total Football". They formed the backbone of the great Holland team of the 1974 World Cup with stars like Johan Cruyff, Johnny Rep and Johan Neeskens.

Burkinshaw was told they were on the verge of a revival. "They had a side that people warned would emerge to be one of the great European powers," he said. "They had Jesper Olsen, Soren Lerby and many Dutch youngsters in their team. Instead of thrashing us as we feared, we went out and gave them a footballing lesson." It was the start of a brave new era for Spurs.

Keith Burkinshaw sees his squad start to flourish in European competition

Mark Falco after scoring two goals on his European debut in Amsterdam

LOOKING BACK WITH
MARK FALCO

Mark Falco joined Spurs straight from school and watched the European games against Hajduk and Lyon in 1967 from the Shelf, his favourite vantage point on the terraces.

"European nights were always special for the fans and for me. They bring out the patriotism in the Spurs crowd. The atmosphere in other matches just isn't the same, no matter what the game."

Falco made his presence felt with two of the goals which saw Spurs take a 3-1 advantage from the first leg in Holland.

"Recall those matches against Ajax? That's no trouble," enthused Falco in 1986. "I'll never forget them. After the glory of winning the FA Cup, we were still on a high when we went into Europe, but we didn't really know what to expect.

"Ray Clemence and Steve Perryman had plenty of experience, while Glenn Hoddle had played in Europe for England, but the rest of us couldn't know what was in store.

"Although we didn't know what to expect, we were keyed up. Everyone was eager to impress. The first half against Feyenoord when we went four goals up, the 2-0 win over Bayern Munich after losing in Germany, and the UEFA Cup Final against Anderlecht I'd select as special performances.

"But we reached heights against Ajax that even surprised us. The fact that I scored two goals as well means so much. We took Ajax apart. My first goal came from a corner. The ball was knocked out, and as Ajax pushed forward to catch us offside Ricky Villa slipped a pass to me and I slipped the ball round the keeper. My second again came from a corner. I slid the ball in at the far post."

Falco was generous with his praise for Tottenham's third goal, scored by the brilliant Ricky Villa. "He ran from the half-way line, beating a few players before going round the keeper and walking the ball in."

Falco was in the middle of a hot run at the start of the season with nine goals in 11 games, keeping his place for Spurs' return to Europe. Spurs comfortably won the second leg and a 6-1 aggregate score was a terrific start to a new European adventure.

Sorry Spurs get the luck of the Irish!

21 October 1981, second round, first leg

DUNDALK 1
TOTTENHAM HOTSPUR 1

Oriel Park, Dundalk, Ireland *Att:* 17,500

After the appetising starter against Ajax came the kind of opposition more typical of the early rounds European football – but Spurs struggled to digest the bread-and-butter fare provided by little Dundalk. The Irish part-timers gave Spurs a fright, combining admirable effort with no little skill. Yet Spurs contributed to their own problems with some slack defending and Dundalk might have been three up within half an hour. Tottenham came to their senses and rallied after half-time, taking the lead through a piece of Garth Crooks opportunism. The striker eluded a flat-footed Dundalk defence and latched onto a Hoddle through ball before rounding goalkeeper Richie Blackmore to score in the 63rd minute. The lead was cancelled out within seconds as the Spurs defence dithered once again, allowing Mick Fairclough to round Graham Roberts and rattle in the equaliser past Ray Clemence.

Clemence, Hughton, Miller, Roberts, Hazard, Perryman, Ardiles, Archibald, Galvin (Smith), Hoddle, **Crooks**

4 November 1981, second round, second leg

TOTTENHAM HOTSPUR 1 (2)
DUNDALK 0 (1)

White Hart Lane *Att:* 33,455

Garth Crooks once again spared Tottenham blushes as Spurs laboured to overcome Dundalk. As *The Guardian's* Robert Armstrong noted: "The night was one that Tottenham will want to forget soon, with Hoddle sadly anonymous and Archibald still bereft of the sharpness that often punished defences last season." In front of a crowd expecting a deluge of goals, Spurs delivered only a flood of ill-taken chances and attacking play that lacked cohesion and precision. As the grumblings from the stands and terraces increased, Tottenham finally made the breakthrough when Crooks struck in the 63rd minute, just as he had in Ireland two weeks before. This time he seized the initiative in a crowded penalty area, stabbing home a Hoddle corner as Dundalk's defenders dithered. It was a victory, but served notice that Tottenham would need to improve if their return to Europe was to be an extended one.

Clemence, Hughton, Miller, Roberts, Hazard, Perryman, Ardiles, Archibald, Galvin, Hoddle, **Crooks**

Ossie Ardiles is outnumbered by Dundalk defenders in the home tie that saw Spurs proceed in the competition but fail to impress

Glenn Hoddle points the way for Spurs at White Hart Lane. He went on to score the decisive goal in the away leg in Frankfurt

Hero Hoddle gets Spurs back in business

3 March 1982, third round, first leg

TOTTENHAM HOTSPUR 2
EINTRACHT FRANKFURT 0

White Hart Lane *Att:* 38,172

By the time the competition resumed, Spurs were flying. Charging ahead on three fronts at home, they re-opened their foreign offensive with a decent if underwhelming victory over a German side that did not offer quite the resolute discipline usually expected of Bundesliga teams. Spurs found it hard going to make the breakthrough, however, and it was left to centre-half Paul Miller to show the London side's misfiring forwards how it should be done. On the hour Micky Hazard fed Ossie Ardiles, and after his shot was blocked Miller rifled in from 20 yards. Suitably inspired and relaxed, Spurs added a vital second in the 83rd minute when Hazard jinked past two defenders and scored from distance. As a reminder that the job was far from complete, however, keeper Ray Clemence needed to make a crucial save to deny Norbert Nachtweih what would have been a vital away goal four minutes from time.

*Clemence, Hughton, **Miller**, Price, **Hazard**, Perryman, Ardiles, Archibald, Galvin, Hoddle, Crooks (Falco)*

17 March 1982, third round, second leg

EINTRACHT FRANKFURT 2 (2)
TOTTENHAM HOTSPUR 1 (3)

Waldstadion, Frankfurt, West Germany
Att: 44,000

All the good work done in London was nearly ruined in 15 mad minutes in West Germany. First, the injured Ossie Ardiles gave the ball away to Norbert Nachtweih who released Ronald Borchers to score after just two minutes. Thirteen minutes later, Paul Price missed a deflected cross and Bum Kun Cha made it 2-2 on aggregate. The season was in danger of unravelling: fresh from defeat in the League Cup Final four days before, Spurs looked set to surrender in Europe. But this team was made of the right stuff and, after Keith Burkinshaw reorganised, played its way back into contention. The revival was completed 10 minutes from the end, when Mark Falco fed Chris Hughton, whose pass opened up a chance for Glenn Hoddle, which he took in style. "It was the most important goal I have scored," Hoddle told *The Sun's* Brian Woolnough.

*Clemence, Hughton, Miller, Price, Hazard, Perryman, Ardiles (Roberts), Archibald, Galvin, **Hoddle**, Falco (Villa)*

7 April 1982, semi-final, first leg

TOTTENHAM HOTSPUR 1
BARCELONA 1

White Hart Lane *Att:* 41,545

The modern Barcelona are synonymous with all that is good about football. Back in 1982, though, they were an altogether different proposition.

Rarely can Spurs have played a more controversial game than this meeting with the Catalans. On an infamous night that shamed one of the most famous names in sport, Barcelona earned the description of "butchers" from the English media, while White Hart Lane resounded to the impassioned accusation of "animals", sung from almost every corner of the ground.

The reason for so much ire was Barcelona's frequently vicious and perpetually cynical attempt to nullify Tottenham's attacking endeavour. Plenty of sides had come to White Hart Lane in the past with the same intention, but none had carried it out with such spite and violence as Barcelona.

With games and injuries mounting up, Spurs were forced to call on the almost forgotten Chris Jones for a surprise substitute appearance. Any hope of a fairytale story was short-lived, though. The match began testily and got worse as a series of Barcelona fouls, sly transgressions and blatant assaults went unpunished. When referee Egbert Mulder finally dismissed Juan Estella in the 57th minute, all hell threatened to break loose; at one point a policeman had to intervene to stop Martinez Manolo from attacking an increasingly incensed Graham Roberts.

Roberts himself had been fortunate to stay on as he was provoked into a series of running battles, but his presence was crucial. He scored a vital equaliser five minutes from time, side-footing home to cancel out Barcelona's opener, scored by Antonio Olmo in the 65th minute when Ray Clemence spilled a 40-yard effort over the line.

It was to prove a costly error, but in the immediate aftermath Keith Burkinshaw told *The Sun's* Brian Woolnough: "If we play in Spain like Barcelona did here, there will be a revolution."

*Clemence, Hughton, Miller (Jones), Price, Hazard, Perryman, **Roberts**, Villa, Galvin, Hoddle, Crooks*

Top: Graham Roberts turns in delight after scoring Spurs' equaliser, but he was also at the centre of several flashpoints on an acrimonious night

Far right: Keith Burkinshaw can barely face the press after a gruelling night and eventual defeat at the Nou Camp

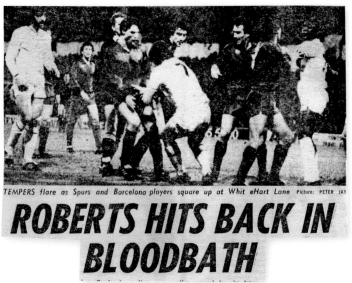

TEMPERS flare as Spurs and Barcelona players square up at White Hart Lane Picture: PETER JAY

ROBERTS HITS BACK IN BLOODBATH

21 April 1982, semi-final, second leg

BARCELONA 1 (2)
TOTTENHAM HOTSPUR 0 (1)

Nou Camp, Barcelona, Spain *Att:* 80,000

Midway into the first half, the floodlights in the cathedral-like Nou Camp went out – the perfect metaphor for the extinguishing of Tottenham's trophy dreams. While Spurs performed valiantly and emerged from the tie with great credit, the huge backlog of fixtures they had played inevitably took its toll.

On the night, Allen Simonsen's goal in the 46th minute, with the Dane stabbing home after Quini's header had looped into the area, secured Barca's passage to the final. For Tottenham, it was not just defeat in one game, but a sure sign that circumstances had finally caught up with them. After a harsh winter had caused a log-jam of fixtures, an exhausted Spurs team that had been in serious contention of winning four trophies was fading away.

"Spurs are the victims of a programme which would tax the physical resources of Superman," wrote Jeff Powell in the *Daily Mail*. To add to the obstacles in Tottenham's way, the imminent conflict with Argentina over the Falklands led to a massive security presence, the tension ratcheted up further by dressing-room warnings from UEFA that the violence of the previous game would not be tolerated. Spurs abided; Barcelona carried on from where they left off, and with that dictated the pattern of play – to the visitors' cost. Spurs tried, but couldn't summon the wit or energy to draw level.

"If this is failure, I want more of it," said a proud and defiant Keith Burkinshaw. They were stirring words but proved prophetic as the season all but withered away at the last; Spurs had to play eight league matches in 17 days alone. The League Cup had been lost, the title challenge was set to crumble, and now the Cup Winners' Cup was gone. But the FA Cup once again provided compensation – and another route back into Europe.

Clemence, Hughton, Price (Falco), Roberts, Hazard, Perryman, Villa, Archibald, Galvin, Hoddle, Crooks

POST-MATCH **REACTION**

STEVE PERRYMAN "Their intimidation against us at home, the way we matched it and overcame it worked against us there. For the return, the ref went in both dressing rooms and said, 'If there's anything like that again, I'll call the game off'. In our naive English way we sort of believed him. The Spanish just went at it. They weren't ever going to call it off!"

PAUL MILLER "We were the best team in Europe that year," says Miller. "Barcelona kicked us out. Maybe we were a bit naive in that home leg, rising to the bait. They got us at it. Which probably stood us in good stead for when we won the UEFA a couple of years later. It was a bad mistake from Clem that gave them it, one of the few mistakes Clem made all year. Not bad for 60-odd games. But that gave them a lifeline. We went out there with a few injured and tired and we weren't really at the races. We tried to change our gameplan but we should've been more physical. We weren't the Spurs side that we should've been. But we were tired and the games were coming thick and fast."

TONY GALVIN "The one that really killed us was the Barcelona game, where Ray [Clemence] let that one shot slip through his hands. We'd outplayed them and they'd kicked us. These days they'd have had eight players sent off. They got away with murder because they were the famous club. I remember talking to Brian Glanville once and he was adamant that it was a set-up because the final was going to be in Barcelona. And the first leg, the referee was so lenient... But we outplayed them. Then we went over there, played well again, but they went 1-0 up and just shut up shop. But you've got to win your home leg. The first leg though, it was a disgrace. That really annoyed me, it sticks with me from that season. Because we deserved to be in that final."

F.A. CUP FINAL
WEMBLEY
1982

THE ROAD TO EUROPE

1982

By the 1982/83 season, Keith Burkinshaw's side had matured into one of the finest footballing sides in England. Despite the ugliness of the previous season's exit from Europe, the players and the fans had revelled in the beauty of being back in competition with the Continent's top teams, gaining valuable experience in the process. In 1981/82 Spurs played 66 games and threatened at one stage to win every competition they were in. In the end, the exhausted Lilywhites lifted just one trophy, retaining the FA Cup. Despite the fine football played throughout the season, the cup final victory was workaday, Glenn Hoddle scoring from the penalty spot in the replay to see off the challenge of Second Division QPR. One heartwarming moment did stand out – the standing ovation given to the sidelined Ricky Villa by the crowd, despite the fact that Argentina and Britain were at war over the Falklands. Hoddle was at the peak of his powers, as was skipper Steve Perryman. Up front, Garth Crooks and Steve Archibald were as deadly a striking combination as could be found. This team fancied its chances to grab some success in Europe.

QPR manager Terry
Venables (far left)
and Spurs boss
Keith Burkinshaw
lead out their teams
at Wembley in 1982

15 September 1982, first round, first leg

COLERAINE 0
TOTTENHAM HOTSPUR 3

The Showgrounds, Coleraine, Ireland
Att: 12,000

The campaign threw up a favourable first challenge in the shape of Irish League part-timers Coleraine. Ricky Villa was back and looked, said Ken Lawrence in the *Daily Star*, "like he came from a different planet from anything the Irish side could offer". Spurs went ahead in the 12th minute, when Gary Mabbutt headed against the post and Steve Archibald nipped in to tuck away the rebound. Just after half-time, Garry Brooke crossed for Garth Crooks to head home. Six minutes from time it was Crooks again, tapping home from close range after Coleraine keeper Vince Magee blocked a Brooke shot. "After this catch-as-catch-can win, the second leg at White Hart Lane in a fortnight is nothing more than a formality," said Lawrence. Keith Burkinshaw said: "We've got to be happy with the win, even though these games often lack pattern."

Clemence, Hughton, Price, Lacy, Brooke, Perryman, Mabbutt (Hazard), **Archibald***, Galvin, Villa,* **Crooks 2**

28 September 1982, first round, first leg

TOTTENHAM HOTSPUR 4 (7)
COLERAINE (0) 0

White Hart Lane *Att:* 20,925

Before the game, the talk was of a "Tottenham goal bonanza" and this seems to have drawn a crowd surprisingly large for the time. As it happened, the Irish defence kept Spurs at bay for large periods of the game. They may have suffered from scoring early again, Garth Crooks racing away from his marker to slot home in the 14th minute. Spurs continued to make chances, but another goal did not come until the 54th minute, when Gary Mabbutt curled a 20-yard shot into the right-hand corner of the net. By the 65th minute, Spurs felt confident enough to withdraw goalkeeper Ray Clemence and give their young reserve keeper his European debut. His name was Tony Parks. Garry Brooke bagged Spurs' third, then in the 86th minute Terry Gibson, another young player given his chance, got his name on the scoresheet. It was, said *The Sun*'s Ian Gibb, "A Euro stroll for Spurs."

Clemence (Parks), Hughton, Price, Lacy, **Brooke***, Perryman,* **Mabbutt***, Archibald, Hazard, Villa,* **Crooks** *(Gibson)*

Garth Crooks makes no mistake, opening the scoring for Spurs in the return leg v Coleraine

SPURS LOST IN THE FOG

Brilliant Bayern smother Burkinshaw ghost squad

Spurs' hopes in the 1983 Cup Winners' Cup campaign disappear into the mist in Munich

20 October 1982, second round, first leg

TOTTENHAM HOTSPUR 1 BAYERN MUNICH 1

White Hart Lane *Att:* 36,488

Tottenham's next opponents could not have provided a greater contrast with the last – the German giants featured Paul Breitner and Karl-Heinz Rummenigge in their ranks. To make things even more difficult, injuries meant Spurs could only field half their first-choice XI. And yet after three minutes, a Steve Archibald goal put Spurs ahead. Bayern's defence was stunned, and only Belgian international Jean-Marie Pfaff in the Bayern goal kept the score down with a string of great saves. But, said David Lacey in *The Guardian*, Bayern came out for the second half "looking as though they had been revived with the beer that refreshes the parts other beers cannot reach". The inexperienced Gary O'Reilly sliced a clearance and Breitner slammed home. Bayern controlled the rest of the game, while Spurs lost Archibald with a pulled muscle.

*Clemence, Price, O'Reilly (Gibson), Miller, Lacy, Hazard, Brooke, **Archibald** (Falco), Mabbutt, Villa, Crooks*

3 November 1982, second round, second leg

BAYERN MUNICH 4 (5) TOTTENHAM HOTSPUR 1 (2)

Olympic Stadium, Munich, Germany
Att: 55,000

Mist delayed the team's departure from Luton Airport, and thick fog greeted them at the Olympic Stadium. Stuart Jones in *The Times* described the "eerie" conditions vividly: "The pass of the ball was often to be traced only through the noise of the crowd nearest to it. With delayed stereophonic sound, the reactions spread to the viewers hidden at the opposite end." At half-time, Keith Burkinshaw and Bayern manager Uli Hoeness spoke to the referee and for a while it seemed the match would be called off. But it went on. Bayern scored twice in the first half, the identity of the scorers only known to most of the crowd when their names appeared on the electronic scoreboard. A third was added 15 minutes from time. Although Chris Hughton pulled one back, a still depleted Spurs were well beaten by the time the fourth went in.

*Clemence, Price, **Hughton**, Miller (Perryman), Lacy, Hazard, Mabbutt, Archibald, Brooke (Hoddle), Villa, Crooks*

THE ROAD TO EUROPE

1983

This was the season in which a great Spurs team bowed out in a European final, just as in 1963 and 1974. Spurs qualified for the UEFA Cup in unlikely fashion after what was looking to be a poor 1982/83 season. Ossie Ardiles decided he could not return to England after the Falklands War, while Glenn Hoddle was absent for a large part of the season due to injury. This meant the team had lost its two most creative players. Early exits from three cups sapped morale further. But a run of nine victories in the final 12 league games secured fourth place and another crack at Europe. This campaign was to throw up new heroes and cathartic victories and, on one unforgettable night, the eclipsing of a genuine legend of world football by one of Tottenham's own in a game described by skipper Steve Perryman as "probably the best Spurs performance I'd ever been involved in". Europe, as it so often does, brought the best out of a team Perryman says was "battle-hardened". It all ended in a climactic game tinged with sadness but one which, despite the less-than-sparkling football played, will be forever secure in its status as one of the true glory glory nights.

Spurs players salute the crowd during a season of mixed fortunes in 1982/83

TOP MARKS FOR FALCO

Spurs superman leads the rout of bewildered Irish

14 September 1983, first round, first leg

DROGHEDA UNITED 0
TOTTENHAM HOTSPUR 6

United Park, Drogheda, Ireland *Att*: 7,000

The campaign began on a rain-soaked night in County Louth in the Republic of Ireland. It was the first foray into Europe for the Irish part-timers, but before the game Spurs manager Keith Burkinshaw had warned his players not to take anything for granted. Spurs started without Steve Archibald, who was involved in an on-going row with Burkinshaw, and with Glenn Hoddle and Alan Brazil on the bench. But as Harry Harris put it in the *Daily Mail*, "They hit the Irish side for six", racking up a club record European away score. Mark Falco, in for Archibald, grabbed two, as did Gary Mabbutt, while Tony Galvin and Garth Crooks also got in on the act. "Drogheda's consolation," said Harris, "is a £65,000 payday and a couple of nights out in London in a fortnight." Burkinshaw said: "The players showed great attitude. But we'll probably get little credit for this win."

Garth Crooks was amongst the goals in an emphatic win for Spurs in Ireland

Clemence, Hughton, O'Reilly, Roberts, Price, Perryman, **Mabbutt 2, Falco 2,** *Galvin, Brooke,* **Crooks**

28 September 1983, second round, second leg

TOTTENHAM HOTSPUR 8 (14)
DROGHEDA UNITED 0 (0)

White Hart Lane *Att*: 19,831

There was little chance Keith Burkinshaw was going to let his players take it easy in the return. Spurs had not won at home since the season started and had picked up only six points from seven games. A confidence boost was needed, and duly secured on a night when, according to Colin Bateman in the *Daily Express*, "Irish defenders were like sitting ducks in a shooting gallery". In the end, Spurs just missed out on bettering their European record 15-1 aggregate score. So eager were the Lilywhites to hit the net that, at one stage, Tony Galvin was penalised for pushing team-mate Chris Hughton off the ball. One who benefitted most from the fillip this goal feast provided was Alan Brazil. When he finally got off the mark for the season in the 50th minute he got one of the biggest cheers of the night, diving in to head home 10 minutes from time to complete the rout.

Clemence, **Hughton** *(O'Reilly), Galvin,* **Roberts 2,** *Price, Perryman, Mabbutt,* **Archibald, Falco 2,** *Hoddle,* **Brazil 2**

1980s AWAY DAYS

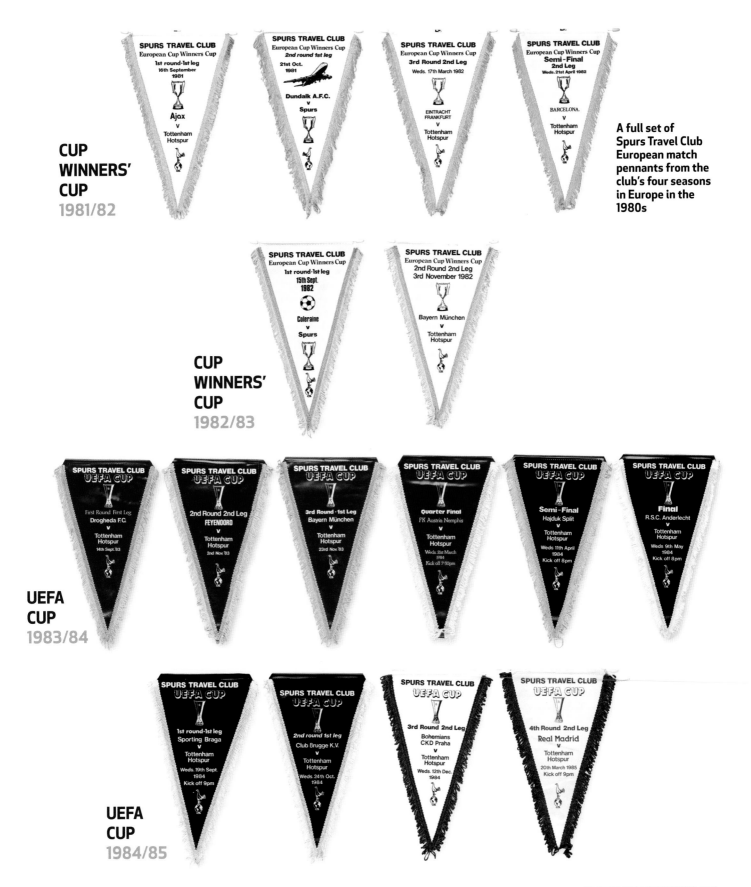

CUP WINNERS' CUP
1981/82

SPURS TRAVEL CLUB
European Cup Winners Cup
1st round·1st leg
16th September
1981
Ajax
v
Tottenham
Hotspur

SPURS TRAVEL CLUB
European Cup Winners Cup
2nd round 1st leg
21st Oct.
1981
Dundalk A.F.C.
v
Spurs

SPURS TRAVEL CLUB
European Cup Winners Cup
3rd Round 2nd Leg
Weds. 17th March 1982
EINTRACHT FRANKFURT
v
Tottenham
Hotspur

SPURS TRAVEL CLUB
European Cup Winners Cup
Semi-Final
2nd Leg
Weds. 21st April 1982
BARCELONA.
v
Tottenham
Hotspur

A full set of
Spurs Travel Club
European match
pennants from the
club's four seasons
in Europe in the
1980s

CUP WINNERS' CUP
1982/83

SPURS TRAVEL CLUB
European Cup Winners Cup
1st round·1st leg
15th Sept.
1982
Coleraine
v
Spurs

SPURS TRAVEL CLUB
European Cup Winners Cup
2nd Round 2nd Leg
3rd November 1982
Bayern München
v
Tottenham
Hotspur

UEFA CUP
1983/84

SPURS TRAVEL CLUB
UEFA CUP
First Round First Leg
Drogheda F.C.
v
Tottenham
Hotspur
14th Sept. '83

SPURS TRAVEL CLUB
UEFA CUP
2nd Round 2nd Leg
FEYENOORD
v
Tottenham
Hotspur
2nd Nov. '83

SPURS TRAVEL CLUB
UEFA CUP
3rd Round·1st Leg
Bayern München
v
Tottenham
Hotspur
23rd Nov. '83

SPURS TRAVEL CLUB
UEFA CUP
Quarter Final
FK Austria Nemphis
v
Tottenham
Hotspur
Weds. 21st March
1984
Kick off 7·30pm

SPURS TRAVEL CLUB
UEFA CUP
Semi-Final
Hajduk Split
v
Tottenham
Hotspur
Weds 11th April
1984
Kick off 8pm

SPURS TRAVEL CLUB
UEFA CUP
Final
R.S.C. Anderlecht
v
Tottenham
Hotspur
Weds 9th May
1984
Kick off 8pm

UEFA CUP
1984/85

SPURS TRAVEL CLUB
UEFA CUP
1st round·1st leg
Sporting Braga
v
Tottenham
Hotspur
Weds. 19th Sept.
1984
Kick off 9pm

SPURS TRAVEL CLUB
UEFA CUP
2nd round 1st leg
Club Brugge K.V.
v
Tottenham
Hotspur
Weds. 24th Oct.
1984

SPURS TRAVEL CLUB
UEFA CUP
3rd Round 2nd Leg
Bohemians
CKD Praha
v
Tottenham
Hotspur
Weds. 12th Dec.
1984

SPURS TRAVEL CLUB
UEFA CUP
4th Round 2nd Leg
Real Madrid
v
Tottenham
Hotspur
20th March 1985
Kick off 9pm

HODDLE'S DODDLE!

19 October 1983, second round, first leg
TOTTENHAM HOTSPUR 4
FEYENOORD 2

White Hart Lane *Att:* 35,404

Johan Cruyff's name ranks with the best, up there with Pelé and Maradona. The Dutchman is a global legend from a time before saturation coverage of football made many players legends – at least for a short time until the next one comes along. Nearing the end of his playing career, he was pulling the strings at Feyenoord and when the draw was made the prospect of a match-up with Glenn Hoddle was almost too delicious to bear.

Steve Perryman remembers Spurs were fired up, their loyalty to and admiration for Hoddle giving them that extra drive to show their man was no mere pretender (*see page 142*). They ripped Feyenoord apart in the first 45 minutes, and Hoddle was at the centre of everything. "Determined that the word 'greatness' should be stamped as permanently as a silver mark [Hoddle] grabbed hold of this game and never let go," marvelled Clive White in *The Times*.

Eight minutes in, Hoddle sent Chris Hughton through to cross for Steve Archibald to open the scoring. Ten minutes later Hoddle's perfect cross was headed home by Tony Galvin. Then another inch-perfect ball sent Mark Falco through. Falco's parried shot was pulled back by Gary Mabbutt and

2 November 1983, second round, second leg

FEYENOORD 0 (2)
TOTTENHAM HOTSPUR 2 (6)

Feyenoord Stadium, Rotterdam, Netherlands *Att*: 49,241

A return to Feyenoord was always going to be something to fill those associated with Spurs with some trepidation. But despite some more ugly scenes in the port city, this would be a night that, in the main, stood out for the right reasons. "The chant 'Super Tottenham' rang out round Rotterdam last night as Keith Burkinshaw's star-studded side asked to be remembered for the quality of their football rather than the fury of their fans," wrote Harry Miller in the *Daily Mirror*.

Feyenoord knew they had to attack, while Spurs had pledged to squeeze the life out of the Dutch league leaders with a tight defensive plan. In the event it was a Spurs defender who made the difference, but not in his own box. With 25 minutes gone, full-back Chris Hughton slammed home a goal that meant Feyenoord would have to go all out to salvage the tie. They did so, pushing two men wide and thrusting Johan Cruyff forward. But Cruyff was not the player he once was, and Feyenoord's shape left them increasingly vulnerable to Tottenham's counter attacks.

Mark Falco had gone close three times before Hughton scored, with that man Glenn Hoddle heavily involved in the build-up to the goal. Skipper Steve Perryman also shone and Ray Clemence pulled off a couple of fine saves when the home side did manage to get something on target. Tony Galvin made sure of the win in the 85th minute, shooting home crisply after picking up a Gary Mabbutt pass.

"We have become used to outstanding performances by Spurs on the foreign field," reported the *Mirror* man. "This one, controlled and exciting, came close to comparison with the best."

Keith Burkinshaw was very pleased, saying, "It was a very professional performance… What pleased me more than anything was that everyone ran for each other."

DUTCH TREAT!

Hoddle the master in Spurs spree

Archibald struck again. Six minutes before half-time Hoddle sent an audacious, beautiful 40-yard ball into Galvin's path and the winger waltzed through the defence to make it four.

In the second half, Spurs let things slip, allowing Cruyff to make his mark with a goal in the 70th minute. A close-range finish from Ivan Neilsen in the 81st minute kept a competitive edge to the tie. But this was Hoddle's night. "It had to happen I suppose," reported *The Times*'s White. "Johan Cruyff placed in the wings by an opposing number 10. But who better to take over the mantle from the great but ageing champion than our own darling, Glenn Hoddle."

Clemence, Hughton, **Galvin 2**, *Roberts, Stevens, Perryman, Mabbutt,* **Archibald 2**, *Falco, Hoddle, Brooke (Crook)*

Left: Glenn Hoddle outwits Johan Cruyff as he masterminds Spurs' home win against Feyenoord

Top: Steve Archibald celebrates one of his two goals at White Hart Lane

Above: Graham Roberts is challenged by young star of the future, Ruud Gullit

Clemence, **Hughton**, *Thomas, Roberts, Stevens, Perryman, Mabbutt, Archibald, Falco (Brazil), Hoddle,* **Galvin**

LOOKING BACK WITH **JOHAN CRUYFF**

Johan Cruyff did not make too many mistakes in his glittering career, but he certainly made one at White Hart Lane in October 1983. For the Dutch master, the man who had led Ajax and Holland to the peak of European and world football, wanted to make one more point.

The place he decided to make the great stand was against Tottenham, at White Hart Lane. The occasion, a UEFA Cup second-round tie. The result: defeat by four goals to two.

For weeks before the tie, Cruyff had been fascinated with the prospect of playing against Glenn Hoddle, the midfield star who was making a name for himself in European terms. Cruyff said: "I wanted to test myself against the young star of the present. I knew I could play. I wanted to see what level I was at. Glenn Hoddle was a great player in my book. He played football the way that I wanted to see it played. He could make great passes and was the best player for Tottenham."

That almost incredible attraction to the Hoddle skill was to prove Feyenoord's downfall. A technical director of the club as well as a player, Cruyff made a poor decision. Despite the pleas of the Feyenoord boss Thijs Libreghts to rethink, Cruyff insisted that he mark Glenn Hoddle. It was an error from which Feyenoord could not recover.

Within 20 minutes Feyenoord were in trouble, and not until Cruyff was finally released from his self-imposed torture did the Dutch side pose a threat.

Cruyff admitted: "It was a bad error of judgement. I thought that I could mark him and keep him quiet. The result shows that I could not.

"He was a player that I had liked, but it was only on the pitch that I realised how good he really was. I was a shadow without any presence.

"We slipped away into the night and I had to admit to the other players that it was all down to me. We had a glimmer of hope, but that was to disappear in the second leg."

TOP: GLENN HODDLE shapes up to do the "Harlem shuffle," while MARK FALCO, TONY GALVIN and GARY O'REILLY are prepared to pose for the camera.

MIDDLE: GARY O'REILLY finds something interesting in a book at the airport before the Feyenoord match, TONY GALVIN can't work it out and MARK FALCO seems to be thinking about something else!

BOTTOM: We're on our way! Happy Spurs fans celebrate our progress in the U.E.F.A. Cup.

IN THE
PROGRAMME

Spurs players and fans arrive in Rotterdam in good spirits. This feature appeared in the club programme for the subsequent home tie v Bayern Munich

Graham Roberts
contests an aerial
ball during the close
fought tie in Munich

23 November 1983, third round, first leg

BAYERN MUNICH 1
TOTTENHAM HOTSPUR 0

Olympic Stadium, Munich, West Germany *Att: 20,000*

Between Spurs and the last eight of the competition stood Bayern Munich, the West German giants who had humbled Spurs in the previous season's Cup Winners' Cup. That night the thick fog had obscured the view at the Olympic Stadium; for this visit it was clear and crisp as Spurs tried to get even for the drubbing they had suffered almost exactly a year before. The temperature was five below zero, which contributed to the fact that only 20,000 were present in the vast stadium.

The match began in encouraging fashion for the visitors, with Mark Falco sending a shot just wide in only the third minute. Then Glenn Hoddle sent Steve Archibald through, only for the striker to hit the side netting when a goal seemed certain. Bayern hauled themselves back into the game, with skipper Karl-Heinz Rummenigge sending over a swerving centre that Hans Pfluger snatched at and sent wide.

The Germans lost their captain to injury at the start of the second half, but this did not stop them applying pressure on Spurs. The visitors dug in, adopting an approach the *Daily Express*'s Steve Curry described as "more associated with Hackney Marshes than White Hart Lane". Ray Clemence and Danny Thomas were booked, and Gary Stevens nearly conceded a penalty, but Spurs hung on.

Then, five minutes from time, Michael Rummenigge – Karl-Heinz's brother – cut inside from the left and lashed a shot past Clemence.

After the game, Keith Burkinshaw said: "It is now an intriguing situation. But we always feel we can score goals, particularly at home." Bayern's Udo Lattek said: "A 1-0 win might just be enough. Spurs need two goals in London but we will be looking to hit them on the break. Frankly, I don't envy Mr Burkinshaw."

Clemence, Hughton, Thomas, Roberts, Stevens, Perryman, Hazard (Brooke), Archibald, Falco, Hoddle, Dick (Brazil)

7 December 1983, third round, second leg

TOTTENHAM HOTSPUR 2 (2)
BAYERN MUNICH 0 (1)

White Hart Lane *Att:* 41,977

Uli Hoeness didn't want to buy Glenn Hoddle. Franz Beckenbauer said he wouldn't get into his all-star team of 40-year-olds. So it was fitting that the Spurs maestro turned in another peerless performance, creating both the goals that bid Bayern *auf wiedersehen.*

While the football was at times a joy to watch, this was a mature and battle-hardened Spurs team. In *The Times*, Stuart Jones wrote: "Tottenham Hotspur, like the majestic team of old, showed that they are learning the continental lesson of combining natural attacking flair with defensive patience to claim a place in the last eight of the UEFA Cup."

Hoddle orchestrated, bringing both wings in to play so that Ally Dick and Richard Cook could stretch the German defence. On 12 minutes, though, it was a trademark Hoddle pass through the middle that opened up a chance for Mark Falco, only for the striker to hit the post. Falco saw a toe-poke tipped away, Steve Perryman's back header was cleared off the line, Hoddle went close with a free-kick, Steve Archibald volleyed just over the bar, Gary Stevens saw a half-volley blocked and another lob, this time from Hoddle, was pushed over the bar.

Then, in the 50th minute, Hoddle floated a free-kick towards Graham Roberts. Roberts headed down in front of a gaggle of white-shirted players and Steve Archibald thrust himself forward to drill home.

Spurs needed just one more goal, without conceding, but their rhythm was broken by injuries to Chris Hughton and Dick. The Rummenigge brothers, "lurking dangerously on the periphery like fireworks that have been lit and forgotten," according to *The Times* reporter Jones, went close. But on 86 minutes, Falco hit the woodwork before ramming home. Tottenham had their revenge, and a quarter-final place.

Clemence, Hughton (O'Reilly), Thomas, Roberts, Stevens, Perryman, Cooke, **Archibald, Falco,** *Hoddle, Dick (Brooke)*

Scorer of the match-winning goal, Mark Falco, and Garry Brooke (no 15), turn to acknowledge Glenn Hoddle on a memorable night for the team

Steve Archibald is in the thick of the action again, shaking off an injury to score Spurs' first goal v Austria Vienna

SPURS DOUBLE SCOTCH

7 March 1984, fourth round, first leg

TOTTENHAM HOTSPUR 2
FK AUSTRIA 0

White Hart Lane *Att:* 34,069

Tottenham were drawn against Austria Vienna, a top side with players of the calibre of Austrian international Herbert Prohaska and the Hungarian star Tibor Nyilasi. With the first leg of the tie at home, the Londoners needed a result, which possibly explains the physical style they adopted. It was an approach, said Harry Harris in the *Daily Mail*, "that eventually shook the Austrian sophisticates out of their silky stride".

Graham Roberts was at the centre of the Spurs approach, imposing his not inconsiderable presence from the start and leading shell-shocked Vienna midfielder Istvan Magyar to describe him after the game as "wrong in the head". But it was striker Steve Archibald who really stood out. Suffering with a knee injury, Archibald declared himself fit just hours before kick-off. He had been embroiled in a long-running dispute with Keith Burkinshaw over his unwillingness to play through injury, a dispute which had led to the

player being placed on the transfer list.

Vienna's defence was well organised, and it was not until the 58th minute that Archibald made the breakthrough, taking the first real chance that fell to him to notch his 23rd goal of the season. Minutes later he headed against the bar, then finished off a commanding display with an intricate pass to Alan Brazil to give Spurs a 2-0 lead. Brazil's 67th-minute strike actually went in off Vienna captain Robert Sara, but Burkinshaw awarded him the goal, saying, "he was looking his old self and was a little unlucky that a goal by him was ruled out in the first half for offside".

Roberts may have been a physical presence but, despite the post-match gripes of the Austrians, his contribution was deemed "dynamic but fair" by Harris.

Parks, Stevens, Hughton, Roberts, Miller, Perryman, Ardiles, **Archibald**, **Brazil**, *Hazard (Hoddle), Dick*

WUNDERBAR, SPURS!

Alan Brazil scores Tottenham's second on the night in Vienna, helping ensure Spurs' safe progress to the semi-finals

21 March 1984, fourth round, second leg

FK AUSTRIA 2 (2)
TOTTENHAM HOTSPUR 2 (4)

Prater Stadium, Vienna, Austria *Att: 21,000*

Spurs turned in one of their best performances of a season that was threatening to turn very sour indeed on this spring night in Vienna's famous Prater Stadium. Out of both domestic cups; out of the race for the league title; riven by disputes with strikers Steve Archibald and now Alan Brazil, who had slapped in a transfer request, and rocked by injuries to influential players such as Ossie Ardiles and Ray Clemence, things were looking bleak for Tottenham. But in a performance dubbed "Spur-fect" by *The Sun*, the team lit a beacon of hope. "It was Tottenham's last chance of glory," said the paper's reporter Brian Woolnough, "and this was not so much a Viennese waltz, but a Sunday afternoon stroll. Spurs were as confident as they have been disappointing in their Jekyll and Hyde season."

After 15 minutes, Gary Stevens picked out Archibald. The Scotsman looked up and played in Brazil, who drove the ball low into the net. Brazil said afterwards: "My goal killed the tie and the Austrians knew then it was all over." The second goal came on 82 minutes, this time from Ardiles who pounced on a half-cleared corner to smash in a goal Keith Burkinshaw described as a "cracker".

Spurs did concede two, the first a penalty when Stevens pushed Tibor Nyilasi – earning Stevens a booking that ruled him out of the semi-final – and the second when Paul Miller appeared to divert Nyalisi's effort into his own goal in a frantic final 10 minutes.

Spurs were through and still in with a chance of glory. Burkinshaw said: "It was our last chance and the players responded perfectly. I was proud of them and it just shows what we can do when we put our minds to it."

*Clemence, Stevens, Hughton, Roberts (Thomas), Miller, Perryman, **Ardiles**, Archibald, **Brazil** (Falco), Mabbutt, Galvin*

THE NEARLY MEN

BATTLE IN EUROPE

Spurs are poised to give Keith final fling

11 April 1984, semi-final, first leg

HAJDUK SPLIT 2
TOTTENHAM HOTSPUR 1

Poljud Stadium, Split, Yugoslavia *Att*: 40,000

By the time the semi-final came around, Spurs were not playing just for silverware. Just over a week before the tie, Keith Burkinshaw announced he would be leaving the club at the end of the season. He had become discontented with what he saw as interference from a new, more commercially minded board. In the *London* Evening *Standard*, Peter Blackman reported: "I've never seen Burkinshaw look so drained. The usually affable man was in a daze; his eyes red-rimmed." The players now had an added incentive – to win the cup "for Keith".

The final push began in Yugoslavia, on a night vividly described by the *Daily Mirror*'s Harry Miller in which "the rain slanted across one of Europe's most picturesque stadiums and the smoke from a stream of multicoloured firecrackers finally dispersed". After 17 minutes, Mark Falco crossed from the left. Under no pressure, Hajduk's Ivan Gudelj handled the ball to concede a penalty.

Falco stepped up to take the spot kick, facing Yugoslavian player of the year, Zoran Simovic. He put the kick straight at the keeper, but the rebound came straight back to Falco. Again he shot, and again Simovic saved, blocking the ball out to Tony Galvin. Galvin pulled it back and Falco scrambled the ball over the line.

As the second half wore on a gritty performance looked like securing a valuable away win. But in the 67th and 77th minutes defensive lapses let Hajduk rise from the dead. Gudelj made amends for his earlier error by bagging the equaliser, then Dusran Pesic levelled the score on the night with a neat header. "Tottenham headed for home knowing their determination to give manager Keith Burkinshaw the farewell gift he wants is still in the balance," wrote Miller.

Parks, Thomas, Hughton, Roberts, Miller, Perryman, Hazard, Archibald, **Falco**, *Mabbutt (Crook), Galvin*

Spurs allow Hajduk Split to get back in the semi-final with the second of two late goals, but the tie was still wide open

GLORY, GLORY
Hazard warning lights up Spurs

25 April 1984, semi-final, second leg

TOTTENHAM HOTSPUR 1 (2)
HAJDUK SPLIT 0 (2) *Spurs won on away goals*

White Hart Lane *Att:* 43,969

Just five days before the second leg, Spurs had lost 3-2 to Arsenal at Highbury, a result that enabled the old rivals to secure a league double and which effectively ended any chance of Tottenham qualifying for Europe through the league. Everything rested on the UEFA Cup, therefore, and over 40,000 turned up to ride the tide of emotion for Spurs and above all for Keith Burkinshaw.

After just six minutes, Micky Hazard stroked a beauty of a free-kick past Hajduk's defensive wall to score his first European goal of the season. Hazard didn't see much of the celebrations – one of his contact lenses had flown out and he had to leave the field for five minutes to get treatment. After the game, he said: "There was a definite mood in the dressing room of winning it for Keith. I particularly owe him a lot for the way he and his assistant Peter Shreeve have helped me."

The crowd roared Spurs on, but despite another excellent performance from Steve Archibald, they failed to add to the score. Late in the second half, stand-in keeper Tony Parks saved another screamer of a free-kick, but only after he'd juggled the ball onto the bar and dropped to smother it. In the end, the away goal in Split proved to be the difference. Spurs were through to their first European final in 10 years. Burkinshaw said afterwards: "The tension was unbearable. It was as emotional a night as I can remember. We were desperate to get through. It's the icing on the cake and if we win the trophy it won't have been such a disastrous season."

Reporting for the *Daily Express*, Colin Bateman said: "The emotion and glory at White Hart Lane last night was all for manager Keith Burkinshaw."

*Parks, Thomas, Hughton, Roberts, Miller, Perryman, **Hazard**, Archibald, Falco, Stevens (Mabbutt), Galvin*

Mark Falco shows his delight as Micky Hazard's early free-kick puts Spurs narrowly ahead in the tie, and so it remained through to full-time. Spurs were in their third UEFA Cup Final in little over a decade

9 May 1984, Final, first leg
ANDERLECHT 1
TOTTENHAM HOTSPUR 1

Constant Vanden Stock Stadium, Brussels, Belgium *Att*: 38,000

So much rested on this game that Spurs opted to incur the wrath of the English football authorities by fielding a reserve team away to Southampton two days before the first leg. Spurs lost 5-0, but all eyes were on the final. Anderlecht had dumped Brian Clough's Nottingham Forest out of the competition in the semi-final, overturning a 2-0 first-leg deficit. "They had an awesome team," remembers Tony Parks. "Munaron in goal, he was outstanding. Franky Vercauteren, Morton Olsen the Danish captain – they had class all over the park. They had the lad [Enzo] Scifo too, who was 17 at the time."

Reporting from Brussels, the *Daily Star*'s Bob Driscoll said: "It was plain from the opening minutes that [Spurs] were determined to make their point by coming home from Brussels with the kind of result to set up victory in the second leg." Spurs began defending the goal behind which their travelling support was congregated, and it was defensive rock Graham Roberts who set the tone five minutes into the game when he made a courageous tackle to deny midfielder Wim Hofkens as he broke clear inside the penalty box. Spurs, said Driscoll, "made no pretence of their intention to absorb whatever Anderlecht could throw at them. The tackling was robust, to say the least."

In the 19th minute, Mark Falco got his head to a Tony Galvin cross at the far post, but failed to make it count. Minutes later the striker was heading out from beneath his own crossbar after a free-kick. As the first half wore on with Spurs still firmly dug in, the Belgians began to show signs of frustration. By half-time their heads were bowed as the worry grew that home advantage was slipping away.

The second half began with Anderlecht piling the pressure on the Spurs goal, but still the English side held out. Then, in the 58th minute, Paul Miller got his head to a Micky Hazard corner. The ball flashed goalwards, pinged off a defender and hit the roof of the net. Spurs had the vital away goal. But 10 minutes later they suffered a blow. Skipper Steve Perryman picked up a yellow card for an innocuous challenge. It was his second yellow of the competition and it meant he would miss the second leg.

Five minutes from time, Frank Arnesen shot, the ball rebounded, and up popped Olsen to poke home the equaliser.

"The lad hit a shot from the edge of the box," says Parks, "and it just took a deflection and bang, it was in the back of the net. I remember feeling really hard done by. I thought we outplayed them. When we came off the pitch the feeling was we'd done a really good job – they know we can play and we've held them at their place, now we can finish them off at ours. European nights at

Below left: Steve Perryman greets his opposite number before the final but picked up a caution, putting him out of the second leg

Below right: Frank Arnesen, Anderlecht's scorer on the night, competes with Spurs' Tony Galvin

Facing page: Galvin this time takes the attack to Anderlecht

White Hart Lane were brilliant – when that Shelf side was packed out it was awesome."

Roberts would now captain Spurs in Perryman's absence and pledged to send the suspended skipper up to collect the trophy if Spurs won. "He is such a good and important player," said Roberts, "and we depend on his leadership. I am so upset for him. He has missed only one game this season and that was at Southampton."

Winning was now even more of a personal crusade – for Keith and for Steve. But no one could have forseen the drama that was to unfold as the tie, the competition, Tottenham's season and an era in the club's history came to a head.

*Parks, Thomas, Hughton, Roberts, **Miller**, Perryman, Hazard, Archibald, Falco, Stevens (Mabbutt), Galvin*

THIS ONE'S ALL FOR YOU, BOSS GOLDEN MILLER!

23 May 1984, Final, second leg

TOTTENHAM HOTSPUR 1 (2)
ANDERLECHT 1 (2) *aet Spurs won 4-3 on penalties*

White Hart Lane A**TT**: 46,258

Below: Graham Roberts celebrates his crucial equaliser on the night

Below right: Danny Thomas is devastated after missing the fifth Spurs spot kick

Top: Tony Parks seals his place in club history with his second and final save in the shoot-out

This may not have been one of the classic displays of football – Steve Curry in the *Daily Express* rather generously described it as "muscular aggression mixed with delicate skill" – but for sheer drama it takes some beating. On this night legends were cemented into club history and stories unfolded that would have seemed fanciful if scripted for a screen drama. the *Daily Telegraph*'s Michael Colvin described "a capacity crowd, enthralled by the personal story at the heart of a collective triumph".

Spurs were without Clemence, Perryman, Hoddle and Ardiles as they started, and the two sides battled through a first half which ended with the score even, but advantage Tottenham. Then, in the 60th minute, Alex Czerniatinski scored the goal that could have pooped the party. A stunned silence hit White Hart Lane. With 14 minutes to go, Keith Burkinshaw rolled the dice and sent on Ossie Ardiles. It acted, said Steve Curry in the *Daily Express*, "like a shot of adrenalin". They pushed forward and, with six minutes to go, who else but Graham Roberts summoned his last vestiges of energy

to surge through a ruck of defenders to shoot home. It was all even.

Both sides were exhausted, and the 30 minutes of extra-time proved to be a stalemate, with neither conceding any ground nor being able to snatch the advantage. And so it came to penalties.

Six months before, Tony Parks was, said Curry, "the anonymous reserve in the shadow of England's veteran Ray Clemence. Now… young Parks, fresh-faced and a novice in the hard world of professional football, had five eyeball-to-eyeball confrontations with Belgian marksmen in the space of just a few anxious, almost unbearable minutes".

Lionheart Roberts stepped up first to slam his spot-kick home. Morten Olsen placed the ball for Anderlecht's first kick. Parks says: "He just looked into the bottom corner by my left hand and I thought, 'That's it, I'm going there'. I chucked myself at it and just got it round the post." Advantage Spurs.

Mark Falco scored for Spurs, then Kenneth Brylle for the Belgians. Gary Stevens converted, as did Enzo Scifo, then Steve Archibald, then Franky Vercauteren. If Danny

WHITE HART HEROES

BATTLE IN EUROPE

Thomas scored his penalty, the trophy was won. But Jacques Munaron saved Thomas's shot. Thomas looked crushed. Then a crowd so often unfairly criticised for being fickle sent forth a mighty chant – "There's only one Danny Thomas". The moment is still incredibly moving when watched again.

Now the pressure was on Arnor Gudjohnson, father of Eidur. Gudjohnson Snr. stepped up, placed the ball and struck his shot. "It was the worst penalty in the world," says Parks. "It was just a shocker, my mum would have saved it." Parks got his hands to the ball, rolled twice and – as the stadium erupted – ran at full pelt until he was flattened by his jubilant team-mates. "I genuinely did not know what to do," he says. "If that gate in the corner had been open I would've been down at Seven Sisters in seconds."

It looked a brilliant save, for all Parks's modesty, and the magnitude of his performance was succinctly summed up later by Spurs author Bob Goodwin who observed that "never can a man have become such a legend on the basis of just one game".

Perryman got his hands on the cup during the lap og honour, Ardiles gave him his medal, and Burkinshaw was unusually emotional. "The fighting spirit of the lads was tremendous," he said. "This was one of those nights which makes you feel lucky to be involved in football. Somebody up there must have taken a liking to me. It was the sort of night you dream about forever."

*Parks, Thomas, Hughton, **Roberts**, Miller (Ardiles), Mabbutt (Dick), Hazard, Archibald, Falco, Stevens, Galvin*

LOOKING BACK WITH **STEVE PERRYMAN**

Steve Perryman missed Keith Burkinshaw's farewell game as manager of Spurs, the UEFA Cup Final second leg when stand-in skipper Graham Roberts lifted the trophy on an emotional European glory night.

For Perryman it was one of the biggest disappointments in his long and distinguished career. "In all my years in Europe for Spurs, this was the campaign in which I felt I had more command over the direction of the Tottenham team and had done more to keep us in the competition.

"I had played right through the season and throughout the European campaign, working hard with a young side in Munich and playing alongside Micky Hazard against Hajduk."

Perryman's annoyance with the decision to book him for an innocuous challenge late in the first leg of the final in Belgium is tempered by the realisation that he deserved his first yellow card of the competition against Austria Vienna.

He recalls: "I fully deserved to get booked in the home tie against Austria Vienna. We were up against some very good footballers and even our crowd were appreciative of their skills. And that can be annoying. We would not expect warm applause if we played well away from home! We were confronted by a majestic midfield player who burst clear and I felt I had to bring him down.

"Yes, it was a professional foul, which is another word for cheating. I'm not proud of what I did, but I felt it had to be done for the good of the team, and to keep the club in Europe.

"Bill Nick would talk about controlled aggression. We'd learn that away goals are vital. As a player, you build yourself up to do well and progress in Europe. You cannot weigh all that up in the split second it takes to commit such an act. It's all relevant to how the team is playing at the time. We were struggling. They were stringing good passes together and moving sweetly from one end of the pitch to the other.

"The frustration at not being able to control this team, the tension of the night, and faced by a quality player… you live and die by your commitment.

"I tripped him. But there was no intent to hurt him. There have been a lot of cases in Europe where I deserved to get booked and didn't. Here I deserved it, and I got it.

"But there was absolutely no way I deserved a booking against Anderlecht. We were hanging on at 1-1 and I put my foot up to go for the ball. My only aim was to get the ball as far away from our goal as possible.

"I missed the ball, but I also missed the player. The Swiss referee must have felt it was dangerous play because I went in with my studs showing.

"A player has few opportunities to play in cup finals. To miss any final is a dampner, but it was so disappointing to know I would miss the match at Spurs after such a good performance in Belgium against the UEFA Cup holders.

"The Anderlecht players were delighted that I was booked. They were only too aware that I'd be ruled out of the second leg.

"They boasted that they would now slaughter us at Tottenham. But it didn't quite work out that way, even though I wasn't playing."

Steve Perryman gets his hands on the Cup but missed out on playing in the victory at White Hart Lane

Keith Burkinshaw's final night as Spurs manager ends in perfect fashion

SPOTLIGHT ON THE DRAMA AT WHITE HART LANE

BURKY'S FINAL GLORY!

LOOKING BACK WITH
KEITH BURKINSHAW

It was 12.15 in Tottenham High Road on a wet Thursday morning. The rain was still falling, but it did not bother Keith Burkinshaw. He was being hailed by the remains of a White Hart Lane full house.

From the club offices in White Hart Lane's famous Red House, he looked down for the last time on the Spurs fans. It was his swansong – and what a swansong.

Burkinshaw remembers: "It was a wonderful feeling. I had thought from the semi-final stage when we played so well at Hajduk Split in Yugoslavia that we could win the competition. I never lost that feeling until just before Graham Roberts scored his late equaliser for us against Anderlecht at home. We had played some magnificent football in Brussels and deserved a lot more than the 1-1 draw with which we came away.

"The team knew that Anderlecht were an outstanding team and that they would come at us in London. They scored a superb goal and for a long time looked as though they would beat us. Then Graham scored only the sort of goal that he could score to earn us extra-time. Then I knew it was our cup again."

But not before the drama of a penalty shoot-out. Burkinshaw remembers: "When Tony made his save the place went wild. There were people jumping around on the bench. That was not my style though. I just sat calmly through it. I thought at the moment the save was made that I was better sitting back and enjoying the moment. Some people found it hard to watch the penalties. I felt better watching them than not.

"It was a very emotional moment when I picked up the trophy and I am not usually an emotional person. There was a great feeling of satisfaction. It was a nostalgic moment. It was a wonderful way to finish."

Looking back on the response of the crowd, Burkinshaw said: "It was wonderful. I had a great affinity with the Tottenham public; they always seemed to appreciate the type of team that I was trying to produce for them.

"I remember standing there thinking how wonderful everything was. Everything had gelled at the right moment."

LOOKING BACK WITH
TONY PARKS

"I just knew I could save those penalties," recalls Parks. And when they handed him the massive trophy, there was absolutely no chance he would drop it.

Parks had played in a major final, emerging from the obscurity of reserve team football to take over the goalkeeper's jersey from the great Ray Clemence.

"The funny thing was, I was very nervous throughout the whole of the 90 minutes and extra-time. While the final had been an ordeal of nerves, the penalty shoot-out filled me with confidence. I could actually feel the confidence flooding through me.

"I loved penalty competitions in training. I'd stay behind with one of my mates and see how many I could save or my mate could score. Ian Crook and Mike Hazard were my deadly rivals, and I'd usually win quite a few. I just loved diving about going for penalties.

"When it came to the penalties in the final, I knew if I didn't save any, no one would say it was my fault. You can't blame the goalkeeper for conceding a penalty.

"When any keeper goes for a penalty he must move a little, there's no other way. Wait for the ball to be kicked and you've got no chance.

"Everyone talks about my second penalty save. But I felt my first save was the more difficult.

"I watched Morten Olsen when he put the ball on the spot. I watched his eyes. He was looking to the right. That's where I thought he would place the ball.

"I guessed right and pushed the shot around the post. The noise from the crowd was deafening. It sent shivers down my spine.

"It was now up to the lads to score and I was hoping everything would go alright, and it did, until Danny Thomas missed his penalty.

"When it came to the last penalty, I still felt sure I could save it.

"It came at me at the right height, a lovely height to make it look a spectacular save. We all like a bit of glory, and I must admit I made it look a better save than it was...I took a leaf out of Bruce Grobbelaar's book."

LOOKING BACK WITH **GRAHAM ROBERTS**

Ask Graham Roberts which was the most memorable week in his footballing career and he will tell you immediately. "It was in May 1984."

For in that week Roberts, the famously tough former Tottenham defender, became a television hero for millions of soccer fans up and down the country.

It was in a pulsating UEFA Cup Final second leg at White Hart Lane against the Belgian artists of Anderlecht that Roberts's determination reaped its rewards.

"It was an amazing week," said Roberts. "Steve Perryman had been suspended for the second leg after he had been booked in Brussels.

"Immediately after the first leg Steve had told the lads in the dressing room that he was out of the return and I had an inkling that I would be captain.

"It was an honour that I had only dreamt about. I had always wanted to be the captain of a major club and here was the chance in one of the European finals."

Graham was officially told by manager Keith Burkinshaw on the Monday of the game that he was to lead the side.

"That was a special moment for me," he remembers. "Captaining the side is something really different and I decided to play it the only way I know. I wanted to lead the lads by example.

"At the time I think I was at the peak of my career and I was playing as well as anyone but my game was based on giving all I had.

"With it being Keith Burkinshaw's last match as well there was just as great a determination among the players to do well for him. I don't think that we ever mentioned it as a team, but we all knew that we had to make the day special."

Roberts did more than anyone else in the Spurs team to make sure that Burkinshaw's dream of leaving White Hart Lane with a major trophy came true.

There were only a few minutes left when Steve Archibald's shot was turned away for a corner. The cross came in and the ball fell to substitute Ossie Ardiles who shot against the bar.

Roberts takes up the story. "Micky Hazard normally liked to beat a player before crossing but this time he crossed early and the ball cannoned off my chest.

"There were two Anderlecht defenders close by but by taking the ball on the chest, I went away from them.

"That I think was the hard bit. I simply hit the ball then and hoped. It was an incredible feeling of ecstasy and pain. As soon as I ran to the crowd my legs went.

"Hazard jumped on me immediately and he would not let go. The noise was terrific. I was in a total daze."

Roberts also took the responsibility of taking the first penalty for Tottenham in the important penalty shoot-out.

He admits he was in a quandary about what to do after the victory. "I desperately wanted Steve Perryman to be a part of the occasion and when it came to collecting the cup I was thinking of dragging Steve up with me. I mentioned it to Keith Burkinshaw, but he was not sure if we could get into trouble because Steve was suspended and not supposed to be playing a part in the event.

"Steve also said that he wanted the 11 players who had played in the final to get the final accolade. It was a very emotional moment.

"The whole thing seems a blur now. I had tears in my eyes and I can remember desperately searching the crowd for my then wife, Anne. It was a wonderful moment."

Even now, the man who was snatched from non-league football at Weymouth by Burkinshaw plays tapes of that famous night: "It certainly helps to lift me in the bad times."

SAVE OF THE CENTURY!

EURO SOCCER SPECIAL

Parks wins Cup for Spurs

SPURS v ANDERLECHT
IN PICTURES

Three steps to football heaven...

Above: Tony Parks gets some last-minute advice from Ray Clemence

Centre: Parks leaps to his left to save

Anderlecht's first penalty of the night, from Morten Olsen

Bottom: Parks can only watch as Danny Thomas's potentially match-winning penalty is saved by Jacky Munaron

Right: How Parks's subsequent final cup-winning save felt – emotions are written large on the faces of Ossie Ardiles, Gary Stevens, Graham Roberts and Chris Hughton

TOTTENHAM v ANDERLECHT
IN PICTURES

UEFA CUP 1983/84
COUPE D' UEFA
1984
9-5   23-5
Anderlecht
FINAL
FINALE
R.S.C. ANDERLECHT
TOTTENHAM HOTSPUR

R.S.C. ANDERLECHT - TOTTENHAM HOTSPUR
STADE Constant VANDEN STOCK STADION
te ANDERLECHT
PLACE DEBOUT
STAANPLAATS
350 F BLOC
BLOK N

Memories of a famous fortnight in May 1984

Above: A fans' pennant, a ticket from the game in Brussels and a souvenir badge

Right: How *Spurs News*, the club's monthly newspaper, recorded the memorable ongoing celebrations after the trophy was presented at White Hart Lane

● Above, left: Mark Falco more champagne than he m to drink from the massive Cup!

PICTURE MICK EASON

● Left: Ray Clemence and Perryman — who both playe roles from the sidelines — Spurs success.

● Manager Keith Burkinshaw looks on as Ossie Ardiles and Dr Brian Curtin, the club's medical officer, reach champagne.

S GLORY NIGHT

● **Above:** The victorous Spurs squad show off the UEFA Cup after their marathon success.

● **Above, right:** Steve Archibald lifts the cup.

● **Right:** The champers flows afterwards at the end of a thrilling game.

...rving Scholar, injured in a recent Spurs Staff match, enjoys the dressing room ...rations from his wheelchair.

● Tottenham's Three Degrees — Garth Crooks, Chris Hughton and Danny Thomas — on a high note.

U.E.F.A. 1983-84
FINAL

THE ROAD TO EUROPE

1984

Victory in the 1984 UEFA Cup Final came with the added bonus of earning Spurs another crack at the competition the following season. Domestic league and cup form had fallen away as Burkinshaw's reign drew to a close, hinting at longer-term difficulties to come as the club tried to steer an uncertain course to a more commercial goal.

In the summer of 1984, however, there was an atmosphere of renewed confidence. The club was firmly established in the"'Big Five". Peter Shreeve had stepped up from the position of assistant manager to take over as boss. His appointment combined a degree of continuity with the promise engendered by a fresh start. While Steve Archibald had left to join Barcelona, new signings Clive Allen and John Chiedozie joined the established stars and those players becoming integral to the team, such as Gary Mabbutt, Gary Stevens and Danny Thomas.

The side was to make the most credible title challenge of any Spurs side for a generation. But both at home and in Europe, the team fell just short. No one was to know, however, that it would be the last chance for Spurs or indeed any English side to make an impression in European competition for the rest of the decade.

The Spurs squad pose on the terraces during their pre-match inspection of the stadium in Prague prior to their controversial tie with Bohemians

A BUNCH OF CROOKS!
EUROPE SOCCER SPECIAL
Hat-trick hero again

Glenn Hoddle, who came on as a sub, struts his stuff at White Hart Lane as Spurs breezed through their UEFA Cup first-round tie v Braga

19 September 1984, first round, first leg

SC BRAGA 0
TOTTENHAM HOTSPUR 3

Estadio Primeiro de Maio, Braga, Portugal *Att*: 26,000

The tie against Braga featured a neat little twist on north London rivalry. Playing in the same colour kit as the Gunners, the Portuguese side are nicknamed the "Arsenalistas", thanks to a connection dating back to the 1930s and an Arsenal-admiring coach. Braga did not pose quite the same strength of opposition as the team from Highbury often did, however, and were brushed aside with relative ease. The Spurs of the Eighties were becoming old hands at the European game and, after containing an early Braga flurry, took control. Mark Falco was the star performer. "There is no more modest hero in the English game," wrote Brian Scovell in the *Daily Mail*, and Falco scored twice before half-time to prove it, first from a Chris Hughton centre and then a Mickey Hazard through ball. Tony Galvin completed an excellent first half with Tottenham's third.

*Clemence, Mabbutt, Hughton, Roberts, Miller, Perryman, Chiedozie, **Falco 2**, Allen (Crooks), Hazard (Thomas), **Galvin***

3 October 1984, first round, second leg

TOTTENHAM HOTSPUR 6 (9)
SC BRAGA 0 (0)

White Hart Lane *Att*: 22,478

It was one of those nights when everything seemed to go right. Spurs purred, Garth Crooks notched a second hat-trick in a week after hitting three against lowly Halifax Town in the cup, and Glenn Hoddle returned from injury as a second-half substitute after six months on the sidelines. Hoddle soon showed what the fans had been missing, feeding Crooks a beautiful ball to score his second in the 57th minute. Spurs were already three goals to the good by then, thanks to Gary Stevens's long-range shot from a poorly cleared corner in the 10th minute, a second five minutes later from a suspiciously offside-looking Chris Hughton, and a first from an unmarked Crooks on 26 minutes when he headed home a Tony Galvin cross. Mark Falco made it 5-0 in the 65th minute, before Crooks latched on to a weakly hit backpass to score his third, and Tottenham's sixth, eight minutes from time.

*Clemence, **Stevens**, **Hughton**, Roberts, Miller (Hoddle), Perryman, Chiedozie, **Falco** (Cooke), Galvin, Hazard, **Crooks 3***

HODDLE SENT OFF

Spurs's shock night

CLUB BRUGGE K.V. 1891

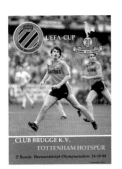

24 October 1984, second round, second leg

FC BRUGES 2
TOTTENHAM HOTSPUR 1

Olympiastadion, Bruges, Belgium *Att:* 27,000

Spurs made a swift return to Belgium, but the fonder memories of the draw with Anderlecht the previous May were not to be repeated against Bruges. A feisty performance from the visitors saw a sending off for Glenn Hoddle, a caution and a ban for Chris Hughton, and numerous other indiscretions. The punishment Tottenham suffered should perhaps have been greater than what turned out to be a surmountable 2-1 deficit. Bruges had taken the lead after six minutes when Jan Cuelemans finished off a swift break. Tottenham were the better side, but in the 83rd minute the home side's goalkeeper, Birger Jensen, ran the length of the field to convert a penalty, given away when Steve Perryman fouled Mark Degryse (who would play for Sheffield Wednesday in the 1990s). Spurs had created chances but looked to be leaving empty handed until sub Clive Allen scored just before the final whistle.

*Clemence, Stevens, Hughton, Roberts, Miller, Perryman, Chiedozie, Falco Galvin, Hazard (Hoddle), Crooks (**Allen**)*

7 November 1984, second round, second leg

TOTTENHAM HOTSPUR 3 (4)
FC BRUGES 0 (2)

White Hart Lane *Att:* 34,356

Spurs made amends for the showing in Bruges with a comprehensive win – though not everyone was pleased. For *The Times*'s David Miller, "it was clear that [Bruges'] superior level of coordinated skill might have carried them through", while for Spurs "there are areas in which their lack of refinement… suggest they will always be in difficulties against teams capable of attacking them through the middle". The judgement seemed harsh. Spurs made a brilliant start, equalising on aggregate within five minutes when a John Chiedozie corner found Micky Hazard lurking on the edge of the area to score with a superb left-foot strike. Graham Roberts' hefty tackle on Jan Ceulemans negated the Belgian's influence and Spurs took control. Clive Allen made it 2-0 on 27 minutes when he tapped in after goalkeeper Birger Jensen spilled a cross, before Roberts smashed in a third 11 minutes before half-time.

*Clemence, Stevens, Mabbutt, **Roberts**, Miller, Perryman, Chiedozie (Brooke), Falco (Thomas), **Allen**, **Hazard**, Galvin*

Gary Mabbut is in action as Spurs comfortably overturn a first-leg deficit v Bruges

THANK THE CZECH MATES!

28 November 1984, third round, first leg

TOTTENHAM HOTSPUR 2
BOHEMIANS PRAGUE 0

White Hart Lane *Att: 27,971*

The meeting with Bohemians was a definitive tie of two matches. In the second, the Czechs resorted to a level of physical intimidation Spurs had not experienced since the clash with Barcelona in 1982. But at White Hart Lane, Bohemians presented a wholly different face, and their imaginative football deserved better reward than a 2-0 reverse.

"The Tottenham public," wrote Jeff Powell in the *Daily Mail*, "were treated last night to an exhibition of superlative skills, reminiscent of the glory, glory days… But the performance which took the breath away was given by 11 footballers anonymous this side of the iron curtain… Tottenham were out-thought, out-paced, out-manoeuvred, outclassed and frequently out on their feet."

Powell's assessment was scathing but brutally honest. Spurs chased Czech shadows for much of the game, with Jakubec Sloup conducting the play and opening up Spurs almost at will. But for wasteful finishing, and some outstanding goalkeeping from Ray Clemence, Spurs would surely have suffered their first-ever home defeat in Europe. Instead, a rare opening in the 25th minute gave Tottenham a fortunate lead, when John Chiedozie's cross was sliced into his own net by Jiri Ondra.

It was Tottenham's first effort on goal, and they barely fashioned another until the final minute of the game, when Gary Stevens gave Spurs a scarcely credible 2-0 advantage with a 25-yard drive. It was telling that Stevens had been Tottenham's best player. Glenn Hoddle and Micky Hazard, the creative heartbeat of the home team, had been either subdued or given the run-around. The Spurs attack had been blunt and ineffective. Tottenham would need a significant improvement if they were to progress further in the competition and hold onto their trophy.

Clemence, **Stevens**, *Mabbutt (Hughton), Roberts, Miller, Perryman, Chiedozie, Falco, Allen, Hoddle, Hazard (Cooke)* [og Ondra]

Clive Allen duels with a Prague opponent on a subdued night for the Spurs strikeforce, despite the scoreline

BLOODY MARVELS

Shreeves salute to Spurs after Bohemian battle

Peter Shreeves

12 December 1984, third round, second leg

BOHEMIANS PRAGUE 1 (1)
TOTTENHAM HOTSPUR 1 (3)

Stadion Vrsovice, Prague, Czechoslovakia *Att: 17,500*

The contrast between the Bohemians of the first leg and the return in Prague could not have been more marked. The Czechs had been fluent, elegant and refined visitors in London, and had received applause from the more sporting sections of the White Hart Lane crowd. Any of those Tottenham fans who made the trip to Prague, however, were in no mood to congratulate their hosts after seeing their side survive a violent physical test.

At the height of the Cold War, trips to Eastern Bloc countries carried a tang of intrigue, daring, and a sense of the unknown. Few supporters would have predicted Bohemians would turn so nasty, though manager Peter Shreeve and the players were well briefed. Even then the severity of Bohemians' play was an eye-opener – almost literally in Glenn Hoddle's case. The midfielder was subjected to a terrible first-half challenge from Jakubec Sloup. The Czech playmaker bared his Mr Hyde teeth after his nice-guy Dr Jekyll display

two weeks before, giving Hoddle a nasty cut eye, concussion and a bad thigh strain.

Graham Roberts was also on the receiving end as Bohemians tried to bully Spurs into submission. It was to Tottenham's credit that they resisted. They took the lead on seven minutes when Mark Falco's header topped off fine work by Garth Crooks and Tony Galvin. The lead was cancelled out by Zdeněk Proke's 50th-minute equaliser, but Spurs saw off the combined intimidation of opponents and a hostile crowd to win through on aggregate.

At the airport that night, Spurs players received a standing ovation from the fans returning home, with the compliment returned in kind. A dazed Hoddle, however, his head swathed in bandages, was clearly in no fit state to know what was going on. It had been quite an experience.

*Clemence, Stevens, Hughton, Roberts, Miller, Perryman, Chiedozie, **Falco**, Galvin, Hoddle (Mabbutt), Crooks (Thomas)*

Glenn Hoddle is poleaxed by Sloup, but Spurs held firm in an attritional contest in Prague

LOOKING BACK WITH **GLENN HODDLE**

The games against Bruges and Bohemians had certainly been eventful for Glenn Hoddle. He admitted it was sheer stupidity that got him sent off against Brugge. It was a tough time for the England international, back in the first team after an extended lay-off.

He said: "After my Achilles operation, I was keyed-up to do well as I made my comeback after a frustrating seven months out.

"I came on for Micky Hazard and straight away Bruges scored from a penalty. Somebody brought Tony Galvin down. It's not normally like me to get involved. But I did. I was only on the field for a few minutes, and here I was getting booked.

"The referee blew his whistle, and as he did the ball rolled to me. I clipped it down the wing. The next minute I was sitting in the dressing room. I couldn't believe I'd been sent off.

"I'd waited so long for my return. I suppose all the frustration simply built up and spilled over. It was such a silly incident. It wasn't just as if I'd gone up and kicked someone. Just two very silly incidents, all very harmless, but there I was back in the dressing room."

Hoddle had been sent off once before in his career. And on that occasion too it was a harmless incident that proved to be his downfall.

"It was a game against Crystal Palace. I had broken down their offside trap but Jerry Murphy pulled me back by my shirt. To push him off I caught him with my arm. The referee must have thought it was a punch."

In fact, the 1984/85 season's UEFA Cup campaign was a personal nightmare for Glenn Hoddle. After the frustration of the sending off in the second round against Bruges, in Prague he was carried off after one of the ugliest tackles imaginable.

"I've never experienced an incident like it, and I hope I never do again," he says.

"I shouted for the ball from our goalkeeper Ray Clemence, and he threw the ball toward me, in the centre of the pitch.

"I heard Garth Crooks shout, 'He's coming.' In the videos before the game we all knew that Sloup was a little 'naughty' in his tackling. I guessed that Garth meant that this fellow was coming after me.

"I went to flick the ball to one side of him and run around to collect it. I thought he was coming at me from behind. As it turned out he came to my left.

"I flicked the ball and turned and he hit me full-on on the thigh with his foot while, at the same time, his elbow caught me on the forehead and caused a massive cut."

Hoddle didn't pass out, but he didn't remember too much more about the game.

"It was the thigh injury that caused me more concern, although my split forehead looked the worst of my injuries."

Graham Roberts and Glenn Hoddle compare injuries after the game in Prague

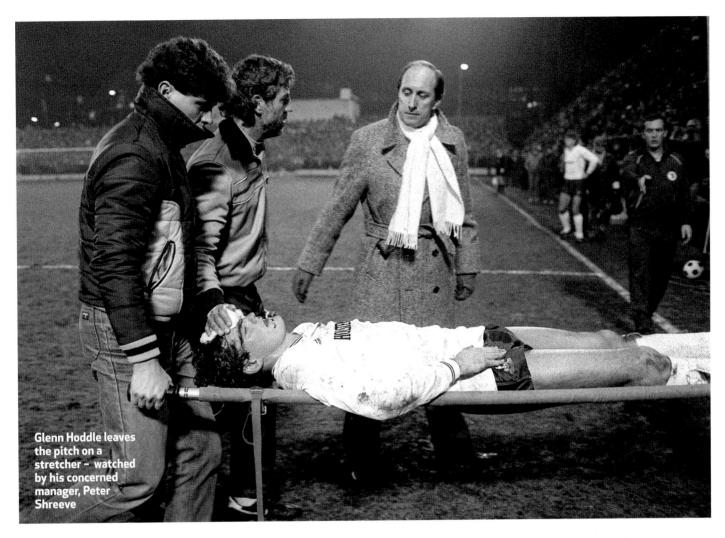

Glenn Hoddle leaves the pitch on a stretcher – watched by his concerned manager, Peter Shreeve

LOOKING BACK WITH **PETER SHREEVE**

When Tottenham Hotspur beat Bruges 3-0 in the second leg of the UEFA Cup at White Hart Lane in November 1984, the Belgian coach put his finger on the difference in European football.

Peter Shreeve sat in his office at the club and the Bruges coach shook his hand and said simply: "I wish that we could generate the spirit that English players show."

That match had seen Spurs start 2-1 down after a stormy first leg in Belgium, but Shreeve said: "We beat them by sheer heart.

"They looked so confident in that first leg, but they could not cope with the blood-and-thunder type of football that English teams play. Even the great teams like Bayern Munich never liked playing English teams because, no matter what the score, they knew they could not relax.

"When we played them on the way to the final in 1984 we lost 1-0 on one of the coldest

nights I can remember. When a television commentator asked me for my comments on the match I was so cold I could not talk.

"But they thought that they had it all tied up, and in the second leg they could not cope either. It was strange that other countries just could not produce that special type of game."

But the match that sticks in Shreeve's memory the most from that season was the battle in Prague in December:

"It showed how deceptive appearances could be. In the first match they came to London, they murdered us playing some delightful football and lost 2-0. They looked a gentle little football team.

"Then I spoke with Aad de Mos, the Ajax coach whose team had lost to them in the previous round. He told me exactly what we could expect when we got to Prague, and to be honest we did not believe it. Then I got a videotape of the match.

"The players watched it after training one day and they were shocked. They did not think that it was the same team they had played."

But the same team it was and in Prague the battle was fierce. Glenn Hoddle came home with a damaged thigh and a cut eye. Other players suffered cuts and bruises.

Shreeve said: "I don't think that I have ever been prouder of a Spurs team. They were intimidated in every way, but they stood shoulder to shoulder and fought hard.

"They tried to intimidate us so much, but the lads still kept their heads. It reminded me very much of the Barcelona attitude some years before. They needed to win at all costs. I will never forget the pre-Terry Venables days at Barcelona. When they played us they fielded eight defenders at home.

"They did not care about the feelings of their fans. They just wanted a result. They had drawn 1-1 in Tottenham and knew 0-0 was good enough. The game does not prosper from things like that."

Ray Clemence is helpless as Steve Perryman accidentally diverts the ball into his own net. The goal condemned Spurs to a first home defeat in Europe

STEVIE BLUNDER

Perryman own goal puts Spurs on ropes

6 March 1985, fourth round, first leg

TOTTENHAM HOTSPUR 0
REAL MADRID 1

White Hart Lane *Att:* 39,914

Tottenham's first meeting with arguably the grandest name in club football was a watershed. It was the last glory glory glamour night at White Hart Lane for 25 years. It also ended Spurs' long and proud unbeaten home record and was the first time they had failed to score at home in Europe.

Stretching back 24 years and 44 matches, the records were bound to be broken at some point. But despite a substantial increase in one-off ticket prices, Spurs fans turned up in their droves.

It was a heady night dripping with expectation and history. Spurs wore the all-white kit that had been chosen in Real's honour. The Spanish were clad in purple, the regal colour of kings, and they delivered an imperious performance. Real may have been struggling in the league and had not dominated Europe for a generation, but they were a formidable side packed with world-class talent including Emilio Butragueno, Michel, Uli Stielike and Jorge Valdano.

Real were developing an attack dubbed *La Quinta del Buitre*, or 'The Vulture's Cohort', named after Butragueno. Its leader proved key to Tottenham's undoing. After holding Spurs' early flurry at bay, Real sprang into action in the 15th minute when Michel released Butragueno down the right. He outpaced Gary Stevens and Paul Miller, and drilled a hard centre low into the Tottenham area. With Valdano lurking, Ray Clemence got a touch onto the ball, only to see it rebound off Steve Perryman and into the net.

It was a desperately unlucky setback, but while Tottenham's effort could not be faulted, they lacked the nous to undo Madrid's defence. Glenn Hoddle was subdued, while, as *The Guardian*'s David Lacey noted, Spurs "badly missed the power of the suspended [Graham] Roberts".

Clemence, Stevens, Hughton, Hazard, Miller (Dick), Perryman, Chiedozie (Brooks), Falco, Galvin, Hoddle, Crooks

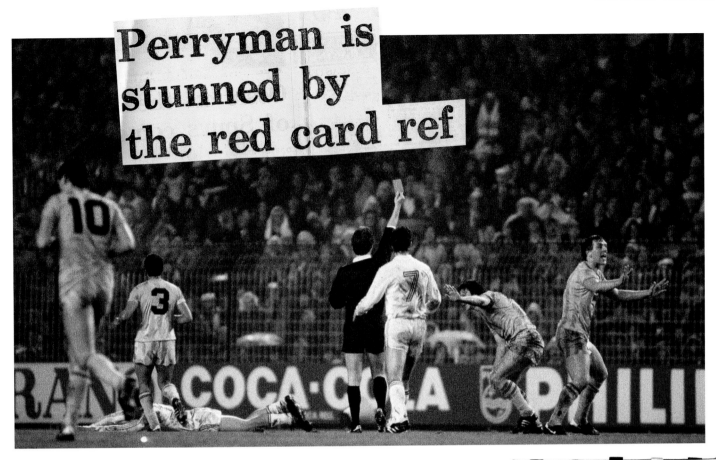

Perryman is stunned by the red card ref

20 March 1985, fourth round, second leg

REAL MADRID 0 (1)
TOTTENHAM HOTSPUR 0 (0)

Santiago Bernabeu, Madrid, Spain *Att: 90,000*

Steve Perryman's misery is complete as he picks up a red card at the Bernabeu. It would be his last appearance for Spurs in Europe and a sad end to a fourth consecutive campaign for the successful Eighties side

Tottenham's grip on the UEFA Cup was removed at the quarter-final stage in a clear case of what might have been. Spurs played well in a tight and tense match, but a controversial disallowed goal rankled long after the campaign was over.

When Mark Falco rose to head home late on, it appeared the tie was heading for extra-time. But, to the anger of the Tottenham players and the bewilderment of Madrid's, referee Bruno Galler ruled the goal out, supposedly for a foul by Falco.

It was a maddening decision on a night of huge frustration. Despite the din of a vast and partisan home crowd, Spurs refused to be cowed in such a vaunted arena as the Bernabeu and seized the initiative. The returning Graham Roberts twice went close, firstly through a searing 25-yard drive saved by Angel and then a header the goalkeeper kept out at the foot of the post. At the other end Ray Clemence used all his experience to deny Real when Michel threatened.

For Tottenham's principal leader, however, the tie was one to forget. Having conceded an unlucky own goal in the first leg, Steve Perryman was then sent off for a foul on Jorge Valdano as the Argentinian was poised to break through in the 79th minute.

It was only the third time in his long and distinguished career that Perryman had been dismissed and signalled a sad close to his and the club's participation in Europe. The awful events in Heysel that year enforced an exile on all English clubs. With nine of the remaining 14 domestic league games remaining at White Hart Lane, hopes were high that Tottenham would finally end their long wait for a Championship, but with mounting injuries the title was lost. It was a season of disappointment both abroad and at home.

Clemence, Thomas, Hughton, Roberts, Miller, Perryman, Hazard, Falco, Galvin (Dick), Hoddle, Crooks (Brooke)

LOOKING BACK WITH **STEVE PERRYMAN**

For Steve Perryman the nightmare of Spurs' first home defeat in Europe was multiplied by his own peculiar miseries… an own goal to contribute to Spurs' downfall in front of their own fans, and then a sending off in the return tie.

"The repercussions of that own goal were immense," recalls Perryman, "it was a piece of history… gone – the first home defeat. But I've no recriminations. There was absolutely nothing I could have done to avoid that. There was a cross from the by-line, Ray Clemence got a touch, and as I was coming back to cover, the ball struck me on the knee and flew in.

"It would have required quicksilver thinking to have got out of the way."

Spurs, the UEFA Cup holders, crashed out of the competition with that goalless draw in Madrid.

"It was a niggly game. Graham Roberts was having problems with Real's Argentinian player, Valdano. I was playing in midfield with Glenn Hoddle and this was one of our better performances, although it didn't work out for us on the night.

"They didn't seem to be looking too much for goals, while we played some good football. Then, Valdano came across me, kicking out and connecting with my calf and Achilles, an area of the body I detest being injured.

"The worst injury any athlete can have is an Achilles. This tackle made my blood boil. Ossie told me after the match that the guy thought I was Roberts and that's why he made the challenge.

"But I was convinced he was out to get me. I got him first. I really went for him, it was repayment for that tackle 10 minutes earlier.

"There was also a lot of frustration. Mark Falco seemed to score a perfectly good goal, but it was disallowed. We watched the replay on Spanish TV, but it just confirmed what we thought at the time – there was no foul. The referee must have thought that Mark had climbed on the back of the defender to make his far-post header."

Perryman recalled in *The Times* in 2011, "At the end we were pushing up and leaving ourselves open. The ball broke and I was the last man, so I stopped Valdano and got sent off for it. I'm not proud. It was a selfish act and it didn't benefit the team, but I was trying to level out an injustice over the officiating and foul play."

In the Bernabeu changing rooms, there was no hot water for Perryman to take an early shower until Cliff Speight, the assistant physio, complained long and loudly enough to get the plumbing sorted. Perryman's team-mates, meanwhile, offered their captain commiserations.

"I was thinking, 'Nothing to do with bad luck, I deserved it,'" Perryman said. "But later, Bill Nicholson said to me, 'You silly sod, why'd you do that?'

"We might have equalised and then we would have needed 11 men in extra-time. He was right."

Steve Perryman captains Spurs in Europe for the last time in Madrid

LOOKING BACK WITH
PETER SHREEVE

It was 3am in a Sydney hotel on 30 May 1985. The Spurs players were gathering around their sandwiches and beer waiting for the live screening of the European Cup final from Brussels. They were on a tour of Australia and as Peter Shreeve said: "Suddenly the world was turned upside down. We felt sick to our stomachs." What made Shreeve and his squad so upset were the pictures of the carnage in the Heysel stadium. Pictures showing English fans on the rampage and Italian fans dying under the crush of a broken wall.

Shreeve said: "There had been a general decline of standards in society and football reflected it. It was a sad day. It hit the clubs dramatically. We knew that we would be banned from European football.

"Tottenham had qualified and yet we knew from that moment that we were not going to play for a long, long time. In the context of people losing their lives, though, that was a minor consideration."

Tottenham had been faced in that season with the problems of hooligans in Europe. There had been trouble in the previous seasons in Holland and Belgium.

Indeed in Bruges that year the club had gone as far as banning their supporters from travelling to the game to prevent trouble. Shreeve said: "We try to be professional at all times, and when our opposition would not listen we asked our fans not to travel.

"We felt that we had almost come to terms with the problem but a lot of the difficulties were making the local club and police face up to the problems. We went to Hajduk Split in the semi-final of the UEFA Cup and they seemed shocked when we suggested segregation in the ground.

"We knew that the penalty for any more misbehaviour by the fans would be hard. We were not shocked at the reaction of UEFA in banning the English clubs after Heysel."

Within two weeks English clubs were ordered home and the FIFA ban on friendlies outside Western Europe was to last until December 1985. In a pre-emptive move the Football Association imposed a ban on English clubs. It was not lifted until 1990.

The glory nights were over – for now.

Farewell to the 80s, Peter Shreeve and Keith Burkinshaw hold aloft the UEFA Cup in 1984 – the undoubted highlight of the decade

IN CONVERSATION WITH
PAUL MILLER & MICKY HAZARD

The third chapter of Tottenham's European story was to feature some the club's finest and most dramatic exploits. Two key figures of the era were Paul Miller and Micky Hazard – home-grown talents inspired by the club's proud traditions to take on Europe's best and succeed.

One of the things that's notable about the 1980s Spurs side is that you were different to other English teams?

Paul Miller Europe was made for us. That team was suited to Europe more, possibly, than the English league.

Micky Hazard That was a bit blood and thunder. We had very gifted, talented players who liked to play in a much more European style. I always looked forward to Europe simply because I thought we'd be brilliant due to the quality and type of player we had.

PM Steve, Clem, Ossie and Ricky in the World Cup – we had a lot of experience, and internationals, so we weren't strangers to that kind of football.

MH For me the heart and soul of every club is the youth that it brings through to the first team. Spurs at that time had Stevie P, Chris Hughton, who was also in my youth team, Paul, Robbo and Tony Galvin, who were more or less home-grown, Mark Falco, Ally Dick, Garry Brooke, Mark Bowen, Ian Crook, Ian Culverhouse, Tony Parks, and of course Glenn Hoddle. So we had a lot of heart and soul out on the pitch and it was supplemented by big-name, talented signings.

How did that team measure up against foreign opposition? Did they have better technique than domestic players – it's something we hear a lot, these days.

MH European players were not necessarily more technical than English ones. Whenever you came up against continentals they could all pass and control, and it was a much shorter game than the English style, which was very long. It was difficult to play against but it wasn't technically *better* than us – it was their style that made them look more technically gifted than the English player.

When you watch Spain they very rarely play a pass over 10-15 yards – it's the simplicity of their passing and the timing of their movement that enables them to be so good. They don't hit Glenn Hoddle-type passes.

I never felt inferior technically. I looked around our team and I never thought any side had more technically gifted players in that era. I would go so far as to say that Glenn was the most technically gifted player I ever saw.

PM We have to remember that at the time we were playing some of the best players in Europe in the English league. English teams had great players and we weren't going to be playing too many players in Europe that were better than them. We'd get briefed on

Paul Miller with a Real Madrid shirt, 1985

the opposition – "We're playing Eintracht Frankfurt and they've got a great centre-forward." Yeah? So what, we're playing against great centre-forwards *every* week. There would always be a special player – when we played Bayern Munich they had Karl-Heinz Rummenigge and Paul Breitner, for example. But we had very good players. We were always positive, it was more about us than them and they weren't happy to play us, because we could mix it *and* play.

You also had a strong club tradition in Europe to live up to. To what extent was that communicated to you?

PM The first time you played at Spurs you met our junior coach Ron Henry. Ron reminded us constantly about how he won the Double and the Cup Winners' Cup, but I was always good on my knowledge of the club's proud history – you couldn't not know it, really.

MH I was fortunate enough to play with Steve Perryman who was our captain and leader. Steve had won in Europe, so, while the club didn't make us specifically aware of our achievements as such, obviously when you talk to Steve – not just about Europe but for instance making your debut – he was only too willing to sit down and talk you through how special the moment is.

PM A midweek game at White Hart Lane always made it special because of the atmosphere – 50-odd thousand, plus the all-white kit. We copied the Spurs Double side, so straight away it seemed different – it made us feel a bit bigger, a bit stronger. Straight away you're connected with the tradition and history. Plus the fans were up for European nights, so it was special all round.

MH I loved it. I loved being at White Hart Lane at night – the lights, dew on the grass… it would suit the short, low-centre-of-gravity

PAUL MILLER
Spurs career:
285 apps, 10 goals
Europe:
23 apps, 2 goals
European honours:
UEFA Cup
Winner 1984

MICKY HAZARD
Spurs career:
170 apps, 25 goals
Europe:
23 apps, 3 goals
European honours:
UEFA Cup
Winner 1984

players like myself. You knew the game was going to be played on the floor rather than in the air. The buzz I used to feel! As soon as the league game on the Saturday was over, within minutes I was looking forward to the European game in midweek. I couldn't wait.

I would drive to the game and I would have this churning in my stomach. I would run the game through my mind, it was so real. I would picture myself scoring the winning goal, running away to the Shelf and standing there elated. I never did that in league games, really. They were going to be battles and some day our skill and technique would win, some days their strength, but in Europe I always felt we were going to win.

PM Actually playing in European football wasn't a mystery, though. I left school, joined Spurs and went straight to a youth tournament in Belgium. We would go on tournament trips every season – I played a lot of foreign teams. So when we played in senior teams we'd had experience; it wasn't a step into the unknown.

And in Keith Burkinshaw, you had a disciple of the "Spurs Way" and that European tradition. Micky, Keith said that Europe enabled you to flourish?
MH On my day in Europe I actually think I was untouchable. I didn't care who I was playing against, I didn't ever feel they could get the ball off me – if it was my day. In England there was always a battle to be won and, even if I won the battle technically I'd still have to compete physically, there was no respite. In Europe, as it was a more technical game I always believed, well, I'm one of the most technical players there was, so if I'm confident and it's my day, nobody's gonna better me. Keith was very astute in recognising that.

Keith was a soulmate in the belief of how the game should be played?
MH Absolutely, but then my beliefs are that any manager of any club should know the history and tradition of that club and abide by them because ultimately that's the way to success. If Cliff Jones walks into a room, I think every current player should stand up and shake his hand, because he and others like him are part of the reason we're there – they were part of the reason why I was earning £700 a week then, we were in Europe and winning cups. It's paramount that the manager knows the history and tradition, and applies them in his thinking of his style for his team. That was what Keith was great at.

PM Tactically we had to get things right, we had to learn about dropping off, letting them have the ball, and saying, "Go on then, what are you going to do about it?" But we were such quick learners it wasn't a problem for us. The tie we played against Ajax [in 1981] we beat them 6-1 on aggregate. 6-1 against one of the big names in Europe. We dropped off, let them have the ball in their own two thirds and then we hit them on the break.

It was simple stuff – knowing where to position ourselves for free-kicks and corners, who would take them, knowing player X is

> **"THE BUZZ I USED TO FEEL! AS SOON AS THE LEAGUE GAME ON THE SATURDAY WAS OVER, WITHIN MINUTES I WAS LOOKING FORWARD TO THE EUROPEAN GAME IN MIDWEEK. I COULDN'T WAIT"**
> MICKY HAZARD

strong on this foot or good with that turn – the main things. We watched short videos, we didn't go over the top but we were very well prepared.

At home, the first four or five balls Clem had he'd smash down the middle. Our opposition would have heard we were a footballing side and suddenly they are seeing us smashing long balls. We did that to stretch them out so Glenn, Ossie and Micky would get more space to play in midfield. We also believed in getting right at them English style; I'd smash the ball above the right-back's head and Tony [Galvin] would come in with a clattering challenge. The full-back would be saying, "Where's he come from?"

A potent combination, strength and flair.
PM We had both, more than others.

Keith also said Europe helped in terms of playing as individuals and a club.
PM It helped enormously. As you get older you get more experience, you travel more, you enjoy the nights out after the games. Seeing other cities and the culture, the great stadiums like the Bernabéu and the Nou Camp. The atmosphere was no different – White Hart Lane could be as noisy as anywhere. I didn't notice it though. Your professional focus is on the game. You don't even hear the booing sometimes! But I've never met a good team that worried about atmosphere.

Team spirit was strong, but to what extent did Europe strengthen bonds?
MH Playing in Europe helped create that wonderful bond that couldn't be broken. It was born out by the away trips, the build-up, the nights out, the celebration after a win, the journey back home. It was just such a bonding experience that it added to the club, and

IN CONVERSATION WITH
PAUL MILLER & MICKY HAZARD

experience that you didn't really get so much in league games. It was a fantastic group and the banter and fun going round the squad at that time was wonderful.

PM Two-thirds of the squad were home-grown, so we had that bond from youth team days and reserves, it was taken as read we all got on well. I roomed with Glenn; I started off with Stevie P, the younger man with the older pro, but from about 19 I was with Glenn. We just got on well; we didn't really talk about football it was more a friendly thing – we were both tidy and clean, the same habits. [laughter]

MH I roomed with Paul Price, Gary Mabbutt, and Ossie quite a bit.

He must have been a real effervescent character to go away with?

MH A very, very close friend of mine. He was inspirational – his thoughts on the game, his ability on the pitch were incredible, you looked at Ossie as a footballer and his brain was just magnificent, so to have an opportunity to sit at the same table as him, share a room with and have a chat with him could only enhance my education in the game.

I was talking to Ossie once and asked, "What would you do if you won the pools and came away with a million?" He asked what I would do. I said: "Well, I'd look after my family, get them all a house, a car, they'd be all rich. What would you do?" Ossie said: "What, if I had another million?" [laughter]

PM We stayed in the best places, we chartered our own plane with the press and some VIP fans; everything was done well. We saw a lot of places and went on visits. It was all very organised. Nothing was left to chance – we took our own chef, even our own food sometimes. But that would have been from the Bill Nick days – everything had to be right and proper. The secretary went out the day before and as a player you drop your bag off with the coach and don't see it till you're in your hotel room – you don't do anything. Funny thing was that when Micky went away

on his own for the first time with his girlfriend he didn't know how to check in his bag at the airport! Yet he'd been around the world twice.

MH You're right, I didn't have a clue. [laughs] I flew everywhere with Spurs and then you go on your holidays and it's "What do I do?" I'd never been on holiday with Mum and Dad, we came from an average background, lovely people but little money, so my experience first time was quite scary. As a footballer, you rarely have to think for yourself outside of the pitch. I didn't know how to register with a doctor.

Going into that first campaign, how confident did you feel?

MH I chatted to Glenn and said to him, "We're going to win the European Cup Winners' Cup. Europe is made for us."

PM We weren't lacking in confidence, but drawing Ajax did give us a boost. But we were just too strong. We had had training drills where we put 10 attackers against five defenders. If they had 30 attacks and scored once there was an enquiry. We started so well and after that it wasn't really a problem. Dundalk in the next round was harder. They were very defensive and made it tough for *us*.

The Ajax result must have made a few in the foreign media sit up and take notice?

PM They would come to the training ground

> ## "OSSIE AND GLENN WERE INJURED. ANYONE WOULD HAVE SAID YOU COULDN'T WIN THE UEFA CUP WITHOUT YOUR TWO BEST PLAYERS BUT WE DID. WE HAD TO CHANGE OUR TACTICS AGAIN, PUTTING IN MICKY HAZARD AS THE PLAYMAKER"
> PAUL MILLER

and do interviews. They viewed Spurs and English football as the guvnors – no other team wanted to play English sides. From 1977 onwards everyone kept winning everything, so they were wary of us.

Eintracht Frankfurt came next and you both scored crackers in the home leg. Whose was the best?

MH Not a doubt me! [laughter] I picked it up on the edge of their box, I beat two men, pulled over from right to left so I dragged the keeper over, then I whipped it back to where he's just come from and scored. I can't remember Paul's goal. [winks]

PM My 25-yarder! ? I suppose it was the best goal I scored for Spurs. Galvin had the ball out wide left, stuck it into Glenn with pace and I just gave Glenn a call to leave it and I smashed it first time – didn't go much higher than two foot and straight into the corner. I was doing them in training. [laughter] But I didn't score that many so it was a great moment.

MH On my first training session at Spurs, I got my picture taken with Paul for *The Weekly Herald* [the local paper]. We joined at the same time, we came through the old system together and we both scored in that game.

The semi-final against Barcelona has become infamous. They basically fouled you out of the competition.

PM I felt we were naïve. We were the better side, they came and said, "We'll spoil this" with all the old tricks. In those days the Spanish were masters of it. We hadn't experienced that before. We lost our heads a bit, we'd been so confident and they tried these tactics – blatant. The ref was very poor, let everyone get away with murder. We started smashing them in retaliation; it became a bit of a battle.

Clem made the mistake, a one-in-a-thousand error that gave them the lead. We were angry with ourselves, allowing them to dictate and spoil it. We should have concentrated on playing a bit more and not gone in for the physical stuff.

MH I actually got the man of the match, but I got kicked from pillar to post. It was our lack of experience at that stage that cost us. We were taken aback by the brutality. We expected a technical game, not to be kicked.
PM It was hard to keep our composure. The crowd as well got us going; the game was full of stops and starts and that's when you do hear the crowd. Today they'd have had seven players after 20 minutes; we'd have had nine. They weren't a top side like they are today; all right, they won the cup. But we were the best side in the tournament.

I was injured for the return. I commentated that night for Radio 2 and I said we had gone out without a fight and that's not like us. It was a good learning curve.

The fixture pile-up that season couldn't have helped?
PM For certain. We'd missed six weeks of football due to the snow and we played 17 games in 50 days , we all carried injuries, it was ridiculous. I had injections to play in the FA Cup Final, four of us did.

The next campaign was short-lived, but by the 1983/84 season to what extent were you better equipped to seriously challenge for the trophy?
MH I honestly believed that going into Europe after that first season, having added a bit of experience , there wasn't a team capable of touching us.

And the squad was deeper.
PM We had more solid players and were set up more defensive; Tony [Galvin] was a great defensive midfielder so we effectively had three defensive midfielders in him, Gary Stevens and Perryman. That made us so solid; Stevie didn't really move out of the centre circle in front of us and with Robbo, Danny [Thomas], Chrissie and me we were solid. The UEFA Cup was our focus. And we wanted to make up for the previous three years as well, as we felt we had a European trophy in us.

Micky Hazard with Ossie Ardiles on the UEFA Cup lap of honour in 1984

We were too cavalier in the league with too many attacking players, but in the UEFA Cup the absence of those players was good for us.
MH We'd played the big guns of Europe and if you can't get experience from playing these teams then you're never going to get it. So that '84 season when we won it, we were actually playing in what I would call the Champions League because we were playing the teams that had finished second, third and fourth in their leagues. It was a mighty tough cup to win.
PM It was the hardest, by far. In the European Cup and Cup Winners' Cup you only have eight decent teams anyway, one decent team from each of the best countries. In the UEFA Cup you had at least three teams from every country, so 24 top sides in it – three from Germany, three from Italy etc. We played three more games and I think the year we won it every team we played won their league or nearly did.

Paul, you missed the start of the campaign?
PM I got injured second game of the season, did my cartilage. I had some complications and didn't come back until the New Year. I was struggling when I came back – fit as a fiddle, but my knee was still a bit puffy. However, the team were struggling injury wise and so I had to come back and I caught the last three ties.

Ossie and Glenn were injured and hardly featured. Anyone would have said you couldn't win the UEFA Cup without your two

best players but we did. We had to change our tactics again, putting in Micky Hazard as the playmaker. We were really set up defensively but strong. It was a different type of Spurs team, more of a robust side, really. Forest were like that when they won their European Cups. So we were a different side, but Micky really did well, he came into his own.

Micky was the star of the show against Hajduk Split – and they were difficult opposition.
PM I thought we played really well out there, we got beat 2-1 – bit unlucky. They were good technically, they had great ability and movement. Bill Nick criticised us on radio, and said we were sloppy. I don't know what game Bill was watching. We got the away goal and at home we fancied ourselves against anybody. Micky scored with a great free-kick and we didn't have a problem after that.
MH In the away leg we may have lost but we pulverised them. I played a fantastic game that night. It was chucking down, Steve Perryman said to me afterwards, "You're the talk of Europe tonight after that performance." And we'd lost!

In the home leg you were the talk of football again for another reason when you lost a contact lens after scoring. What was the story?
MH As we celebrated the goal, Danny Thomas

IN CONVERSATION WITH
PAUL MILLER & MICKY HAZARD

and Chris Hughton jumped on me and one of their fingers flicked my lens out. In those days we were so ill-prepared, we didn't have a spare lens, but luckily we saw it floating through the air. So we all stood back, it landed on the ground and I picked it up and I ran off the pitch. Can you imagine? I'm shaking like a good 'un, I'm excited, I just scored and I'm trying to get this lens in my eye. I kept hitting my forehead, my nose, my ears, my hands were shaking.

Shreevesie came down from the dugout came into the dressing room and told me, "Calm down, calm down" – but he was just as excited as I was! By pure accident the lens flicks into my eye. My thoughts went from worrying about a contact lens to thinking, "What a reception I'm going to get now." [laughter] I'm running down the tunnel, my chest out, my head high and I know what's coming. This cheer erupts, a crescendo of singing of "One Micky Hazard". I mean, eh? Shivers, lumps in my throat. If there's a better moment of elation in my football career – you couldn't write the script any better. I emerged like I've risen from the dead – I felt like Jesus arising from the dead three days later! Well, mine was five minutes later. [laughter] Ah, what a moment. The linesman's holding me back saying, "You can't go straight on." I said, "I don't want to, listen to the noise!"

PM Half-time we gave him some stick, but it would have gone in one ear and out the other with Micky. [laughter]

By the time of the final, you knew Keith Burkinshaw was leaving. What bearing did that have on your motivation?
PM We felt sorry for Keith, but we wanted to do it for ourselves as well. We didn't really take much notice, to be honest. That sounds quite selfish but it was about us wanting to win. It would be nice to send Keith off with the trophy, but it was about us. A lot of us had contracts coming to an end. It was a traumatic time at the club, but with respect to Keith and Peter they kept everything professional. I felt a lot fitter by the final and I didn't want the

season to end. We had unfinished business and felt that we'd underachieved in previous years.
MH In the first leg of the final against Anderlecht we absolutely smashed them. We could have won comfortably.
PM We took a great amount of support. Remember that Anderlecht were one of the finest teams in Europe at that time. Unfortunately a supporter the night before had been shot and killed which made things sour.

When were you aware of that?
PM We knew straight away. It made it very sad for all of us, players and fans. We were very close in those days, so we were determined. We played really well. Archie and Mark missed chances, we should have been 3-0 up at half-time. Then I got my goal. The corner came over from Micky and I scored. Stuff you dream about. But then Tony [Parks] who'd hardly had anything to do, spilled it and they equalised.
MH Irony or fate, call it what you want. We're 1-0 up, there's only one winner, Parksie makes a mistake and it's 1-1 – and then he saves the penalties that win the cup and now he's in Tottenham's folklore.

Not winning the first leg nearly came back to bite you.
PM Absolutely. They came out on our good pitch, maybe we'd been a bit over confident, but for the first half hour we couldn't get the ball off them. We were missing a lot of players including Steve who was a massive leader. I think we really appreciated then how good Anderlecht were.

Take us through the penalty shootout.
PM We had practised penalties. We had good players with a lot of experience.

Micky, you practised penalties in training with Parks, so you played a part in honing his skills?
MH Nah, he never saved any from me! [laughs] Why Tony was so great at saving pens, he had massive thighs and he had such spring that he could leap quickly and powerfully to cover ground better than other keepers. When you took a pen against him you knew it had to be a good one. So I had every confidence in Parksie that night.
PM Parks arguably was a better penalty saver than Clem, he was one of those who had that knack, and he practised a lot. We didn't just

Micky Hazard and Paul Miller with the 1984 UEFA Cup winning Spurs side

throw things together, even Danny [Thomas's] pen wasn't a miss, it was a save.

It's a famous moment when the crowd sang Danny Thomas's name after his penalty to lift his spirits. Did you say anything to him?
MH I was actually down to take Danny's pen but I was suffering from cramp so Keith ruled me out from taking it. I was supposed to be fifth. When Dan had his saved you can imagine the feelings that we're going through. Danny is walking up, we're all celebrating anticipating we've won the UEFA Cup – Danny doesn't score and I go from, "We've won in front of adoring fans" to, "Oh no, I'm next!" If you watch the video of Parksie's save, the first one to arrive to celebrate is me at full pace – and I had cramp! The release of pressure gave me five extra yards.
PM It all happened so fast, we'd won moments later. Danny was brave enough to step forward. It was a magic moment.

You'd got that European trophy you wanted. How did it compare with other triumphs?
PM It's funny. I was so young and I'd won stuff before so it felt like another cup. But what made it special was winning it at home. It was nice to win it in front of the fans. We went upstairs, there were little parties going on all over the club – not like the FA Cup party at the Chanticleer. This was more intimate. I think we felt pleased we'd actually won something in Europe at last. Keith leaving put a dampener on it as well, and a few of us were wondering if this was going to be our last game for Spurs.

You came close to successfully defending the UEFA Cup the next season, '84/85, and had some notable games.
PM Shreevsie had taken over and that was fine, we had a good squad. Braga away was a special occasion. My daughter Charlotte had just been born and in Portugal the club laid on a big party with a cake after the game. A nice touch and an example of how close we were, and of the club doing well by us.

"MICKY HAZARD AND SPURS GO TOGETHER. THERE'S A CHEMISTRY AND WE BOTH HAVE THE SAME BELIEFS. WHAT SPURS FANS STAND FOR IS WHAT I STAND FOR"
MICKY HAZARD

Bohemians of Prague, that was a tale of two teams?
PM Peter had gone out there to see them, said he had never been so cold and had to sit in the bath for 20 minutes to warm up. It was baking hot when we went out there. We took thermals and sheepskin jackets. [laughter]
They were a good footballing side. They came to ours and must have loved London, because they slaughtered us for an hour. Yet we won. I went off the pitch thinking, "How the hell did they not win that game?" Out there they changed tactics completely. They must have thought we outplayed this Spurs side and got beat. So now we're gonna kick the hell out of them. Glenn still has a scar on his head from getting clattered. Today the bloke who did it would have been sent off – or sent to prison for it. It was one of the most physical games I ever played in.

You went out to Real Madrid in the quarter-final, in controversial circumstances. Do you still feel a sense of injustice?
PM We were so unlucky at home, they put 10 behind the ball. Out there we played really well and scored a fantastic goal from Mark Falco but the ref disallowed it. What for to this day I still don't know. No one was near him.
MH It wasn't even a foul.
PM You see the goal and it was perfectly legal. Then Steve Perryman got sent off after Valdano had spat at him. We felt gutted because we had a better side than the year

before, Ossie was fit, John Chiedozie had joined. We should have won the league but games caught up with us.

The Heysel ban meant that side couldn't compete in Europe again.
PM But playing and succeeding in Europe was very special. They were great nights, touching on the history and traditions of the past. The fans were up for it, it was exciting. You played the Saturday knowing you were going away – new places, new experiences. You felt vey proud and it was a British thing as well, we were carrying the flag.
MH To be part of that era for me has been – I find it hard to find the words to describe it – but Spurs and Micky Hazard go together. There's a chemistry and that is that we both have the same beliefs. What Spurs fans stand for is what I stand for.
When you watched me play football I was a risk taker. If I could beat a man or thread a pass through the eye of a needle I went for it. So did Glenn, we took risks – "To dare is to do". That is the Spurs philosophy, and that's mine. I coach kids today and say don't be afraid to try. For me, Spurs and me were made for one another. When I look at my career, Spurs is me. People say, "But you played for Chelsea for five years?" and I did, great, fine, but I never had the chemistry anywhere that I had at Spurs.
My sons are season-ticket holders at Spurs, they cry when we lose and scream when we win. When we played Chelsea in the semi-final of the cup [in 2012] the cameraman zoomed in on two boys shouting and screaming and it was my two sons, singing their hearts out. My granddaughter is seven and went to her first game last season. So listen, my household is Spurs through and *through*. It's in my heart. Forty years I've worked for Spurs, from the age of 12 and I still work there today on a part-time basis. You don't work for someone for 40 years and not let it get in your heart.

SUPPORTING THE CAUSE

1,100 miles … to the loneliest match they'll ever play

Plane, train to Katowice for their first European Cup-tie

60,000 to 1 AGAINST SPURS!

Lone British student will cheer them on

TOTTENHAM HOTSPUR kick off their European Cup crusade here tomorrow with the loneliest match in their history.

Eleven hundred miles from their 50,000 roaring Londoners, they are certain of only one, solitary supporter—a nomadic Southampton student named David Mummery.

"**I**f football is an escape, European trips are The Great Escape," wrote Spurs fan Mel Gomes in his account of following Spurs abroad. At a club where European football has such a special resonance, the fans have followed the team in numbers to some of the most difficult destinations in Europe.

In an era when air travel has made the world a smaller place and top football clubs regard regular European trips as a given, the allure of travelling to see the Spurs has not diminished. While any history of a football club's European participation inevitably focuses on the players, the experiences of the fans are also compelling.

The truth is that Spurs fans, like the team, were European pioneers. Perhaps none more so than David Mummery, a student from Southampton who, according to the *Daily Mail* on 13 September 1961, was the only Spurs fan to travel to Poland when Spurs played their first competitive European game in Katowice against Gornik Zabrze. "The European Cup exhortation of this David will be drowned by the Goliath gathering of at least 60,000 impassioned Poles," wrote the

paper's Ian Wooldridge. But as the Double side embarked on the great adventure that spawned the glory glory nights, more fans were determined to be with them every step of the way. And they forged new ground alongside their heroes. The fans who had been the first in England to fly to an away game (to Sunderland in 1961 for an FA Cup tie) were, within two years, organising flights to the 1963 Cup Winners' Cup Final in Rotterdam. The full story of that remarkable trip is told on page 42. With a further 2,000 travelling to that final by ferry from Harwich to the Hook of Holland, *The Weekly Herald*'s columnist "Fanfare" observed that "not since the big push of 1944 had so many crossed the border".

Spurs fans in fancy dress for the match v Feyenoord in Rotterdam 1961

And it was a Spurs fan, season-ticket holder Chick Shepherd, who co-piloted the aircraft that flew the team to the Netherlands. "I first saw the Spurs play in 1936, and played truant from school to do so," he told the *Daily Mirror*. On that flight also worked steward Jack Gott, the founder of the BEA Stewards XI football team who were dubbed "The Spurs of London Airport". Along with captain Doug Evans and stewards Sylvia Swanepoel and Tony Kernighan, the flight crew ferried the team to all their away games, and in return were guests of the club at every home European tie.

The fans can also take the credit for dubbing Tottenham Hotspur's European nights as "glory glory nights". Stung by criticism of their team as "no angels", three fans, Peter Kirby, Dave Casey and Mike Curly, dressed as angels for the home leg and walked along the touchline in front of the packed stands brandishing placards bearing slogans such as "Hallowed be thy names". On that night, as Gornik were swept aside 8-1, the chorus of "Glory Glory Hallelujah" was first heard as the crowd warmed to the theme. That song has become a part of the club's DNA. While it is much imitated by other fans, only the Spurs version retains "Hallelujah" where others substitute their team's name or colours.

The Tottenham Angels, though, only survived two seasons. In 1963, their appearance on Tottenham High Road prompted the Reverend Clifford Hill, of High Cross Constitutional Church, to send a telegram to the Home Secretary urging action against Spurs under the blasphemy laws. "The idolisation of a football team

by taking quotations from the Bible is wrong and offends Christians," he fumed. The angels decided to retire with their halos intact. "We have apologised to the people who feel offended," said Peter Kirby. "Against the few who object, there are thousands who have welcomed our little performances without taking them in a way in which they were never intended. We are going back to our old costumes of Noddy hats and butcher's aprons."

In those early days of mass air travel, remarkably, the fans organised themselves. They worked with the club, but this was a grassroots operation and it is arguably this which made the tradition so strong. The Spurs Supporters Club was at one time so large that its committee had specialist sections for travel, catering, social and even a sports section. Daphne Edwards was one of the early travellers. She devoted years to running the SSC, and she remembers one early trip to Ibrox in 1962. "We got to the ground for the match, to find that there were no ladies'

toilets there and, as there were a few ladies on the coach, we found a nearby café. But the toilets were outside on the roof. Still, needs must.

"We stood on the terraces in the middle of the Rangers fans – no segregation in those days. They wished us luck in the next round."

Roy Woodward was also involved in running the SSC – whose distinctive oval badges have become prized collectors' items – and he remembers the friendliness of the Glaswegian fans. "We were met by numerous

Top: The legendary Spurs angels prior to the European Cup semi-final v Benfica

Above: Spurs fans at Heathrow airport en route to Lisbon in 1962

Glaswegians, who shook our hand, apologised for the fog and delay as well as the match having been postponed, then took us to the nearest pub to buy us drinks," he says.

Football's ability to break down borders also provided the rare opportunity for fans from the capitalist west to visit the socialist east at the height of the Cold War. Edwards remembers a trip to Bratislava in 1963 when the plane Spurs fans had chartered was "buzzed by Russian MIG fighter planes". The reception was friendlier on the ground, with local fans fascinated by the paraphernalia of the Spurs support. "When one of the Spurs fans started to turn his football rattle they were fascinated by it and kept asking him to spin the rattle again."

There were more exotic visits too, providing new experiences, such as the trip to Lisbon for the game against

Benfica in 1962. Aubrey Morris, whose Riviera Travel company organised the early air trips, remembered it fondly when interviewed in 2004. "We took the opportunity to explore," he said. "It was gorgeous weather. You could sit down to eat at 10 or 11 in the evening, and I remember it was the first time I could choose live fish, including lobster, from a tank in the middle of the room. Kick-off would have been about 10 at night, and that was glorious, nobody had ever experienced that. Warm weather at 10 o'clock."

Of course, things weren't always as peaceful, and no account of Spurs fans in Europe can gloss over the hooliganism that accompanied English clubs onto mainland Europe in the 1970s and 1980s. The trouble in Rotterdam in 1974 marked a low point for the reputation of English clubs in Europe and the end of Bill Nicholson's love affair with football. Spurs were ordered to play the next two games at a ground at least 150 miles away, but the club was on a downward spiral and there was no need to enforce the punishment. Spurs returned to Europe in 1981, but there was more trouble in Rotterdam in 1983, and a year later in Brussels after a young Spurs fan was shot dead by a barman. A year after that, the horrific events

at Heysel saw all English clubs banned from Europe indefinitely. The ban was not to be lifted for six years. But even at the height of English fans' notoriety in Europe, there were warmer and more friendly moments. Season-ticket holder Bruce Lee remembers a big turnout for a pre-season friendly versus PSV in 1980. "A mate saw it advertised in the local paper and coaches were leaving from Harlow. It was fantastic. It was in a small non-league town called Beilen – you could just wander

onto the pitch and there was a 50-a-side match going on at half-time. As we left the town on the coaches, the locals were out on their front lawns waving."

By the 1980s, mass travel was more commonplace and fans began to organise their own trips. This, combined with the club's move to set up official trips – a move partly prompted by the need to try to control fans abroad – put the squeeze on the SSC's travel activities and this strand of the club's history was allowed to wither away. For the fans who wanted to organise their own trips – sometimes to save money, sometimes to take a longer sightseeing trip – the challenge of doing so became part of the fabric of their support. Elaborate routes to obscure airports and complex transport interconnections formed part of an increasingly ingenious approach that has marked out English football fans, Spurs foremost among them, as some of the most dedicated in the world.

The travel industry was one of the first to be revolutionised by the internet, and this provided even more opportunity for fans to build their own trips. From the late 1990s onwards, sitting in front of a computer late at night, chasing the air fares and hotel bookings while simultaneously consulting with other fans on the multitude of supporter message boards to arrange trips became an increasingly common pursuit for the committed travelling fan.

The club's official trips still remain popular, in large part due to the dedication of the team

Top: The dash for tickets for Spurs' 1962 match with Glasgow Rangers

Above: Spurs supporters group in Oslo for the 1972 UEFA Cup tie

of club stewards who make every effort to ensure fans get to and from the match in the safest and most enjoyable way possible. The logistics of transporting large numbers of fans are challenging, but it's only rarely that the club has not been able to help the fans follow the team.

But listen to the campaign stories of European tours in the bars around the ground on matchdays and you'll get a rich array. You'll hear about the mass street football match in Kaiserslautern in 2000; the trips to the Prater Park funfair in Vienna in 1991, the lifts on the cliff face that the ground at Sporting Braga is built into ridden by Spurs fans in 2007 humming the theme tune to *Are You Being Served*; the warm welcome given to the doughty crew who went to Istanbul in 2006 to see Spurs play Besiktas. And neither fog in Munich in 1983, high winds taking down train power lines before the game in Eindhoven in 2008 nor freezing conditions in Enschede in 2010 could stop Spurs fans turning out.

In Seville in 2007, a fantastic pre-match atmosphere which saw English and Spanish fans eating and drinking together in the town's squares threatened to turn sour when over-zealous local police began to baton charge Spurs fans inside the stadium. Match commentators at first believed this was another outbreak of English hooliganism, until TV presenter Clare Tomlinson – a Spurs home and away season-ticket holder who was sitting with the travelling support – called her station to give the real story. Her on-the-spot report that "this was not caused by Spurs fans" did much to defend their reputation, and the club filed an official complaint with the Spanish authorities. The club's stewards also

won praise for the way they had helped calm the situation and protected the fans.

But the testing times make the good times even more enjoyable, and there have been few more enjoyable trips than those to Milan and Madrid during the Champions League run. In Milan, in the 24 hours leading up to the game, it was difficult to go anywhere without bumping into a fellow Spurs fan, and in Madrid the sheer number of fans congregated in the sunshine-drenched city squares took the breath away. It's days like these that fuel the passion of fans as much as the exploits of the team on the pitch. Back to Mel Gomes, who says: "Football has given me the excuse to visit some great cities and have some great experiences. I have ridden on gondolas in Venice, attended a spectacular Easter festival in Seville, sat in the Gaudi Park in Barcelona, been to the ruins in Rome… drunk Coln beer and visited the Christmas markets in Bruges and Cologne."

But those days abroad, however inspiring, can only ever be the warm-up for the main event, for those glory glory nights under the floodlights. As Mel Gomes says: "Ultimately it is the football that makes the trip".

Top: At Luton Airport before the 1982 Cup Winners' Cup match in Frankfurt

Above: In Cyprus for the 2007 UEFA Cup game v Anorthosis Famagusta

Above: Fans in the Madrid sun prior to the 2011 Champions League tie

The 1990s

UEFA lifted the ban on English football clubs competing in Europe in 1990. One year later, a Paul Gascoigne-inspired Spurs reached Wembley and won the FA Cup in a dramatic game, securing a return to competition on the mainland. The return of European football to White Hart Lane after an absence of six years attracted a crowd of over 30,000, despite the opposition being Austrian Second Division side SV Stockerau.

But much had changed. The English game had suffered from the lack of opportunity for its top sides to test themselves against the best of the rest, with Italian teams dominant both on the pitch and financially. The summer before Tottenham Hotspur entered this new world, Gascoigne's tears in Italy during the World Cup proved to be the catalyst for an extraordinary change. Football, once a pariah sport, was being refashioned into a marketable entertainment business. Spurs were one of the clubs at the forefront of the push to form a new English Premier League in 1992. The money and prestige this eventually generated put English sides back firmly at the centre of the footballing world.

But while the first phase of the club's relationship with European competition had seen it set new standards and establish a tradition that defined the club, this second phase presented Spurs with the challenge of trying to make the most of the opportunity it had helped create.

The bid for the Cup Winners' Cup in the year following the Wembley win over Nottingham Forest ended all too quickly as the club's new ownership structure unravelled and a long period of consolidation began as Tottenham went through 10 coaches in as many years.

As this long transitional period stretched out, so the realities of European competition changed. The European Cup became the Champions League, a competition that put the UEFA Cup and Cup Winners' Cup in the shade, both in terms of prestige and financial benefit to clubs who qualified. A gap between the regular qualifiers and the rest began to grow – and Spurs were not qualifying.

In a curious aside, Spurs entered the Intertoto Cup in 1995, a competition first dreamed up to generate money for pools companies during the summer break as far back as 1961, and later embraced by UEFA to give teams who hadn't otherwise qualified for a Europe a chance to play European football. Spurs played only four ties and, with the first-team squad on tour in Denmark, fielded a side made up of young professionals and loan players, including a certain Alan Pardew, and playing at Brighton's old Goldstone Ground.

By the end of the Nineties, Spurs were back in Europe again after winning the League Cup, but a largely uninspiring UEFA Cup campaign fizzled out in the second round on a November night in Germany when the cautious approach of then Spurs manager George Graham was blown apart in two dramatic minutes at the close of the night. It would be five seasons before Spurs returned.

Left to right: Gordon Durie and Erik Thorstedvt celebrate Spurs' win over Porto in 1991; Gary Lineker, the bone fide star player in the club's last-ever Cup Winners' Cup campaign; David Ginola, in typical swashbuckling style, takes on FC Zimbru in 1999

CUP WINNERS' CUP
1991/92
SV STOCKERAU
HAJDUK SPLIT
PORTO
FEYENOORD

UEFA CUP
1999/2000
FC ZIMBRU
1FC KAISERSLAUTERN

THE ROAD TO EUROPE
1991

A year after the post-Heysel ban on English clubs was lifted, Spurs were back in Europe. The club had qualified due to an eighth FA Cup victory secured almost singlehandedly by the extraordinary talent of Paul Gascoigne. That cup victory was almost impossibly romantic. The clowning genius Gascoigne was the central character in a story that featured a sumptuous swatting aside of a top Arsenal team in the first semi-final to be played at Wembley and the high drama of Gascoigne's adrenalin-fuelled antics in a final that swung first one way and then the other before Spurs finally prevailed to deny Nottingham Forest manager Brian Clough his last chance to win the only trophy he'd never secured.

But the glory and the romance concealed some hard realities. Gascoigne was gone, new chief executive Terry Venables moved upstairs, breaking the training ground link with the players that had been so effective the year before. The popular Peter Shreeve was given a one-year contract to work with a team built by Venables. It was a new European era, not just for Spurs but for all English clubs. But compared with times past, this Spurs team was not in as good shape to take on the task.

David Howells, Steve Sedgley, Paul Gascoigne and Paul Stewart celebrate the 1991 FA Cup semi-final win over Arsenal that sent Spurs towards a cup win, and back on the road to Europe

THANK GORD!

Durie spares Spurs' blushes

Stadion Zeitung

EUROPA CUP EXTRA

21.8. 19.30

SV STOCKERAU : TOTTENHAM

Sparkasse Stockerau
"Wir fördern den Sport"

21 August 1991, preliminary round, first leg

SV STOCKERAU 0
TOTTENHAM HOTSPUR 1

Praterstadion, Vienna, Austria *Att:* 15,500

The Austrians were described by Alex Montgomery in *The Sun* as "painters, plumbers, civil servants, a student and just three full-time professionals". But, he wrote, "shame-faced Spurs had to thank keeper Erik Thorstvedt's penalty save for denying their rag-bag opponents a draw". Spurs had gone ahead in the 38th minute when Gary Lineker flicked on for club-record signing Gordon Durie – inevitably already nicknamed "Jukebox" – to fire home. Then, on 66 minutes, skipper Gary Mabbutt conceded a penalty. Michael Keller took the kick, but "Erik the Viking" dived low to his left to palm the ball out. Spurs had set up cautiously and after the game Peter Shreeve said: "The blueprint for playing these games away from home in Europe is to keep possession, even if that means boring everyone to tears." A case of power before glory.

Thorstvedt, Fenwick, Van den Hauwe, Nayim, Howells, Mabbutt, Stewart, Durie, Samways (Hendon), Lineker, P. Allen

4 September 1991, preliminary round, second leg

TOTTENHAM HOTSPUR 1 (2)
SV STOCKERAU 0 (0)

White Hart Lane *Att:* 28,072

A near-30,000 crowd turned up to welcome European football back to N17, but it was no carnival. The Austrian Second Division side adopted a physical approach and Spurs' strikeforce stuttered. Gary Mabbutt scored in the 43rd minute to wrap the game up, but the talk afterwards was about Gary Lineker. The England striker had been carrying a hamstring strain and was substituted in the 72nd minute after having been subjected to some robust challenges. The player who stood out, according to the *Daily Mirror*'s Harry Harris, was Paul Stewart – "growing in confidence with every game after taking over the mantle vacated by Paul Gascoigne" and turning in "a performance of enormous stature". But, observed *The Sun*'s Alex Montgomery: "Spurs will have to find more inventiveness and more flair and goal sense when they face the Yugoslavs of Hajduk Split in two weeks' time."

Walker, Fenwick, Van den Hauwe, Nayim, Howells (Sedgley), Mabbutt, Stewart, Durie, Samways, Lineker (Moran), Bergsson

Top Left: Terry Venables has lots to ponder as Spurs return to European football in Austria in 1991

Top right: Gordon Durie strikes to seal an away win in Vienna

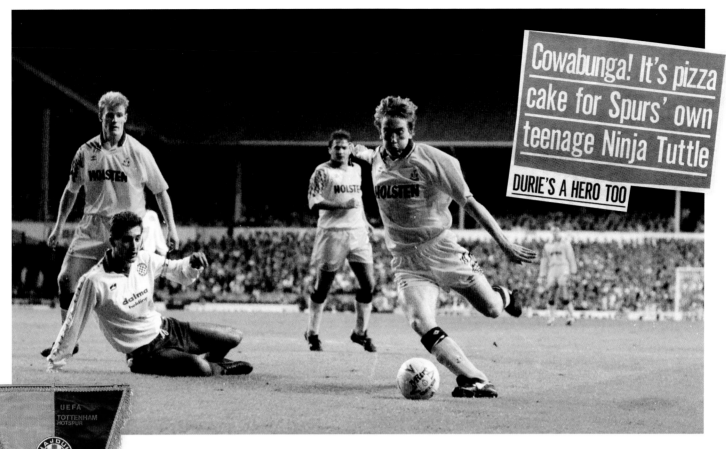

Cowabunga! It's pizza cake for Spurs' own teenage Ninja Tuttle

DURIE'S A HERO TOO

17 September 1991, first round, first leg

HAJDUK SPLIT 1
TOTTENHAM HOTSPUR 0

Linzer Stadion, Linz, Austria *Att*: 7,000

Armed conflict in Yugoslavia meant this game was played in Austria, in front of a sparse crowd brandishing banners proclaiming the Croatian cause. For 19-year-old goalkeeper Ian Walker, making his European away debut, it was a night to forget. He fumbled the ball in the second minute and then, in the 30th, let a tame 30-yard effort from Mario Novakovic slip under his body to guarantee a place in the headlines for all the wrong reasons. But Walker did make some outstanding saves as Hajduk put Spurs under intense pressure in the first 30 minutes. The *Daily Mirror*'s Nigel Clarke wrote that "Spurs battled away to hold out, but produced little in the way of attacking menace". In *The Evening Standard*, Steve Stammers described the Spurs perfomance as "sluggish". Peter Shreeve said: "It was not a vintage Spurs performance, but at 1-0 down we are still in the tie."

Walker, Fenwick, Van den Hauwe, Nayim, Howells (P. Allen), Mabbutt, Stewart, Durie, Samways, Lineker (Sedgley), Bergsson

2 October 1991, first round, second leg

TOTTENHAM HOTSPUR 2 (2)
HAJDUK SPLIT 0 (1)

White Hart Lane *Att*: 24,297

At 2.30pm on the day of the game, Gary Lineker became a father for the first time. That evening, wrote the *Daily Mirror*'s Nigel Clarke, "another Spurs baby became a hero of White Hart Lane". It was 19-year-old David Tuttle whose explosive left-foot goal in the sixth minute levelled the tie. Eight minutes later, Gordon Durie volleyed the winner. Peter Shreeve praised Durie's performance, saying it was his "best game since he joined us". *The Evening Standard*'s Steve Stammers agreed, calling Durie "Tottenham's lethal weapon in their search for European glory". Keeper Erik Thorstvedt also drew praise, turning in a faultless performance despite only being drafted in an hour before the game when the luckless Ian Walker went down with tonsillitis. But it was still a nervy second half as Hajduk pressed for the away goal despite going down to 10 men after Mario Novakovic was sent off.

*Thorstvedt, Bergsson, Sedgley, Nayim, **Tuttle**, Mabbutt, Stewart, **Durie**, Samways, Lineker (Hendon), P. Allen*

David Tuttle opens the scoring against Hajduk as Spurs overturn a first-leg deficit in the first 15 minutes at White Hart Lane

SPUR-FECT!

Tottenham toast a nice drop of Porto

23 October 1991, second round, first leg

TOTTENHAM HOTSPUR 3
PORTO 1

White Hart Lane *Att:* 23,621

Perhaps spurred on by UEFA's decision to switch the first leg to White Hart Lane to avoid a clash with Arsenal who were playing Benfica in Portugal, the Lilywhites served up a real footballing treat. In the 14th minute Porto fell behind to a stunning passing move that finished with Gary Lineker taking the ball down on his knee to prod home. It was, said Brian Woolnough in *The Sun*, "a goal of simplicity yet pure genius as the one-touch move carried the ball through the bewildered Portuguese defence". On 32 minutes, Gordon Durie added a second. Then, in the 51st minute, substitute Antonio Toze ran 40 yards into the box and crashed a shot against the post for Emil Kostadinov to fire home. But that consummate goalscorer Lineker popped up again with eight minutes left, controlling a Durie throw on his chest before spinning to finish.

Thorstvedt, Edinburgh, Van den Hauwe, Sedgley, Walsh (Houghton), Mabbutt, Stewart, **Durie***, Samways (Bergsson),* **Lineker 2***, P. Allen*

7 November 1991, second round, second leg

PORTO 0 (1)
TOTTENHAM HOTSPUR 0 (3)

Estádio das Antas, Porto, Portugal
Att: 55,000

Only four of the squad had been involved in games this high profile before, and there were worries before the match that the occasion and the setting would prove too much. In the event, according to *The Sun*'s Brian Woolnough: "Spurs kept London's European flag flying here last night with a display of courage and character." It was all the more satisfying coming after Arsenal's humiliating exit from the European Cup. Porto had not conceded at home all season, and went for Spurs from the off. Late in the first half Emil Kostadinov hit the post, the ball rebounding to Ion Timofte who fired into the side netting. There were more chances and two penalty appeals but Spurs, with Paul Stewart and David Howells in front of the back four, held firm. It was, said Woolnough, "a superb performance with reliance and English pride".

Thorstvedt, Edinburgh, Van den Hauwe, Bergsson, Howells, Mabbutt, Stewart, Durie (Sedgley), Samways, Lineker (Walsh), P. Allen

Top left: Gordon Durie celebrates his strike as Spurs run out impressive winners at home to Porto

Top right: Skipper Gary Mabbut can reflect on a job well done after the goalless return leg in Portugal

4 March 1992, third round, first leg

FEYENOORD 1
TOTTENHAM HOTSPUR 0

Feyenoord Stadium, Rotterdam, Netherlands
Att: 38,385

Spurs were reacquainted with old rivals Feyenoord on a night described by *The Sun*'s Alex Montgomery as "sheer torture". The game was no spectacle, with Feyenoord set up to maximise the effectiveness of a defence yet to concede in the competition. "It was European chess on grass," sighed Montgomery, "a nightmare for the public but a great night out for the coaches". Spurs too were cautious, Gary Lineker playing the lone striker. Feyenoord won courtesy of a mix-up between Paul Allen and Erik Thorstvedt. In the 56th minute Allen underhit a back pass and Joszef Kiprich nipped in to fire home. "It was a crazy goal to give away," said a distraught Allen afterwards. Both Spurs full-backs were booked too, ruling them out of a must-win game back at White Hart Lane, where Spurs had already lost 10 times that season.

Thorstvedt, Fenwick, Van Den Hauwe, Sedgley, Howells (Samways), Mabbutt, Stewart, Durie, Nayim, Lineker (Walsh), P. Allen

18 March 1992, third round, second leg

TOTTENHAM HOTSPUR 0 (0)
FEYENOORD 0 (1)

White Hart Lane *Att:* 29,834

The European dream died as Tottenham's season fell apart in sharp-focus slow motion. Out of the cups and in a relegation dogfight, the rumour was that Peter Shreeve was to be replaced. The truth was that Spurs were too reliant on the goals of Gary Lineker and Gordon Durie, and with John "Wolfman" De Wolf and former Spur Johnny Metgod stifling the strikeforce, Spurs had nothing else to offer in this tie. "The Dutch masters of defensive football strangled the life out of Spurs," wrote Nigel Clarke and Harry Harris in the *Daily Mirror*. It was, said *The Sun*'s Alex Montgomery, "a frustrating and bitterly disappointing end". The disappointment was not just felt from a football point of view. As the game became more commercialised, and with Spurs still not financially robust, the loss of a potential £2 million from a semi-final hurt too. It was all a long way from glory.

Thorstvedt, Bergsson, Edinburgh, Sedgely, Howells (Houghton), Mabbutt, Stewart, Durie, Nayim (Walsh), Lineker, P. Allen

The dramatic spectacle that greeted the teams before the narrow defeat in Rotterdam

THE ROAD TO EUROPE
1999

Tottenham's return to serious European competition had been long overdue – and the gap of seven years had come at precisely the wrong time. The advent of the Premier League and the Champions League had seen football at home and abroad enjoy a massive revival. Attendances and revenues were booming, English clubs were becoming powerhouses once again, and the good times were rolling.

The problem for Spurs was that they were missing the party. Having been one of the key protagonists in establishing the Premier League, thanks at least in part to the initiative of chairman Alan Sugar, the team had lagged behind other clubs that had seized the new opportunities, and a rapid turnover of managers and considerable spending had done little to restore the fortunes of a club that was losing touch with the top table.

So in 1999 Sugar turned to former Arsenal legend George Graham. It was a bold but risky appointment to bring in a manager with such clear associations with the old rivals. Yet within months, it bore fruit, as Graham led Spurs to a 1-0 win over Leicester in the League Cup Final. Along with a first trophy in eight years, it meant Spurs were also back in Europe. But problems lay in wait.

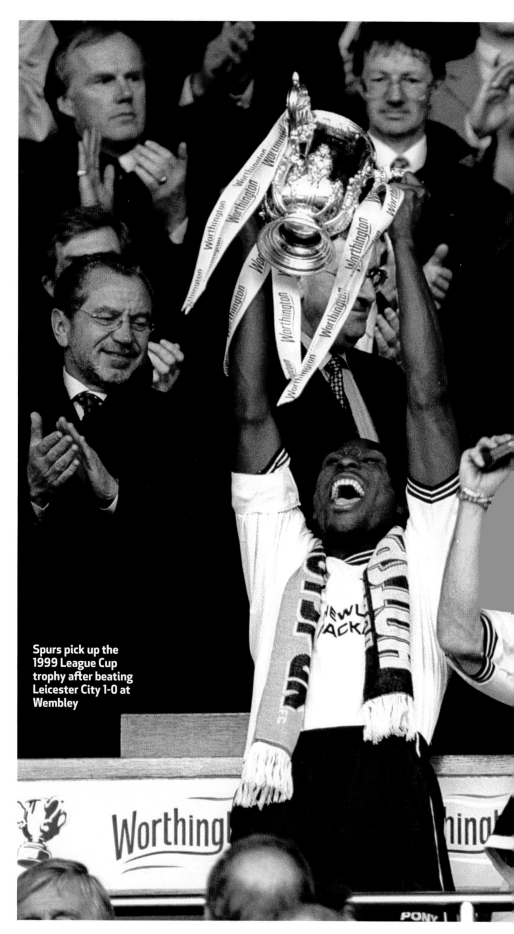

Spurs pick up the 1999 League Cup trophy after beating Leicester City 1-0 at Wembley

GEORGE MAKES IT LOOK ZIMPLE

Graham's boys roll over Moldovans

Tim Sherwood acknowledges team-mate Chris Perry after they combine for Spurs' third goal v FC Zimbru

16 September 1999, first round, first leg

TOTTENHAM HOTSPUR 3
FC ZIMBRU 0

White Hart Lane *Att:* 32,660

David Ginola was the shining light in a Spurs side short of star quality in the late 1990s, and he illuminated a comfortable victory over generous opposition as Spurs made a winning return to Europe. While the Frenchman did not score, he was instrumental in much of Tottenham's attacking endeavour. Spurs were ahead after just three minutes. Steffen Iversen picked himself off the floor after being fouled and played a swift free-kick to Oyvind Leonhardsen, who scored with a firm drive. On 33 minutes Leonhardsen turned provider, floating in a free-kick for Chris Perry to head in. Ten minutes after the restart, Zimbru allowed Ginola the time to find Perry, whose knockdown was despatched by Tim Sherwood. "We're going forward, playing good, exciting football, and that's something the fans can be pleased with," said George Graham, belying his reputation for tactical caution – at least for now.

Walker, Carr, Taricco (Edinburgh), Freund, Young, **Perry, Leonhardsen,** *Sherwood, Armstrong (Dominguez), Iversen, Ginola*

30 September 1999, first round, second leg

FC ZIMBRU 0 (0)
TOTTENHAM HOTSPUR 0 (3)

Republican Stadium, Chisinau, Moldova
Att: 7,000

Tottenham's venture into Moldova was a triumph for George Graham's organisational skills, and for Chris Perry. The defender was made captain in the absence of Sol Campbell and Tim Sherwood, and produced "a superb all-round display as Tottenham completed the professional job against Zimbru that Graham had demanded," said Gerry Cox in *The Guardian.* Graham ventured that Perry deserved an England call up for his fine form. Hit by a lengthening injury list, Spurs did what was required. In a strangely subdued stadium with around 500 Spurs fans in attendance, Tottenham fended off Zimbru's largely ineffectual attacks and, but for a goal-line clearance from Perry in the last minute, were rarely troubled. With better finishing they would have added to their 3-0 aggregate, as Perry, Steffen Iversen, Chris Armstrong and Stephen Clemence all went close.

Walker, Carr, Taricco (Edinburgh), Freund, Young, Perry, Leonhardsen, Clemence, Armstrong (Dominguez), Iversen, Nielsen

AN UTTER CARR-LAMITY

28 October 1999, second round, first leg

TOTTENHAM HOTSPUR 1
1FC KAISERSLAUTERN 0

White Hart Lane *Att:* 35,177

When George Graham was first appointed as Tottenham boss, it was widely accepted that David Ginola would be the first player to be ushered toward the exit. The two seemed polar opposites – one a free-spirited artist who prided self-expression over rigid conformity, the other a strict disciplinarian with little time for fripperies and a focus on workrate and physical commitment. The two portrayals were caricatures, but revealed a wider clash of ideals, never better illustrated than in the tie with Kaiserslautern. In the home leg, Ginola took centre stage and delivered, cracking a hard defensive nut with a succession of penetrating runs, crosses, passes and shots. It was his run in the 34th minute that earned Spurs victory, when he tumbled under goalkeeper Andreas Reinke's challenge. The Germans protested, but the resulting spot kick was converted by Steffen Iversen for a precious 1-0 advantage.

Walker, Carr, Taricco, Freund, Campbell, Perry, Leonhardsen, Sherwood, Fox, (Clemence), **Iversen**, *Ginola*

4 November 1999, second round, second leg

1FC KAISERSLAUTERN 2 (2)
TOTTENHAM HOTSPUR 0 (1)

Fritz-Walter Stadium, Kaiserslautern, Germany *Att:* 29,044

Two minutes into injury time at the end of a gruelling examination of their mettle, Spurs looked to have survived. With a mixture of superb saves from Ian Walker, woeful finishing from the home side, and large slices of luck, Tottenham had kept Kaiserslautern at bay. Then disaster struck. Youri Djorkaeff fed Andreas Buck and his angled drive beat Walker. Extra-time loomed but, seconds later, calamity befell Stephen Carr as he deflected a Buck shot into his own net. Spurs fans despaired but there were recriminations amid the agony. George Graham had left Ginola, his most potent attacking threat, on the bench until too late in the game, by which time Spurs were camped in their own half. The manager's instinctive caution was much criticised, with an impact not just on immediate European participation but his own long-term future. Within 18 months, Graham was gone.

Walker, Carr, Edinburgh (Young), Freund, Campbell, Perry, Leonhardsen, Sherwood, Armstrong (Ginola), Iversen, Clemence

The wheels come off for Spurs in Germany as Stephen Carr scores the own goal that meant an aggregate lead with minutes to go turned into a painful 2-1 defeat

The 2000s

After an absence of six years, an attacking, attractive side moulded by Martin Jol qualified for Europe after finishing fifth in the Premiership in May 2006. It was a significant achievement, and with the benefit of hindsight this can be identified as a key moment in modern Spurs history. In fact, the side missed the prize of Champions League qualification in the most stomach-churning of circumstances – and that can be read literally – on the final day of the season.

And so began the latest chapter in Tottenham Hotspur's European story, a chapter which included an almost impossibly romantic canter through the club's first Champions League season which is covered in some depth later in this book.

The new century would see Spurs travel to Turkey, Denmark, Ukraine and Cyprus for the first time in European competition. Somewhat inevitably, Feyenoord also featured too, albeit briefly when the behaviour of the Dutch fans led UEFA to award Spurs a bye in that first season back. And in the way that football often throws up neat connections, the first campaign also saw Dimitar Berbatov – the striking talent who had played such an influential role in returning Spurs to Europe – face his former club, the German side Bayer Leverkusen. Of course, he scored the only goal.

There were three seasons of UEFA Cup football for Spurs to acclimatise to the modern realities of European competition. The UEFA Cup, now with a league stage and soon to be expanded further and renamed the Europa League, had arguably lost some of its prestige as modern managers under pressure for league results had to choose between putting out the best team possible in every game, or keeping players fresh for the ones that mattered more. In the 2000s what mattered most of all was the Champions League, but first you had to qualify and that meant doing well in the league. For Spurs managers in particular, with all that Europe meant to the club, that battle between head and heart was keenly felt.

Harry Redknapp's bluntness when discussing the Europa League may not have been to the taste of many traditionalists – and his comments were certainly a far cry from those of Bill Nicholson – but they accurately reflected the new reality.

What this new reality did mean, under Redknapp in particular, was that younger players more often got the chance to turn out in European competition for Spurs – certainly in the early rounds – than they would previously have done as managers rotated their squads.

European competition may not be as alluring and exotic as it was back in those first, pioneering years when each country visited was a new frontier and each opponent faced was an unknown quantity. But as Spurs have recently rediscovered, and in so doing introduced the magic to a new generation of fans, there's nothing quite like a European tie under the floodlights to set the pulse racing.

Left to right: Dimitar Berbatov celebrates scoring v Braga in the 2006 UEFA Cup; Gareth Bale after his famous hat-trick in the San Siro v Inter Milan in 2010; Aaron Lennon shows off his skills in the Champions League game v FC Twente in 2010

**UEFA CUP
2006/07**
SLAVIA PRAGUE
BESIKTAS
CLUB BRUGGE
BAYER LEVERKUSEN
DINAMO BUCHAREST
SPORTING BRAGA
SEVILLA

2007/08
ANORTHOSIS FAMAGUSTA
GETAFE
HAPOEL TEL AVIV
AALBORG BK
ANDERLECHT
SLAVIA PRAGUE
PSV EINDHOVEN

2008/09
WISLA KRAKOW
UDINESE
DINAMO ZAGREB
NEC NIJMEGEN
SPARTAK MOSCOW
SHAKHTAR DONETSK

**UEFA EUROPA LEAGUE
2011/12**
HEARTS
PAOK
SHAMROCK ROVERS
RUBIN KAZAN

**UEFA CHAMPIONS LEAGUE
2010/11**
YOUNG BOYS
WERDER BREMEN
FC TWENTE
INTER MILAN
AC MILAN
REAL MADRID

THE ROAD TO EUROPE

2006

In 2001, Alan Sugar took his leave of football and sold up to new owners. The English National Investment Company arrived with a plan to get Tottenham back into the domestic elite and then in contention for European participation. But the new regime suffered an immediate blow when star defender Sol Campbell ran down his contract and signed for Arsenal.

The lure of Champions League football had played a major part in Campbell's defection, emphasising how important the reconfigured European Cup was. Playing catch-up and getting into Europe had been a difficult task for Spurs, however, and significant investment and a succession of managers made little impression on the newly emerged "big four" of Manchester United, Liverpool, Chelsea and Arsenal.

The arrival of Frank Arnesen as Director of Football, an improvement in player recruitment, and then the appointment of Martin Jol as manager gave impetus to the Spurs revival. By 2006, Tottenham were challenging for a top-four spot and with it a place in the Champions League. A heartbreaking end-of-season defeat to West Ham ended the dream: key players had been ruled out due to a mystery stomach bug, illustrating Tottenham's poor luck. Qualification for the UEFA Cup, however, provided some compensation.

Spurs are back in Europe! Robbie Keane scores against Slavia Prague in the opening tie of the UEFA Cup campaign at White Hart Lane

Jermaine Jenas is mobbed by team-mates after scoring Spurs' winner in the away tie in Prague that marked the club's return to European competition

JENAS UP 'N AWAY
JJ the main man for Jol

14 September 2006, first round, first leg

SLAVIA PRAGUE 0
TOTTENHAM HOTSPUR 1

Stadion Evzena Rosickeho, Prague, Czech Republic Att: 14,869

Despite fielding a number of players lacking in experience of European football, Tottenham registered a dominant performance in the Czech Republic. Jermaine Jenas's ability to get into goalscoring positions from midfield earned Spurs a first-leg victory. In the 37th minute Didier Zokora surged through the middle before feeding Jenas in space on the right, and his precise low finish from 18 yards did the rest. Spurs were rarely threatened by a Slavia side well below Premier League standard, but the game represented a landmark occasion: it was Tottenham's 100th in Europe.

Robinson, Assou-Ekotto, Chimbonda, Dawson, King, Huddlestone (Davids), **Jenas**, *Tainio, Zokora, Defoe (Keane), Mido*

28 September 2006, first round, second leg

TOTTENHAM HOTSPUR 1 (2)
SLAVIA PRAGUE 0 (0)

White Hart Lane Att: 35,191

Robbie Keane ended a barren run with his first goal in 11 games as Spurs laboured to repeat their first-leg winning margin. Plagued yet again by injuries, the whole side was struggling to find form and the net. For the *Daily Mirror*'s John Cross, Spurs "still seem to be suffering a hangover from last season when they missed out on the fourth Champions League place". Though Tottenham struggled to establish a fluent rhythm they did create chances – all spurned, however, until 10 minutes from time, when stand-in skipper Keane at last broke his duck. It may have been unconvincing, but Spurs were through to the next stage.

Robinson, Chimbonda, Davenport, Dawson, Lee, Jenas, Murphy (Ghaly), Ziegler (Tainio), Zokora, **Keane**, *Mido*

19 October 2006, Group B

BESIKTAS 0
TOTTENHAM HOTSPUR 2

Inonu Stadium, Istanbul, Turkey Att: 26,800

There was a new format and new opposition for Spurs' opening game in the group stage of the reconfigured UEFA Cup, which saw nine groups of five teams each playing each other just once – giving each club two games at home and two away. In their first game Spurs made their first competitive visit to Turkey a highly successful one. Tottenham faced a Turkish crowd making the familiar deafening din, but were not put off their stride. Dimitar Berbatov was the star, setting up Hossam Ghaly in the 32nd minute for the first. Ghaly's shot was blocked by the keeper but then ricocheted back off the Egyptian and into the net. Berbatov made it 2-0 in the 63rd minute, gliding through the Besiktas half before eluding his marker and then dummying the goalkeeper to stroke the ball into the net.

Robinson, Assou-Ekotto, Chimbonda, Dawson, King, **Ghaly** *(Lennon), Huddlestone, Jenas, Murphy (Ziegler),* **Berbatov** *(Defoe), Keane*

Dimitar Berbatov is typically downbeat after scoring against his former team Bayer Leverkusen in Germany

GROUP B	W	D	L	F	A	Pts
TOTTENHAM HOTSPUR	4	0	0	9	2	12
Dinamo Bucharest	2	1	1	6	6	7
Bayer Leverkusen	1	1	2	4	5	4
Besiktas	1	0	3	4	7	3
Club Brugge	0	2	2	4	7	2

2 November 2006, Group B

TOTTENHAM HOTSPUR 3
FC BRUGES 1

White Hart Lane *Att:* 35,716

Dimitar Berbatov again drew comparisons with the great Alan Gilzean with a man of the match performance. The Bulgarian's finishing and his desire to help his team-mates thrive fitted the "Gilly" mould. After Bruges took a surprise 14th-minute lead through Salou Ibrahim, Berbatov took control. He calmed home nerves three minutes later with an assured strike after Pascal Chimbonda had headed down a Jermaine Jenas free-kick. Then in the 63rd minute Berbatov turned provider when he released Robbie Keane to score from a tight angle, before the Bulgarian made sure of the points with a precise 73rd-minute header.

Robinson, Assou-Ekotto, Chimbonda, Dawson, King, Ghaly, Jenas, Lennon, (Murphy), Zokora, **Berbatov 2** *(Mido),* **Keane**

23 November 2006, Group B

BAYER LEVERKUSEN 0
TOTTENHAM HOTSPUR 1

BayArena, Leverkusen, Germany *Att:* 22,500

While Spurs were not at their best, the result made for impressive reading. Tottenham's third away win guaranteed passage to the next round and illustrated that Spurs were firmly in contention for the trophy. Once again it was Dimitar Berbatov who proved decisive to the outcome. "With a certain degree of predictability, Berbatov scored the goal against his former club," reported the *Daily Telegraph's* Martin Smith. The strike came in the 36th minute when Robbie Keane and Aaron Lennon combined to get behind the home defence, and Berbatov scored from close range.

Robinson, Assou-Ekotto, Chimbonda, Dawson, King, Lennon, Malbranque (Huddlestone), Tainio, Zokora, **Berbatov** *(Mido),* **Keane**

14 December 2006, Group B

TOTTENHAM HOTSPUR 3
DINAMO BUCHAREST 1

White Hart Lane *Att:* 34,004

With the pressure of qualification off, Spurs relaxed and gave further credence to the growing belief that they could win the whole competition. "Few sides left in the last 32 look better equipped to reach the final," wrote *The Guardian's* David Ornstein after Tottenham had despatched an in-form Bucharest team. Dimitar Berbatov opened the scoring thanks to a gift from the Dinamo goalkeeper whose fluffed clearance went straight to the Bulgarian who smashed the ball home from 25 yards. A double from Jermain Defoe in the 39th and 50th minutes gave the striker his first-ever European goals.

Robinson, Assou-Ekotto, Chimbonda (Stalteri), Dawson, King (Davenport), Ghaly, Huddlestone (Malbranque), Lennon, Zokora, **Berbatov, Defoe 2**

Aaron Lennon puts pressure on the Braga defence during an entertaining encounter in Portugal that Spurs eventually won 3-2

8 March 2007, fourth round, first leg

SPORTING BRAGA 2
TOTTENHAM HOTSPUR 3

Estadio Municipal de Braga, Portugal
Att: 15,000

With Spurs given a bye after original opponents, Feyenoord, were banned due to crowd trouble in the group stage, luck seemed to be in Tottenham's favour. But it needed Robbie Keane to save their blushes after his dramatic last-minute winner secured a win that should have been wrapped up by half-time. In the spectacular surroundings of the Estádio Municipal de Braga, Tottenham took early control and created chance after chance. The visitors had to wait until the 57th minute, however, before opening the scoring, when Keane latched on to Aaron Lennon's pass and shot into the top-right corner. Steed Malbranque made it two when he seized on the rebound from Lennon's parried shot 18 minutes from time. That should have been enough, but after goals from Paulo Jorge in the 76th minute and Ze Carlos five minutes later, Spurs were thankful for Keane's second.

*Robinson, Chimbonda, Dawson, Gardner, Lee, Lennon, **Malbranque**, Tainio (Huddlestone), Zokora, Berbatov, **Keane 2***

14 March 2007, fourth round second leg

TOTTENHAM HOTSPUR 3 (6)
SPORTING BRAGA 2 (4)

White Hart Lane *Att:* 33,761

Now into the "business end" of the season, Spurs were enjoying a rich vein of form. Once again Braga made a game of it and scored twice, but Spurs were just too strong at the other end of the pitch. Integral to the free-flowing, goal-grabbing style was Dimitar Berbatov. With another brace, he took his tally in the competition that season to seven, and was at the centre of virtually everything good about his team's display. After Braga took a surprise lead when Tom Huddlestone headed into his own net after 24 minutes, Berbatov seized the initiative. He scored the equaliser four minutes later, released into the area by Robbie Keane's flick and notched a second two minutes before the break, chesting Huddlestone's pass before smacking a brilliant volley past Paulo Santos. Braga drew level via Joao Amaral but Berbatov's sublime pass enabled Steed Malbranque to make it 3-2 14 minutes from time.

*Cerny, Chimbonda, Dawson, Lee, Stalteri, Huddlestone, Lennon (Ghaly), **Malbranque**, Zokora, **Berbatov 2**, Keane (Defoe)*

Robbo's rant as sad Spurs are done by joke penalty

Left: Spurs keeper Paul Robinson saves at the feet of Sevilla's Brazilian forward Adriano Correia, but a penalty is controversially given against him

Right: Despite a late rally Spurs go out of the UEFA Cup after a draw in the second leg at White Hart Lane

5 April 2007, quarter-final, first leg

SEVILLA 2
TOTTENHAM HOTSPUR 1

Estadio Ramon Sanchez Pizjuan, Seville, Spain *Att*: 32,738

An old spectre of times past reared its head as Spurs went down to an unfortunate defeat. Having taken the lead after just 73 seconds, it seemed Tottenham were set for one of the great nights abroad. Sadly, it became a game to forget. Dimitar Berbatov threaded a pass for Robbie Keane to put Spurs one up, but Tottenham were stunned when referee Alain Hamer awarded a penalty for Paul Robinson's challenge on Adriano after 19 minutes. Ex-Spur Freddie Kanoute equalised from the spot, before Alexander Kerzhakov gave Sevilla the lead with a 37th-minute header. But the papers were dominated by reports of crowd violence. The old narrative of "hooligans" was inappropriate this time, however: the police had launched an unprovoked attack on Spurs fans in the away section and, while the players had some metaphorical wounds to lick, a number of supporters had real injuries to treat.

Robinson, Chimbonda, Dawson, Lee, Stalteri, Jenas, Lennon (Malbranque), Tainio (Ghaly), Zokora, Berbatov, **Keane**

12 April 2007, quarter-final, second leg

TOTTENHAM HOTSPUR 2 (3)
SEVILLA 2 (4)

White Hart Lane *Att*: 35,284

A brave but ultimately fruitless draw was to have an impact wider than the end of that year's UEFA Cup for Spurs. Sevilla would go on to retain the trophy and their tactically astute manager, Juande Ramos, would go on to replace Martin Jol as Tottenham boss. Spurs had expected a rearguard action from the Spanish side; instead they tore into Tottenham and raced into a 2-0 lead – first through Steed Malbranque's miskicked goal-line clearance in the 2nd minute, then with Freddie Kanoute's brilliant denouement to a sweeping move five minutes later. Spurs rallied with second-half goals from Jermain Defoe and Aaron Lennon, but it was not enough. Instead, as the *Daily Mirror's* Darren Lewis reported: "Spurs fans are this morning reflecting on what might have been after a thriller down at the Lane which saw their team recover magnificently from being butchered in the first half by the barbers of Seville."

Robinson, Chimbonda, Dawson, King, Jenas, **Lennon,** *Malbranque, Tainio Zokora* **(Defoe)**, *Berbatov, Keane*

White Hart Lane
April 12, 2007 7.45pm
Official Matchday Programme £3.00

THE ROAD TO EUROPE
2007

The good times were back. Spurs, having finished fifth in the Premier League for the second season running, were in the UEFA Cup again. If the Nineties had proved a low point for the club's belief in its abilities in Europe, the Noughties were marked out by a new confidence. With Dimitar Berbatov and Robbie Keane forming one of the club's deadliest strike forces in years, and a sprinkling of eye-catching talent in a side that Martin Jol had playing attractive, organised football, fans dared to dream of going all the way to the final in Manchester.

But despite Jol's success, questions were being asked about whether he had taken the team as far as he could. The Spurs board were certainly aware of Sevilla coach Juande Ramos, whose consecutive UEFA Cup successes and impact in the Spanish League had made him a hot property. And more rumours surrounded the future of Berbatov, a player of immense ability who, it was said, felt he needed to move on from Spurs. As it turned out, the UEFA Cup campaign would provide the mood music for the latest dramatic turn of events in the Tottenham Hotspur story.

Spurs boss Martin Jol congratulates his players after a victory against Manchester City on the last day of the 2006/07 season ensured a return to European competition

DEFOE'S SO SIXY
Now Jol has problem

Didier Zokora grabs hold of Jermain Defoe as they celebrate the emphatic victory over Cypriot side Anorthosis Famagusta

20 September 2007, first round, first leg

TOTTENHAM HOTSPUR 6
ANORTHOSIS FAMAGUSTA 1

White Hart Lane *Att:* 35,780

Jermain Defoe stole the show with two goals from the subs' bench to complete Tottenham's goal harvest against the Cypriot visitors. Jol, with four strikers to keep happy, played down rumours of a feud after opting to leave Defoe on the bench. Not that this stopped the press focusing on the off-field drama in the absence of much more than a routine win on the pitch. Younes Kaboul headed Spurs in front on five minutes, with three goals in three minutes just before half-time from Michael Dawson, Robbie Keane and Darren Bent wrapping things up before Defoe's late double.

*Cerny, Chimbonda, **Kaboul**, **Dawson**, Assou-Ekotto (Bale), Lennon, Zokora, Huddlestone, Malbranque (Taarabt), **Bent**, Keane (Defoe 2)*

4 October 2007, first round, second leg

ANORTHOSIS FAMAGUSTA 1 (2)
TOTTENHAM HOTSPUR 1 (7)

Antonis Papadopoulos Stadium, Larnaca, Cyprus *Att:* 6,606

Robbie Keane's 78th-minute goal saved Spurs from what *The Independent*'s Mike McGrathin wrote would have been "an embarrassing defeat". Spurs created chances but failed to convert them, then in the 54th minute the home side's Fabinho volleyed home after Nikolaos Frousos pulled back a high ball he appeared to have controlled with his arm. Jol had to bring Keane off the bench to spare Spurs' blushes. After the game, as the rumours about his job continued to swirl, Jol told the press: "I'm sick of talking about it. The most important thing is we're through to the next round, so we go home happy."

*Robinson, Lee (**Keane**), Dawson, Gardner, Stalteri, Malbranque, Zokora, Huddlestone, Boateng (Bale), Bent (Taarabt), Defoe*

25 October 2007, Group G

TOTTENHAM HOTSPUR 1
GETAFE 2

White Hart Lane *Att:* 26,122

This was another extraordinary night at White Hart Lane. Spurs had been poor in the league, with the pressure on Martin Jol growing, and just before kick-off news spread through the stands that he had been sacked. The strange atmosphere spread to the pitch where Spurs were unable to despatch a team lying third from bottom in La Liga. Dominic Fifield in *The Guardian* observed that "a vital group game was surrendered with barely a whimper". The Spurs defence was jittery, Radek Cerny gifted Getafe a goal and, while Jermain Defoe equalised, a late winner condemned the club to only its second home defeat in European competition.

*Cerny, Chimbonda, Kaboul, Gardner (Dawson), Lee, Lennon, Huddlestone, Zokora (Tainio) Malbranque (Keane), Berbatov, **Defoe***

Dimitar Berbatov heads home for Spurs against Hapoel Tel Aviv during the club's first competitive game in Israel

SPOT-ON DIMI DOES THE JOB

Spurs through after penalty avoids Goor fest

GROUP G	W	D	L	F	A	Pts
Getafe	3	0	1	7	5	9
TOTTENHAM HOTSPUR	2	1	1	7	5	7
Anderlecht	1	2	1	5	4	5
Aalborg BK	1	1	2	7	7	4
Hapoel Tel Aviv	1	0	3	3	8	3

8 November 2007, Group G

HAPOEL TEL AVIV 0
TOTTENHAM HOTSPUR 2

Bloomfield Stadium, Tel Aviv, Israel *Att:* 10,000

Unbeaten in his first three games in charge, new boss Juande Ramos looked to have stopped the rot in the league. Now it was time to get the European campaign back on track. And on this occasion in Tel Aviv the result was never in doubt against a poor Israeli side. Livewire striker Robbie Keane volleyed the opener on 26 minutes, and five minutes later Steed Malbranque crossed for Dimitar Berbatov to head home. His muted celebration fuelled more "want away" talk in the press, but the Bulgarian told *The Sun*: "I don't always smile but that does not make me a bad person." Spurs were now second in the group table.

Robinson, Chimbonda, Lee, Stalteri, Dawson, Malbranque (Defoe), Jenas (Boateng), Zokora, Lennon, **Berbatov**, **Keane** *(Bent)*

29 November 2007, Group G

TOTTENHAM HOTSPUR 3
AALBORG 2

White Hart Lane *Att:* 29,758

Spurs diced with disaster against the Danes, as another bout of shambolic defending helped the visitors go 1-0 up after just five minutes. By the break Spurs were two down, White Hart Lane was in shock and Ramos rang the changes. On came Darren Bent and Tom Huddlestone, the latter setting up Dimitar Berbatov to score 40 seconds after he had come on. Six minutes later Steed Malbranque levelled, and on 66 minutes Bent tapped home from close range. "Tottenham have an embarrassment of riches in attack," wrote the *Daily Mail*'s Simon Cass, "Which is just as well, given that they simply remain an embarrassment at the back".

Robinson, Lee (Bent), Chimbonda, Dawson, Bale, Lennon, Jenas (Huddlestone), Zokora, **Malbranque**, *Keane,* **Berbatov** *(Boateng)*

6 December 2007, Group G

ANDERLECHT 1
TOTTENHAM HOTSPUR 1

Constant Vanden Stock Stadium, Brussels, Belgium *Att:* 22,500

A late wobble from Jelle gave Spurs the penalty they needed to secure a draw and with it qualification to the knockout stages on a night when the torrential rain, that had finally broken through after subjecting the sizeable travelling support to an insidious drizzle all day, threatened to wash away the club's dreams. Jelle van Damme fouled Jermaine Jenas in the box, allowing Dimitar Berbatov to convert just three minutes after a Michael Dawson blunder had given the Belgians the lead. It was, wrote *The Sun*'s Antony Kastrinakis, "mission accomplished" for Juande Ramos but, observed the *Daily Mirror*'s Neil McLeman, "the Spaniard has a long winter of work ahead if he is to turn this team into European contenders".

Robinson, Chimbonda, Dawson, Zokora, Lee (Stalteri), Lennon, Jenas, Huddlestone, Malbranque, Keane (Berbatov), Bent (Defoe)

Dimitar Berbatov is amongst the goals again, this time on a chilly night in Prague where Spurs played, and won, for the second time in consecutive seasons

TOV TO A FLIER

Berba 'n Robbie fire in but Spurs suffer late jitters

14 February 2008, third round, first leg

SLAVIA PRAGUE 1
TOTTENHAM HOTSPUR 2

Stadion Evzena Rosickeho, Prague, Czech Republic *Att:* 11,134

In temperatures several degrees below freezing on a rock hard pitch, Spurs faced a side who had not played a competitive game for two months because of the winter break. What's more, Spurs had secured a League Cup Final place against Chelsea, and when Dimitar Berbatov drilled home in the fourth minute thoughts of a cup double surfaced. Jermaine Jenas was running riot in midfield and, having made the first goal, set up Robbie Keane who chipped home Spurs' second. But on 69 minutes keeper Radek Cerny fumbled a cross and David Strihavka poked home. Six minutes from time, Erich Brabec hit the bar from eight yards. Spurs still had work to do. Before the game, Juande Ramos had talked about changing the players' diet to make them leaner and fitter. *The Independent*'s Jason Burt wrote: "Never mind the cream cakes, this threatened to be a custard pie in the face."

*Cerny, Tainio (O'Hara), Woodgate, Zokora, Chimbonda, Lennon, Huddlestone, Jenas, Malbranque, **Keane** (Bent), **Berbatov***

21 February 2008, third round, second leg

TOTTENHAM HOTSPUR 1 (3)
SLAVIA PRAGUE 1 (2)

White Hart Lane *Att:* 34,224

This tie was the tale of two keepers. After Radek Cerny's blunder a week before, the recalled Paul Robinson "completed a journey from zero to hero", according to *The Independent*'s Mike Rowbottom, pulling off two top-class saves in a display that lit up a performance the same paper dubbed "insipid". Several first-team regulars were rested ahead of the League Cup Final three days later, and it was young Jamie O'Hara who scored on seven minutes. But after that chances went begging and, five minutes into the second half, Matej Krajcik equalised. Jermaine Jenas, Steed Malbranque and Robbie Keane were brought on, but the whistles emanating from the stands indicated the nervousness around the ground. Darren Bent hit the bar late on but, said Rowbottom, "Spurs were still living dangerously. Then again – when was it ever different?"

*Robinson, Tainio, Kaboul, Woodgate, Chimbonda (Malbranque), Lennon (Jenas), Huddlestone, Zokora, **O'Hara**, Berbatov (Keane), Bent*

Spurs suffer spot of Euro bother

6 March 2008, fourth round, first leg

TOTTENHAM HOTSPUR 0
PSV EINDHOVEN 1

White Hart Lane *Att:* 33,259

The League Cup, secured in a famous 2-1 win over Chelsea the preceding weekend, was paraded around the ground before this match, but as soon as the play began "the hangover from Wembley was maintained," thought *The Guardian's* Dominic Fifield. It was, he wrote, "a lacklustre display, limp and uninspired". For the visitors, Jefferson Farfan posed a constant threat, with Timmy Simons running the midfield. Just after the half hour, Spurs debutant Gilberto dawdled, Farfan stole the ball and lashed home. Substitute Jamie O'Hara volleyed wide but, like Aaron Lennon on the opposite flank, was unable to deliver the killer ball after getting into some good positions. A well-organised PSV kept Spurs shackled for the rest of the game, leaving Juande Ramos "a livid figure on the touchline as Spurs subsided to only a third defeat in 59 European home games," wrote Fifield.

Robinson, Chimbonda, Gilberto, (O'Hara), Woodgate, King (Taarabt), Lennon, Zokora, Jenas (Huddlestone), Malbranque, Berbatov, Keane

12 March 2008, fourth round, second leg

PSV EINDHOVEN 0 (1)
TOTTENHAM HOTSPUR 1 (1)

aet Spurs lost 6-5 on penalties
Philips Stadion, Eindhoven, Netherlands
Att: 33,000

PSV were far less impressive in the return but once again the men in white failed to convert their chances. The momentum looked to have swung Spurs' way when Dimitar Berbatov fired home a sensational volley nine minutes from time to square things up. In extra-time Darren Bent volleyed wide, and Steed Malbranque saw his effort brilliantly tipped over by PSV keeper Heurelho Gomes. And so it went to penalties. Paul Robinson saved PSV's second while Spurs scored their first four. But Gomes saved from Jermaine Jenas, both sides converted their sixth kick and PSV got number seven. Pascal Chimbonda stepped up for Spurs and scuffed wide. The truth was, wrote Simon Johnson in the *Evening Standard*, "Spurs didn't play well enough to deserve success at this level". It was all over.

*Robinson, Chimbonda, Woodgate, King (Lennon), Lee (Bent), Jenas, Zokora, Huddlestone, Malbranque, **Berbatov**, Keane (O'Hara)*

Spurs go out of Europe on penalties after a Pascal Chimbonda miss. Didier Zadora, second right standing, and Dimitar Berbatov, far right crouching, can't bear to watch

THE ROAD TO EUROPE
2008

Sevilla's removal of Spurs from the 2006/07 UEFA Cup may have effectively served as an audition for the Andalucian side's manager Juande Ramos. For in the autumn of 2007 the Spurs board sacked Martin Jol and installed the Spaniard in his place.

Spurs were taking a chance, but in Ramos's first full season the decision found its reward with Tottenham's first trophy in nine years, thanks to a memorable League Cup campaign in 2007/08. After a magnificent win over Arsenal in the semi-final, including a famous 5-1 thrashing in the home leg, a rejuvenated Spurs took on a Chelsea team riding the wave of their chairman Roman Abramovich's unprecedented spending.

The odds were stacked against Spurs, and when Didier Drogba gave Chelsea the lead the final at the new Wembley appeared to be sticking to the script. But this new Spurs team was made of spirit to go with the craft, and after Dimitar Berbatov equalised from the spot, Tottenham won through thanks to Jonathan Woodgate's ricocheted goal in extra-time. Tottenham's noisy support roared their approval: despite modest league form, Spurs were back in Europe again but this time with a trophy under their belt. With a team and manager seemingly in sync, confidence was high.

Elation for Spurs after defeating Chelsea in the League Cup Final at Wembley in 2008 and returning to Europe for a third consecutive season

Fraizer Campbell causes distraction in the Wisla Krakow defence and Gareth Bale's cross is diverted into the net by defender Arkadiusz Glowacki

Fragile Spurs fail to lift gloom for Ramos

18 September 2008, first round, first leg

TOTTENHAM HOTSPUR 2
WISLA KRAKOW 1

White Hart Lane *Att:* 35,751

For all the enthusiasm for the new season, Spurs made a worrying start, failing to win a single one of their first four games. They found solace in the UEFA Cup, with a hard-earned victory over sturdy Polish opposition. Record signing Darren Bent had found it tough going to win over the Spurs fans, and the departure of Dimitar Berbatov right at the end of the summer transfer window had heaped more pressure on Bent to provide goals. His 73rd-minute strike was a blessed relief for both player and team-mates. Spurs had taken a short-lived lead when David Bentley finished off a chance created by the fleet-footed Aaron Lennon in the 33rd minute. Just a minute later however, the Poles drew level, when Tomas Jirsak chipped over Heurelho Gomes. Spurs betrayed the fragility and nervousness that had plagued them that season, until Bent's goal settled both his side and the outcome.

*Gomes, Gunter (O'Hara), Woodgate, King, Bale, **Bentley**, Jenas, Zokora, Lennon (Campbell), Giovani (Assou-Ekotto), **Bent***

2 October 2008, first round, second leg

WISLA KRAKOW 1 (2)
TOTTENHAM HOTSPUR 1 (3)

Stadion Miejski, Krakow, Poland *Att:* 12,900

By the time of the return leg, matters had worsened. Dreadful league form at home was clearly weighing heavy on management and players, and the anxiety was transferred to Europe. This was a tense, apprehensive performance as Tottenham struggled to cling onto their first-leg advantage. They were thankful that Gareth Bale's cross was deflected by Arkadiusz Glowacki into his own net in the 58th minute to give Spurs a 3-1 aggregate advantage, but that was cut to just a single goal with Pawel Brozek's long-range lob seven minutes from time. Spurs were increasingly vulnerable, and but for the heroics of goalkeeper Heurelho Gomes may have faced the agony of extra-time. "I think the team is playing OK," Juande Ramos told the BBC's Sam Lyon. But things were far from OK: Ramos's fate was about to be sealed.

Gomes, Gunter, King, Woodgate, Bale, Lennon (Dawson), Zokora, Jenas, Modric (Huddlestone), Campbell (O'Hara), Bent [Glowacki og]

HARRY'S HELL-BENT ON RAPID REVIVAL

Striker does trick for new boss

Left: Gareth Bale battles with a Udinese defender

Above: Darren Bent celebrates the first goal in his hat-trick v Dinamo Zagreb as Spurs refind their European form

23 October 2008, Group D

UDINESE 2
TOTTENHAM HOTSPUR 0

Stadio Friuli, Udine, Italy *Att:* 22,000

In the aftermath of this dispiriting defeat, Jonathan Woodgate was asked if Spurs could take anything positive from the game. "No. Not at all," was the blunt response from the League Cup hero. It was only October, yet Tottenham's season was fast unravelling, betraying the growing mood of crisis. Within hours Juande Ramos paid the price. Familiar lapses cost Spurs dear. All the problems of their desperate league form – a lack of confidence, discipline, leadership and cohesion – surfaced once the Italians took the lead through Antonio di Natale's penalty after 24 minutes. Simone Pepe's adroit finish four minutes from time underlined Tottenham's desperate plight. With just two points from eight games, problems at home were now infecting Spurs on their travels; Ramos had made his name in the UEFA Cup, but now it was to prove his final undoing.

Gomes, Hutton, King, Woodgate (Giovani), Assou-Ekotto (Modric), Lennon, Zokora, Jenas, O'Hara, Bale, Bent

6 November 2008, Group D

TOTTENHAM HOTSPUR 4
DINAMO ZAGREB 0

White Hart Lane *Att:* 32,788

With Ramos gone, Tottenham chairman Daniel Levy decided to bypass the Director of Football system and not so much ring the changes as call on the tried and tested. He turned to Harry Redknapp to rescue the situation, hoping that the 61-year-old's experience, nous and gift for motivation would rescue Tottenham's parlous state. Redknapp had an immediate effect, restoring first domestic form and then performances in the UEFA Cup. Suddenly the goals were flowing to mirror the uplift in mood. Darren Bent gave a man of the match display against Zagreb, notching his first on the half hour, adding a second three minutes later and completing his hat-trick in the 69th minute, with Huddlestone getting the fourth. With 11 minutes left, substitute John Bostock became Tottenham's youngest-ever player in a first-team competitive match at 16 years and 295 days.

Gomes, Hutton, Dawson, Woodgate (Gunter), Bale, Bentley, (Bostock), **Huddlestone**, *Zokora, Lennon, Modric (Campbell),* **Bent 3**

GROUP D	W	D	L	F	A	Pts
Udinese	3	0	1	6	4	9
TOTTENHAM HOTSPUR	2	1	1	7	4	7
NEC Nijmegen	2	0	2	6	5	6
Spartak Moscow	1	1	2	5	6	4
Dinamo Zagreb	1	0	3	4	9	3

27 November 2008, Group D

NEC NIJMEGEN 0
TOTTENHAM HOTSPUR 1

McDOS Goffertstadion, Nijmegen, Netherlands *Att*: 12,500

The upward swing in form was maintained as Spurs gained another commendable away win. While Harry Redknapp took the likelihood of Spurs being one of the three sides qualifying from a group of five almost as a given, the *Daily Telegraph*'s Sandy Macaskill was more impressed, waxing lyrical in colourfully militaristic terms. "Ears prick up at the mention of Nijmegen, the one before the bridge too far. Just weeks ago, Tottenham resembled a forlorn, routed force. But… with seven wins now from nine games, their revolution is rolling inexorably onwards." Jamie O'Hara was the hero of the hour – or at least the 14th minute – latching onto a rebounded Fraizer Campbell shot that had struck the bar. Goalkeeper Heurelho Gomes had been much criticised in recent weeks, but he and Spurs were rarely troubled.

Gomes, Gunter, Dawson, Woodgate, Bale, Huddlestone, Zokora, **O'Hara***, Bentley (Mason), Bent (Lennon), Campbell (Obika)*

18 December 2008, Group D

TOTTENHAM HOTSPUR 2
SPARTAK MOSCOW 2

White Hart Lane *Att*: 28,906

While Spurs had made considerable progress after the dreadful form at the start of the season, Harry Redknapp was less than enthused with the modern version of the UEFA Cup. Even after this draw ensured progress to the next round, Redknapp was unmoved. "The UEFA Cup is on the back burner," he told the *Daily Mail*'s Simon Cass. "I won't be sitting in the social club with a pint of beer jumping up and down hoping for a big draw." Spurs were stunned as one of the great names of Russian football took a 2-0 lead thanks to Artem Dzyuba's brace, aided by a horror show from Gilberto, whose nervousness spread panic in the defence. But Croatian maestro Luka Modric's first goal for Tottenham and a Tom Huddlestone header spared Spurs' blushes. The manager might not be getting excited, but Spurs were through to the knockout stage.

Gomes, Gunter, Dawson, Zokora, Gilberto (Lennon), Bentley, **Huddlestone***, O'Hara, Bale,* **Modric***, Campbell*

Left: Jamie O'Hara bravely converts a rebound to secure a win for Spurs in Nijmegen

Right: Luka Modric scores his first goal for Spurs and helps secure a draw in the final group game v Spartak Moscow

GIO FORCE STILL NOT ENOUGH
Harry's kids go down

19 February 2009, third round, first leg

SHAKHTAR DONETSK 2
TOTTENHAM HOTSPUR 0

RSK Olimpiyskyi, Donetsk, Ukraine *Att:* 25,500

Spurs hardly got the big draw Harry Redknapp had alluded to. Instead they were paired with a side from one of the farther-flung corners of Europe, newly enriched with the finance of a seriously rich and ambitious owner and cheered on by a vocal crowd in which every fan seemed to be waving an orange flag. Off the back of a poor run of away form that had returned six straight defeats in all competitions, an under-strength Spurs battled gamely but ultimately without reward. Faced with having to utilise thin resources for a busy run of games, Redknapp gave a debut to 17-year-old Dean Parrett and had five youth-team players on the bench. The scratch side performed well enough, but succumbed at the end. Yevgen Seleznyov's 79th-minute header caught Gomes out of position and Rodrigues Jadson weaved through a static defence to make it 2-0 nine minutes later.

Gomes, Gunter, Huddlestone, Dawson, Chimbonda, Jenas, Zokora, Parrett (Bostock), Bentley, Giovani (Bent), Campbell

26 February 2009, third round, second leg

TOTTENHAM HOTSPUR 1 (1)
SHAKHTAR DONETSK 1 (3)

White Hart Lane *Att:* 30,595

Harry Redknapp gave youth its head again and the junior players did their manager and club proud. While the combination of kids and more senior players could not quite do enough to prolong what had been one of Tottenham's less-glorious European campaigns, their skill and effort gave hope for the future. Giovani Dos Santos had arrived from Barcelona's academy heralding great promise, but his Spurs career had been one of fits and starts. He gave an indication of his quality with a brilliant opener, curling a shot past Andriy Pyatov in the 55th minute. Spurs battled away to the end with full debutant Jonathan Obika showing plenty of enterprise, but Fernandinho's 86th-minute leveller brought down the curtain on that year's European participation. Tottenham would play the next season focusing on a bigger, more enticing European prize.

Gomes, Gunter, Chimbonda, Huddlestone, Gilberto (Bostock), Giovani, Palacios, O'Hara (Parrett), Bale, Campbell, Obika

Giovani Dos Santos takes the plaudits after his goal but it's not enough to keep Spurs in Europe. A 1-1 draw saw Shakhtar Donetsk progress

THE ROAD TO EUROPE
2010

Spurs left it late to secure their first crack at the Champions League. The battle for fourth place had been between Manchester City, Liverpool, Aston Villa and Spurs since August. The team had played some great football all season. But as the season's end neared, the spectre of falling at the last was raised again as the Lilywhites faltered. In the first of three key games over one week in April, an FA Cup semi-final was surrendered to Portsmouth. Three days later Arsenal came to White Hart Lane. Danny Rose's wonderful volley put Spurs on the way to a first league win over their old rivals in 11 years. Next came Chelsea. They were swept aside 2-1. By the penultimate game of the season the race for fourth was between Spurs and City, with the two sides squaring up at Eastlands for what was essentially a play-off for a place in the Champions League. Spurs took the game to the Blues but could not find the vital goal. Then, eight minutes from time, Younes Kaboul crossed, City keeper (and former Spur) Marton Fulop parried, and up popped Peter Crouch to head home. Spurs were back at the top table in Europe.

Spurs players celebrate after the 1-0 win at Manchester City that put them into the Champions League

"THIS IS A BIG THING FOR US. IF WE QUALIFY FOR THE GROUP STAGES OF THE CHAMPIONS LEAGUE I'M SURE THIS CLUB WILL GO ON TO ANOTHER LEVEL. THIS CLUB DESERVES TO PLAY FOOTBALL AT THAT LEVEL"
LUKA MODRIC

17 August 2010, qualifying round, first leg

YOUNG BOYS 3
TOTTENHAM HOTSPUR 2

Stade de Suisse, Berne, Switzerland *Att:* 30,166

Fourth place in the Premier League earned Spurs a one-off, winner-takes-all tie in the Champions League qualifying round. Swiss side Young Boys appeared to be the easiest name in the draw, but Spurs were in for an almighty shock. They were 1-0 down inside four minutes as the home side ripped into them. On half an hour Spurs were 3-0 down. The whole team appeared utterly unable to cope with Young Boys' players, formation or the artificial surface. "It had looked like boys against Boys," observed *The Telegraph*'s Jason Burt. "Having waited 48 years for another tilt at Europe's premier club competition, Spurs were almost swept out of it inside 30 chaotic minutes last night."

Harry Redknapp shuffled the pack, withdrawing Benoit Assou-Ekotto and sending on Tom Huddlestone. Spurs began to make an impression on the game. Just before half-time, Sebastian Bassong rose to head home a Gareth Bale corner. Shortly afterwards,

Jermain Defoe missed a headed chance. Redknapp went down the tunnel with a face like thunder. Whatever he said at half-time, it had some effect as Spurs started the second half with more poise and determination. Huddlestone in particular began to assert himself, and Defoe and Roman Pavlyuchenko started to look more dangerous. But Spurs had lost creative spark Luka Modric to injury at half-time, and when Defoe limped off it seemed as if the bad luck would never stop.

Young Boys were now trying to hit a dominant Spurs on the break. But on 82 minutes Pavlyuchenko, so often the scorer of vital late goals, hammered home from a Robbie Keane pass. "Spurs," said *The Guardian*'s David Hytner, "had flirted with disaster".

Gomes, Assou-Ekotto (Huddlestone), **Bassong***, Dawson, Corluka, Bale, Palacios, Modric (Kranjcar), Giovani, Defoe (Keane),* **Pavlyuchenko**

Tom Huddlestone embraces Roman Pavlyuchenko after the Russian's late goal turned this tie back in Spurs' favour

EU BEAUTY, CROUCHIE

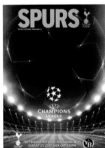

25 August 2010, qualifying round, second leg
TOTTENHAM HOTSPUR 4 (6)
YOUNG BOYS 0 (3)
White Hart Lane *Att:* 34,709

The rain fell hard but this was no humdrum night in London town as Spurs washed away any doubts about their right to be in Europe with a deluge of goals.

Fittingly, it was Peter Crouch's night. The striker whose goal had put Spurs in the qualifying round scored a hat-trick to take them into the competition proper. His first came just five minutes in, when he had the time and confidence to tell Michael Dawson to leave a Gareth Bale cross so he could head home. Jermain Defoe made it 2-0 on 32 minutes, although everyone except the match officials saw that he appeared to control the ball with his arm before firing home. This was a long way from the shambolic Spurs of the first leg, with the *Daily Mirror*'s Darren Lewis observing, "The ruthless precision of Tottenham's finishing showed they had learned their lesson."

On the hour, Crouch headed home Bale's corner, and he completed his hat-trick on 77 minutes with a penalty after the outstanding Bale had been felled in the box by Senad Lulic. While it was undoubtedly Crouch's night, Bale also stood out, creating all four goals in a display the *London Evening Standard*'s James Olley described as "brimming with energy and confidence".

After the game, Harry Redknapp said: "As a kid I used to come training here and watched the games with Benfica in those great days, and at that time it was amazing to see European football and the way this place was jumping. To bring it back was great for the fans – and that is what it is all about." Skipper Ledley King thought, "Spurs have the quality to beat any other team in Europe." As for Crouch, he said: "We want Inter or Real next."

Gomes (Cudicini), Corluka, Dawson, King, Assou-Ekotto, Bale (Kranjcar), Huddlestone, Lennon, Palacios, **Crouch 3**, **Defoe** (Pavlyuchenko)

Hat-trick hero Peter Crouch runs to the home crowd on a memorable night for players and fans at White Hart Lane

HANG ON HARRY

Thrilling Spurs have lots to learn

Peter Crouch, scorer of Spurs' second goal against Bremen is the man behind the mask, but Spurs let a two-goal lead slip in Germany

14 September 2010, Group A

WERDER BREMEN 2
TOTTENHAM HOTSPUR 2

Weserstadion, Bremen, Germany *Att:* 30,344

The first game in Europe proper took the team and a large contingent of fans to the pretty German town of Bremen. Werder had made quite an impression on the Bundesliga in the last few seasons and this looked a potentially tough game. But Spurs, buoyed by the late transfer-window signing of Dutchman Rafael van der Vaart, were to set the template for a sensational maiden campaign in the Champions League.

It was van der Vaart who orchestrated a first 30 minutes in which Spurs swept the German side before them. With Rafa running the show, Tom Huddlestone and Jermaine Jenas controlling the midfield, Ledley King imperious at the back and Gareth Bale simply terrorising the Bremen defence, the home side could not live with Spurs. It was Bale whose 12th-minute cross from the left so panicked the Bremen defence that Petri Pasanen put the ball into his own net. On 18 minutes, Peter Crouch headed van der Vaart's cross into the top corner.

Spurs were cruising and, high in the corner of the Weserstadion, the ecstatic travelling support were dancing in the aisles and singing, "Champions League and we're having a laugh." But, as Martin Lipton wrote in the *Daily Mirror*: "They never do it the easy way. It's not in Tottenham's DNA. Never has been, never will be." On 43 minutes, Benoit Assou-Ekotto miskicked to concede a throw-in, and from the set piece Hugo Almeida ghosted in and headed home. Two minutes after the restart, Spurs stood off the increasingly influential Marko Marin and he made it 2-2. Tottenham looked to be losing their composure, with Carlo Cudicini forced into some vital saves. The introduction of Wilson Palacios helped them settle, and Crouch went close with a late effort. A draw felt like a chance squandered, but it was a fair result.

Cudicini, Assou-Ekotto, Kaboul, King, Corluka, Huddlestone, Bale, Jenas, Lennon (Palacios), van der Vaart (Keane), **Crouch** *[Pasanen og]*

ROMAN HAS THE VAA VAA VROOM

Pav and Gareth bail out 'brilliant & brainless' Rafa

29 September 2010, Group A

TOTTENHAM HOTSPUR 4
FC TWENTE 1

White Hart Lane *Att*: 32,518

"Spurs are making sure that, however this Champions League campaign eventually concludes, they will be remembered as Europe's great entertainers," wrote *The Sun*'s Shaun Custis after another dramatic night in north London. It seemed each one of Spurs' games in the competition would feature a single player on song and tonight it was the turn of Rafael van der Vaart to hit the right note – although not necessarily for all the right reasons.

From the off this was a pulsating, open game. Twente's Bryan Ruiz broke through early on, forcing Spurs keeper Heurelho Gomes to brilliantly claw away an attempted chipped goal. Soon after, van der Vaart forced a super save from Twente keeper Nikolay Mihalyov. The duel between these two men continued through the half. Just before the break, the Dutchman's pass to Crouch prompted Twente skipper Peter Wisgerhof to wrestle the striker to the ground and the referee pointed to the spot. Mihalyov was

booked for time-wasting as he sledged van der Vaart, who had stepped up to take the kick. The tactic worked. Mihalyov turned the kick around the post. A frustrated van der Vaart was then booked for a foul on Nicky Kuiper, but got his revenge two minutes after the break when he slammed home an absolutely glorious volley.

On 50 minutes, Gareth Bale was brought down in the box. Pavlyuchenko converted. But six minutes later Nacer Chadli pulled one back. Then van der Vaart saw red for a silly foul. Things looked ominous, but Spurs earned another, admittedly debatable, penalty, which Pavlyuchenko again converted, and five minutes from time the rampant Bale burst into the box to sidefoot home. Spurs were now joint group leaders with their next opponents, Inter Milan.

Gomes, Hutton, Bassong, King, Assou-Ekotto, ***van der Vaart****, Huddlestone, Modric (Lennon),* ***Bale****, **Pavlyuchenko 2** (Keane), Crouch (Jenas)*

Rafael van der Vaart scores the opening goal on an eventful Champions League night at White Hart Lane. It was a mixed night for van der Vaart, he missed a penalty and was red-carded in the second half

20 October 2010, Group A

INTER MILAN 4
TOTTENHAM HOTSPUR 3

San Siro, Milan, Italy *Att*: 49,551

Milan is one of the world's great football cities, the stadium that football fans will always know as the San Siro is one of the great cathedrals of world football. So from the moment the draw was made, this was the game everyone wanted to be at, the one that stood out as evidence that Spurs were back and competing on the very biggest of stages. While the official ticket allocation was 6,000, estimates that 15,000 Spurs fans travelled to the city cannot be far off the mark. In the days before the match, the number of travelling supporters enjoying the sights and atmosphere of a beautiful late autumn sunny spell grew. From the city parks to the roof of the stunning Duomo and through the restaurants and bars of the city centre there were groups of Spurs fans enjoying every minute.

Inside the ground, the 6,000 found themselves high in the gods. Away to the right was a whole block of travelling support, and all around the ground small pockets of Spurs fans could be seen. Aside from one isolated incident the fans behaved. On and off the pitch, a new chapter was being forged. As for the game itself, well, it was to be one of the most extraordinary nights of European football in many a year.

The players seemed unnerved as soon as they stepped out into the famous old stadium, with the flags and flares of the noisy home support testing their resolve. The line-up was missing the injured Ledley King, Michael Dawson, Jermain Defoe and the suspended Rafael van der Vaart. And it told. Spurs were humiliated in the first half. They were three goals down, reduced to 10 men and had barely touched the ball after just 14 minutes.

Just 67 seconds after the start, Samuel Eto'o split the Spurs defence for Javier Zanetti to take advantage of right-back Alan Hutton's poor positioning and slam home. On eight minutes, Jonathan Biabany ran into a gap vacated by left-back Benoit Assou-Ekotto and was brought crashing down by Heurelho Gomes. Slovenian referee Damir Skomina gave the penalty and showed Assou-Ekotto the red card, before realising his mistake and ordering Gomes off. Luka Modric was sacrificed so that Carlo Cudicini could come on in goal. Eto'o converted. The very next attack brought Inter a third, Dejan Stankovic finishing a fine move. Just before half-time, Eto'o made it four.

In the *London Evening Standard*, James Olley wrote: "Spurs fans were right to fear an utter thrashing after the break."

Above: The first half in the San Siro goes from bad to worse for Spurs's keeper Heurelho Gomes, having conceded a penalty he is sent off after just eight minutes

Right: Gareth Bale scores a wonderful solo goal to pull one back for Spurs, the first of three for Bale in a dramatic second half

Seven minutes after the restart Jermaine Jenas dispossessed Wesley Sneijder deep in the Spurs half and Gareth Bale picked up the loose ball. He began to run, and run. In a stunning 60-yard sprint with the ball at his feet he jinked past three Inter players and slammed a shot into the bottom corner of the net across keeper Julio Cesar. Spurs looked more organised in defence, and were taking more possession. But Inter still looked safe. Then on 89 minutes Bale launched another turbo-charged run to score an almost exact replica of his first goal. You could feel the fear in the home side and its support. In injury time, Aaron Lennon ran at the heart of Inter's defence before laying the ball off to Bale. The Welshman steadied himself before driving home to complete his hat-trick. "We're gonna win 5-4" sang the wildly celebrating travelling support. Never can a team have been as relieved to hear the final whistle as Inter. Given another five minutes, Spurs looked more than capable of snatching a win. "Do not doubt," wrote the *Daily Mirror*'s Martin Lipton, "Gareth Bale could walk into any team on the planet".

*Gomes, Hutton, **Bale 3**, Gallas, Bassong, Huddlestone (Palacios), Lennon, Jenas, Crouch (Keane), Modric (Cudicini), Assou-Ekotto*

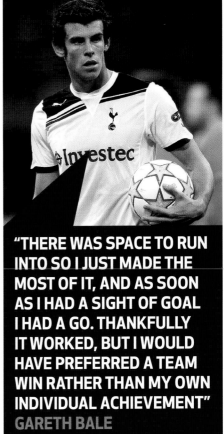

"THERE WAS SPACE TO RUN INTO SO I JUST MADE THE MOST OF IT, AND AS SOON AS I HAD A SIGHT OF GOAL I HAD A GO. THANKFULLY IT WORKED, BUT I WOULD HAVE PREFERRED A TEAM WIN RATHER THAN MY OWN INDIVIDUAL ACHIEVEMENT"
GARETH BALE

2 November 2010, Group A
TOTTENHAM HOTSPUR 3
INTER MILAN 1

White Hart Lane *Att:* 34,103

Almost as one the crowd seized on the chant that had begun deep in the stands. Thousands of voices took up the mantra and propelled it around the ground. "Taxi for Maicon" was the gleeful chorus, a reference to the fact that Maicon, one of the best right-backs in the world, playing for the champions of Europe, had been utterly taken apart by Gareth Bale. In Milan, Bale had been superb for half the game. On this night, he was the star from start to finish.

The headlines the next morning said it all. "Balissimo" in the *Daily Mirror;* "Bale Force" and "Bale is Intergalactic" in *The Sun.* The *Daily Telegraph*'s Henry Winter said it was "the sort of exhilarating performance to intoxicate younger minds amongst the Lane faithful and remind older heads of the glory, glory nights". the *Daily Mirror*'s Darren Lewis wrote of Bale: "The 90 minutes he produced last night must be up there with the greatest by a British winger for some time." *The Sun*'s Steven Howard wrote: "Magnificent, irrepressible Spurs were the talk of the town as they turned the clock back almost half a century."

Both teams set up to attack, but Inter's decision to put two men on Bale left space for the likes of Rafael van der Vaart and Luka Modric to exploit. On 18 minutes, Modric picked up the ball, swayed past a challenge and slipped a pass between Javier Zanetti and Lucio for van der Vaart. The Dutchman read Modric's intention perfectly and was ideally placed to smash home a left-footed shot. White Hart Lane erupted. From the restart, Spurs were off again, leaving no opportunity for the pulsating atmosphere to drop. Aaron Lennon was giving Christian Chivu all kinds of problems down the right, while on the left Bale was tying Maicon in knots. With his by now familiar powerful runs down the flank, he was going past the Brazilian defender time after time and when he crossed for Peter Crouch late in the half another goal seemed certain. But the big man's volley flew just past the post. Just

Gareth Bale gives Inter defender Maicon a torrid time at White Hart Lane, beating him time after time in a scintillating performance

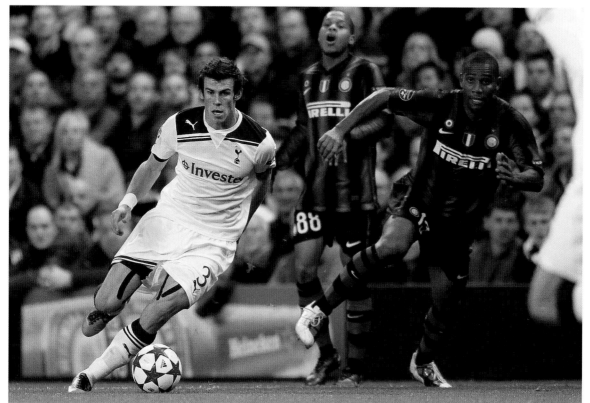

Rafael van der Vaart runs to the Spurs fans ecstatically after opening the scoring on the night

before half-time Carlo Cudicini, whose father had played for Inter's great rivals AC Milan, saved wonderfully from a superb 25-yard free-kick taken by Wesley Sneijder.

At half-time, van der Vaart's niggling hamstring injury led to his withdrawal, with Jermaine Jenas coming on to replace him. But Spurs carried on where they had left off. Bale's overhead kick from 20 yards out went narrowly wide. The whole team was whirring like a perfectly tuned machine, turning defence into attack in the blink of an eye. Benoit Assou-Ekotto instigated one move from his own corner flag which saw Spurs sweep across the pitch to set up Crouch for a header that went just over. On 61 minutes Younes Kaboul won the ball on the edge of the Spurs box and fed it to Modric. The Croatian playmaker stroked it to Bale who powered off

from the halfway line to cross for Crouch to score from close range. Spurs were not only beating the European champions, they were outclassing them.

With 10 minutes left. Samuel Eto'o got one back with a fine strike from the edge of the box. But Bale was not finished. He sprinted past Lucio to set Roman Pavlyuchenko up with what's probably the most perfect assist he'll ever have in his career. Spurs had won 3-1 and White Hart Lane rose to acclaim the team at the final whistle.

But it was Bale's night. After the game, the legendary Luis Figo, now on the staff at Inter, said simply: "He killed us."

Cudicini, Hutton, Gallas, Kaboul, Assou-Ekotto, Lennon (Palacios), Huddlestone, Modric, Bale, **van der Vaart** *(Jenas),* **Crouch** *(Pavlyuchenko)*

> "IT WAS AN OUTSTANDING PERFORMANCE AND ONE OF THE GREAT NIGHTS AT WHITE HART LANE. FROM THE FIRST TO THE LAST WE PLAYED UNBELIEVABLY. WE PRESSED THEM, OUTWORKED THEM AND OUTPLAYED THEM ALL NIGHT. YOU HAVE TO PUT INTO PERSPECTIVE WHO WE WERE PLAYING: INTER MILAN, THE CHAMPIONS LEAGUE HOLDERS"
> **HARRY REDKNAPP**

BALE FORCE
Gareth blows champs away

'BALE'S HE'S

SPURS v INTER
IN THE HEADLINES

Gareth Bale's performances in
the two Champions League group
matches against Inter Milan had
the football world in raptures
and sent the newspaper headline
writers into a frenzy

BOYOS TO

Spurs can dare to dream

JUST UNSTOPPABLE'

INTERGALACTIC

BALISSIMO

Bale's brilliance destroys Benitez

SUPERMEN

after a night of glory

Livewire Lennon lights the way for for Tottenham

24 November 2010, Group A

TOTTENHAM HOTSPUR 3
WERDER BREMEN 0

White Hart Lane *Att:* 33,546

Qualification for the knock-out stages was sealed on an evening when Spurs swatted their opponents aside with another of the confident and attacking displays that were turning even the stoniest-hearted critics into confirmed fans. This time it was Aaron Lennon's chance to shine, his fine wing play creating two goals and drawing some of the spotlight away from Gareth Bale on the other wing.

It had not gone unnoticed that this was the kind of game, one with something important at stake, that Spurs had a reputation for choking on. "But these Spurs are different," wrote the *Daily Mirror*'s Martin Lipton. "They actually expect to win." It took just six minutes for Spurs to get on their way.

Lennon skipped down the wing and sent in a pinpoint cross for Younes Kaboul to volley home. Defender Kaboul was enjoying a purple patch as a goalscorer, having bagged the winner in the derby victory over Arsenal just a week before. Spurs continued to

pour forward, with Luka Modric pulling the strings in midfield. Just before half-time he picked the ball up on the left and played it inside to Bale. Bale swung it wide to Hutton, who crossed for Crouch to head down. And there was Modric, taking Crouch's cushioned header down with his left foot while turning to chip home between two defenders with his right. A breathtaking goal to wrap up the half. Spurs created more chances in the second half, and Bale even missed a penalty, prompting reporters to wonder whether "he is human after all". With 11 minutes to go, Lennon once again destroyed his marker to set up Crouch for an easy finish. Spurs had qualified. "Nobody in Europe saw them coming. But now everyone will want to avoid them," wrote the *Mirror*'s Lipton.

Gomes, Hutton, Gallas, **Kaboul***, Assou-Ekotto, Lennon, Jenas (Palacios),* **Modric***, Bale (Kranjcar), Pavlyuchenko (Defoe),* **Crouch**

Younes Kaboul gets on the score sheet with Spurs' first goal in a comfortable win against Werder Bremen

BISH BASH BOSCH!
Harry stays on top after keeper's nightmare

GROUP A	W	D	L	F	A	Pts
TOTTENHAM HOTSPUR	3	2	1	18	11	11
Inter Milan	3	1	2	12	11	10
FC Twente	1	3	2	9	11	6
Werder Bremen	1	2	3	6	12	5

7 December 2010, Group A

FC TWENTE 3
TOTTENHAM HOTSPUR 3

FC Twente Stadion, Enschede, Netherlands *Att*: 24,000

On a freezing night in the far north east of the Netherlands, Spurs became the first team in Champions League history to score two goals or more in every one of their group games. "When it comes to goals, excitement and entertainment among Europe's elite," wrote *The Sun*'s Paul Jiggins, "there is no team quite like Harry Redknapp's at the moment."

Proceedings started in bizarre fashion when Twente keeper Sander Boschker swung his boot at a gentle back pass from Peter Wisgerhof but connected only with fresh air. As his foot followed through, the ball trickled into the net. On 22 minutes, Benoit Assou-Ekotto was harshly adjudged to have handled. Danny Landzaat converted the pemalty kick, but had to retake after the referee blew for encroachment. At the second time of asking, Landzaat made it 1-1.

Harry Redknapp had opted to leave Aaron Lennon on the bench ahead of the forthcoming game against Chelsea, but had to bring him on when Jermaine Jenas hobbled off. Just after half-time a smart reverse pass from Lennon set Jermain Defoe up to score from 10 yards. But seven minutes later Twente were level again through a Rosales header. Just before the hour Defoe prodded home the rebound after Boschker had blocked a shot from Wilson Palacios, but five minutes later Nacer Chadli evened it up again.

Both sides had chances to win the game, but in the end it was the score from the other group game that mattered most. Inter had been beaten 3-0 by Bremen, meaning that Spurs topped the group.

"They are fast becoming THE English team to watch in the Champions League," wrote Darren Lewis in the *Daily Mirror*.

Gomes, Assou-Ekotto, Bassong, Gallas, Corluka, Palacios, Jenas (Lennon), Bale, Kranjcar (Crouch) **Defoe 2**, *Pavlyuchenko (Keane)* **[Wisgerhof og]**

Jermain Defoe is amongst the goals again in another high-scoring match in the Netherlands

15 February 2011, round of 16, first leg

AC MILAN 0
TOTTENHAM HOTSPUR 1

San Siro, Milan, Italy *Att*: 75,652

The draw for the knockout stages took Tottenham back to Milan for what was to be a very different game, but one which would ensure that the city was remembered with affection in Spurs circles for many years. The sun of October had given way to a grey late winter drizzle and while there was still a healthy number of travelling supporters, the numbers were not as great as had descended on the stadium for the match against Inter. Absent too were the injured Gareth Bale and Luka Modric (who only made the bench). Rafael van der Vaart's calf injury was still a worry, and striker Peter Crouch needed a painkillling injection in his spine to play.

Spurs set up with Sandro and Wilson Palacios protecting the back four, with Aaron Lennon and Stephen Pienaar out wide and van der Vaart operating in the hole behind lone forward Crouch. It was a set-up designed to counter the theory that Spurs simply relied on scoring more than a suspect defence would let in. "A Tottenham team noted for the attacking style which had brought them 24 goals in eight European ties this season produced the kind of disciplined performance

which gives them a solid foundation to make it another outstanding night at home," wrote Frank Wiechula in the *Daily Express*. In the *London Evening Standard*, James Olley wrote: "This was the quintessential European away performance that English clubs have spent years perfecting – gain an early foothold in the match by retaining possession, break up the home team's rhythm which, in turn, will stifle the home crowd, defend with resilience and nick a goal on the break."

Spurs had a legitimate claim for a penalty in the first minute when Alessandro Nesta handled after van der Vaart's backheel had sent Pienaar through. But referee Stephen Laney waved the appeals away. Crouch just failed to get enough purchase to put away a cross from Vedran Corluka, then had a cross swiped almost off his head by keeper Christian Abbiati. A Lennon centre drew another penalty appeal, van der Vaart deflected one into Abbiati's hands before the keeper fell awkwardly and had to be substituted… Spurs were making the most of the play, and Milan looked unimpressive when they did get the ball. The home side did come

Left: Vedran Corluka feels the pain after being on the end of a terrible challenge from Milan's Mathieu Flamini

Above: Peter Crouch slots home Spurs' vital away goal and winner on the night

Right: Crouch salutes the travelling Spurs fans in the San Siro after his goal

CROUCH IS THE SAN SIRO HERO

into the game a little more just before the break, but rarely threatened. van der Vaart rounded the half off with a long-range effort that replacement keeper Marco Amelia had to tip over the bar.

At the start of the second half the Dutchman thought he'd made the breakthrough after a delightful turn and chip, but the ball fell just wide of the post. Milan were going nowhere and getting rattled. Mathieu Flamini somehow escaped a sending off for an X-rated two-footed challenge on Corluka which saw the defender carried off. Then, after a foul by Pienaar, Milan skipper Gennaro Gattuso exchanged words with Spurs coach Joe Jordan on the touchline before grabbing him by the throat and slapping his face. The temperature was rising, but Spurs held firm.

Then, with 10 minutes to go, Lennon burst clear and ran at the heart of the Rossoneri defence, before squaring to Crouch. The big man pounced, sending the ball into the net off his shin. Spurs held out to secure what is one of the club's greatest away victories in Europe with a performance that owed much to Redknapp's tactical acumen. As the teams left the pitch, Gattuso and Jordan continued their argument, with the Italian appearing to headbutt the Spurs man. Jordan barely flinched. Afterwards, Redknapp said: "He picked the wrong man there. I know who I'd pick between Joe and Gattuso…"

Gomes, Assou-Ekotto, Dawson, Gallas, Corluka (Woodgate), Pienaar (Kranjcar), Sandro, Palacios, Lennon, van der Vaart (Modric), **Crouch**

9 March 2011, round of 16, second leg

TOTTENHAM HOTSPUR 0 (1)
AC MILAN 0 (0)

White Hart Lane *Att:* 34,320

"Sometimes you don't need goals for glory. Sometimes you just need guts," wrote Martin Lipton in the *Daily Mirror* after a game the paper said was "the greatest, er, 0-0 in their history". A glorious 0-0 is perhaps the most un-Spurslike of concepts, but this was a magnificent performance against opposition which remembered it was the most successful club in the history of the Champions League and turned in a display that befitted their pedigree. Throughout the game they had more than 50 per cent of the possession, played some wonderful football… but could not find a way to get the goal that would have opened the tie up.

The campaign so far had made stars of Tottenham's attacking talent, but on the night it was the turn of the defence to shine. Heurelho Gomes pulled off some fine saves, but with William Gallas and Michael Dawson outstanding in front of him he was well protected. But it was the shield in front of the back four who really stood out. Sandro had been great in the first game; in this one he was magnificent. He needed to be too. Milan played with no width, so the threat was all through the centre. Sandro matched anything they could muster, prompting Lipton to write that "this was the night that Sandro came of age as a top midfielder".

For Milan, Clarence Seedorf and former Spurs man Kevin Prince-Boateng ran the show in midfield, while Zlatan Ibrahimovic and Alexandre Pato were backed up by Robinho to form an attacking trident that threatened Spurs all night long. For Spurs Luka Modric, Rafael van der Vaart and Aaron Lennon could barely get into the game. On 26 minutes Pato rounded Gomes and pulled the ball back for Robinho. It looked a certain goal, but Robinho scuffed his shot against a grounded Benoit Assou-Ekotto. The ball looped up and in darted Gallas to hook it off the line.

Left: William Gallas makes a crucial goal-line clearance

Above: Joy in the Spurs players ranks as the 0-0 draw sees them through to the next round

Right: Gareth Bale acknowledges the home crowd on another memorable European night

HARRYVEDERCI!

Battling Spurs wave goodbye to Italian giants

In the second half, Gomes denied Pato, Mathieu Flamini shot across goal, and Pato prompted celebrations from the travelling Italian fans until they realised his shot had gone into the side netting. As the half went on, Milan's belief began to slip away and Spurs began to run down the clock. Robinho went close again late on, but this was the last of the danger. The tension began to lift as Spurs stayed focused and unruffled. On the final whistle the joy rolled down from the stands. The previous evening, Arsenal had been dumped out of the competition by Barcelona. Spurs had got further in the competition than their old rivals, and there was only one choice of song for the crowd to serenade the team with – "Are you watching, Arsenal?"

The Sun had it down as a case of "Harryverderci", while the *Daily Mirror* stretched the pun to breaking point with the strap-line: "European greats are Harried out of it by England's finest boss." Oliver Holt pointed out that, "Redknapp is the first English manager to lead a club to the last eight of the European Cup since Terry Venables did it with Barcelona in 1986. The last English manager to lead an English club to the quarter-finals was Joe Fagan with Liverpool a year earlier." Of Spurs, Holt wrote: "This is a club with a tradition of excellence. Redknapp's role has been to revive it, to start to restore it to its former glories."

In the *Evening Standard*, James Olley wrote: "From such inauspicious beginnings now grow the most unimaginable outcomes, with a place in the Champions League quarter-finals raising intriguing possibilities as to where this upward curve will end."

Gomes, Corluka, Gallas, Dawson, Assou-Ekotto, Sandro, Lennon, Modric, Pienaar (Jenas), van der Vaart (Bale), Crouch (Pavlyuchenko)

No reprieve for Spurs this time after another shocking start

5 April 2011, quarter-final, first leg

REAL MADRID 4
TOTTENHAM HOTSPUR 0

Estadio Santiago Bernabeu, Madrid, Spain *Att: 71,657*

Spurs had wanted to avoid Barcelona. They did, landing a tie against Real Madrid instead. It was another trip to a footballing cathedral that drew enormous numbers to the Spanish capital. But this was one of those great trips spoiled by a game of football.

Just before the game began, Aaron Lennon succumbed to a bug, forcing a reshuffle of the team. Then, five minutes into the match, Spurs went behind when Emmanuel Adebayor rose to head home Mesut Ozil's corner. Spurs were all at sea and Peter Crouch, in particular, was making some wild tackles. On 15 minutes he made another rash challenge to earn a second yellow, and Spurs were down to 10 men against one of the best teams in the world.

With Sami Khedira and Xabi Alonso providing a defensive shield, Adebayor, Ozil, Angel di Maria and Cristiano Ronaldo had a licence to interchange at will. Spurs dug in, with Michael Dawson blocking a volley on the line and narrowly escaping conceding a penalty for handball. Rafael van der Vaart and Gareth Bale could only flicker, snatching at half-chances.

Real boss Jose Mourinho couldn't have been pleased that half-time came without his team having killed the tie, but it didn't take long to come. In the 57th minute, Adebayor headed another. Then Angel di Maria fired home a screamer in the 66th minute. Real were utterly in control. Four minutes from time, Ronaldo volleyed home a peach of a goal to get his 38th of the season.

In the return, wrote *The Sun*'s Shaun Custis, "there is only pride left to play for". the *London Evening Standard*'s James Olley wrote, "Spurs' endearing adventure into the Champions League is all but over."

Gomes, Assou-Ekotto, Dawson, Gallas, Corluka (Bassong), Bale, Modric, Sandro, Jenas, van der Vaart (Defoe), Crouch

Left: Peter Crouch leaves the field after being red-carded on 15 mins, a blow Spurs never recovered from in the Bernabeu

Right: William Gallas shakes hands with Emmanuel Adebayor, scorer of Real's first goal on the night

HARRY'S DREAM ENDS IN REALITY CHECK

..now the hard work begins

13 April 2011, quarter-final, second leg

TOTTENHAM HOTSPUR 0 (0)
REAL MADRID 1 (5)

White Hart Lane *Att*: 34,311

Such had been the drama of the campaign that it was not entirely beyond the imagination of more than a few Spurs fans to wonder if, just maybe, what would have been the most extraordinary turnaround in football history was possible. But most turned up in hope rather than expectation, and even the hope was tempered. As it turned out, Spurs never looked like making an impression on one of the most impressive sides ever to play at White Hart Lane. And when, just after the break, Heurelho Gomes fumbled a long-range shot from Cristiano Ronaldo and the ball squirmed over the line, there could be no doubt that Spurs were out. The crowd did manage, though, to muster a rousing chorus of "We're gonna win 6-1".

Gareth Bale and Aaron Lennon did show signs of the wingplay that had taken Spurs so far, but, although Roman Pavlyuchenko and Jermain Defoe might have made more of the chances created, Spurs didn't really threaten.

At the final whistle the crowd rose to its feet, applauding a magnificent performance by Real Madrid and showing their appreciation for what had been a wonderful first Champions League campaign. Everyone knew it had been very special. "They were thanking Harry Redknapp and his players for the magic carpet ride that saw them stun the San Siro twice, made them the side all of Europe wanted to see, and brought a revitalizing approach to a competition that is so often stifled and dull in its initial phase," wrote Martin Lipton in the *Daily Mirror*. While Dan Jones, in the *London Evening Standard* reflected that, "we have seen things that even the most one-eyed Tottenham diehard wouldn't have considered possible."

Gomes, Corluka, Gallas, Dawson, Assou-Ekotto, Lennon (Defoe), Huddlestone (Sandro), Modric (Kranjcar), Bale, van der Vaart, Pavlyuchenko

Cristiano Ronaldo, Real's scorer on the night, rises above Heurelho Gomes and the combined Spurs defence

Above: Spurs take the field for their first Champions League game at home v Young Boys
Right: Fans enjoy the moment

"IT'S BEEN FANTASTIC. THE KEY FOR ME WAS TO GET THROUGH THAT FIRST STAGE AGAINST YOUNG BOYS. I DIDN'T WANT TO GO OUT THERE. I THOUGHT 'WE'VE COME THIS FAR', IT WAS ABOUT GETTING TO THE GROUP STAGE AND GIVING THE FANS SIX MATCHES THEY'D ALL ENJOY."
HARRY REDKNAPP

THE CHAMPIONS LEAGUE
IN PICTURES

Left: Vedran Corluka and Harry Redknapp are in good spirits on the first away trip in the group to Bremen, Germany

Below: An exhausted Gareth Bale after his extraordinary efforts in the San Siro v Inter Milan

Top: The Spurs players huddle before their victory v Milan in the San Siro

Left: William Gallas's clearance keeps the aggregate score at 1-0 in the second leg

"I'VE LOVED EVERY MINUTE OF IT, PREPARING FOR THE MATCHES, GOING OUT TO WATCH MILAN AGAINST LAZIO, THE BUILD-UP, THE ATMOSPHERE, THE MATCHES. IT'S WHAT YOU ALL DREAM ABOUT"
HARRY REDKNAPP

THE CHAMPIONS LEAGUE
IN PICTURES

Left: Gareth Bale and Michael Dawson acknowledge the fans in the Bernabeu on a night when Spurs were well beaten by Real Madrid – the club whose all-white strip inspired Spurs' own European tradition

Below: Harry Redknapp watches as Real Madrid boss Jose Mourinho substitutes Cristiano Ronaldo at White Hart Lane. By this time the tie was beyond Spurs and the Champions League adventure nearly over

THE ROAD TO EUROPE
2011

Tottenham Hotspur's qualification for the Europa League provided a neat snapshot of what European competition had become. The club had tasted the Champions League and won new friends for the way Spurs had lit it up. After that, qualification for the second tier competition felt anti-climactic. The season had seemed to fall away following the defeat by Real Madrid. Games that looked winnable were drawn, and defeats late in the campaign to Chelsea and Manchester City confirmed that Spurs would miss out on the top four. Bill Nicholson once said that "without Europe, this club is nothing". Now, having Europe was a distraction for a team many believed could make a challenge for the Premier League title.

Manager Harry Redknapp said: "It's one of those competitions that teams get in and they try to get out of. You look at the English teams and they all seem to play the reserve teams in it and change." So the fringe players and reserves limbered up, and the blessing of Europe seemed very mixed indeed. And that, ultimately, was to prove significant.

Spurs celebrate a 3-2 win away at Arsenal during a scintillating run of form in late 2010

Jake Livermore is one of five Spurs goalscorers at Tynecastle where Tottenham found their form and outclassed Hearts on the night

18 August 2011, play-off round, first leg

HEARTS 0
TOTTENHAM HOTSPUR 5

Tynecastle, Edinburgh *Att*: 16,279

Dave Mackay took the applause before the game, but it was the club he left Edinburgh to join that took the plaudits. Hearts were "handed a footballing lesson by slick Spurs" according to Alan Pattullo in *The Scotsman*. The visitors, he said, "moved the ball around with frightening speed and accuracy" on a night when the stark reality of the gulf between English and Scottish football was laid bare. Rafael van der Vaart opened the scoring on four minutes, stepping in smartly to shoot wide of keeper Marian Kello. On 12 minutes Jermain Defoe effectively ended the tie with a precision finish to Aaron Lennon's cross. Jake Livermore nabbed a third on 28 minutes, and in the second half goals from Gareth Bale and Lennon rounded off a fine display. Hearts manager Paolo Sergio said: "My players were like people who had bought a ticket for the match."

*Gomes, Walker, Dawson, Kaboul, Assou-Ekotto, **Lennon**, **Livermore**, Kranjcar, **Bale** (Townsend), **van der Vaart** (Huddlestone), **Defoe** (Pavlyuchenko)*

25 August 2011, play-off round, second leg

TOTTENHAM HOTSPUR 0 (5)
HEARTS 0 (0)

White Hart Lane, London *Att*: 24,053

Harry Redknapp opted to field six academy graduates for a game that was effectively a dead rubber. With Hearts also fielding a weakened line-up it could have been a poor spectacle but, said the BBC's Sam Lyons, "There was enough potential on show to please both sets of supporters. For Spurs, Andros Townsend stood out, and Jake Livermore and Tom Carroll orchestrated some crisp passing. Striker Harry Kane won a penalty, but his spot kick was saved by keeper Jamie Macdonald. MacDonald also did well to keep out a long-range effort from Roman Pavlyuchenko. Spurs were restricted to few chances but Hearts never really threatened, and the game somewhat inevitably petered out in the final stages. Afterwards, Redknapp said, "The youngsters did well." For the group stage, he said, he would "play the kids at times – it's a balancing act".

Cudicini, Bassong, Corluka, Dawson (Kaboul), Livermore (Nicholson), Carroll, Fredericks (Kranjcar), Huddlestone, Townsend, Pavlyuchenko, Kane

Giovani Dos Santos gets the third goal against Shamrock Rovers to cap a late Spurs recovery which saw them eventually overwhelm the Irish champions

15 September 2011, Group A

PAOK 0
TOTTENHAM HOTSPUR 0

Toumba Stadium, Salonika *Att*: 24,645

The Greek side's Toumba Stadium is a notoriously hostile venue, but Harry Redknapp judged his youngsters brave enough to take it on, making 10 changes from the side he had fielded in the last Premier League game in a line-up whose average age was 23. Among those on the pitch was debutant Lago Falqué, a playmaker on loan from Juventus. But it was veteran keeper Carlo Cudicini whose experience would be called upon to make a series of vital saves as PAOK pushed for a breakthrough. Cudicini was booked for bringing down Stefanos Athanasiadis – although he denied making contact – and PAOK scored from the penalty. But the referee ordered a retake and the second effort was sent wide. Harry Kane felt he should have had a penalty on the half hour, but instead got a booking for diving – much to Redknapp's bemusement. In the end, credit went to the Spurs youngsters.

Cudicini, Bassong, Corluka, Walker, Livermore, Townsend, Carroll, Pavlyuchenko, Giovani (Parrett), Falqué (Fredericks), Kane

29 September 2011, Group A

TOTTENHAM HOTSPUR 3
SHAMROCK ROVERS 1

White Hart Lane, London *Att*: 24,730

The Irish side brought 3,000 lively, good-humoured fans to London for a tie which again saw Spurs field a second string, this time with an eye on the upcoming derby against Arsenal. The Rovers fans, observed the *Daily Telegraph*'s Cameron King, were as dominant off the pitch as Spurs were on it – "determined to enjoy their evening". Well, in the 50th minute the green-and-white hordes were in dreamland when Stephen Rice shot them into the lead. The goal shocked Spurs into action, and they responded with three goals in 10 minutes. Roman Pavlyuchenko equalised from Andros Townsend's cross, then Jermain Defoe headed home a Giovani Dos Santos cross. Moments later, Defoe and Giovani combined again for the Mexican to slot home a cool finish after Defoe had run 70 yards. In the end, said King in the *Daily Telegraph*, "for Tottenham and their fans it was only a minor distraction".

Cudicini, Bassong, Corluka, Walker, Lennon (Townsend), Rose (Kane), Livermore, Carroll, **Pavlyuchenko, Giovani, Defoe** *(Falqué)*

20 October 2011, Group A

TOTTENHAM HOTSPUR 1
FC RUBIN KAZAN 0

White Hart Lane, London *Att: 24,058*

A Russian striker found the net on the night a team from the Russian Republic of Tatarstan came to White Hart Lane, but fortunately for Spurs his name was Roman Pavlyuchenko. Pav's strike on 34 minutes was a thing of beauty, a free-kick struck so hard into the top corner of the net the ball threatened to combust. Spurs needed that moment of magic, as this was the toughest opposition yet in the competition. Harry Redknapp continued to juggle his resources, fielding a stronger line-up than previously in the Europa League, but still with a sprinkling of youth. The 19-year-old Tom Carroll once again impressed in midfield and Jake Livermore fared well as an improvised centre-back. It needed three experienced subs in the shape of Younes Kaboul, Luka Modric and Benoit Assou-Ekotto to steady the ship, but the win left Spurs set fair for qualification.

Gomes, Walker, Bassong, Sandro (Kaboul), Rose, Carroll, Lennon (Modric), Livermore, Giovani (Assou-Ekotto), **Pavlyuchenko**, *Defoe*

3 November 2011, Group A

FC RUBIN KAZAN 1
TOTTENHAM HOTSPUR 0

Central Stadium, Kazan *Att: 21, 250*

Spurs travelled to deepest Tatarstan without manager Harry Redknapp, who had undergone heart surgery the day before the tie. What he saw watching on TV from his home in Dorset can't have aided recovery. A second-string side churned out a dour display and only the heroics of Carlo Cudicini between the sticks averted a real hiding for the visitors. As it was, the only goal of the night came after a terrible error by central defender Sebastian Bassong. Ten minutes after the break he tried to dribble out of his area instead of clearing the ball. He lost control and Alexander Ryazantsev stepped in, only for Bassong to hack him down. From the resulting free-kick, Rubin Kazan scored. Spurs struggled to muster a shot, and the result now meant qualification was on a knife-edge. Four points from the remaining two games were needed to ensure progress.

Cudicini, Gallas (Parrett), Bassong, Livermore, Townsend, Pienaar, Fredericks, Carroll, Pavlyuchenko (Kane), Defoe, Falqué

Spurs' own Russian, Roman Pavlyuchenko, scores the only goal of the night with a ferocious free-kick against Rubin Kazan

GROUP A	W	D	L	F	A	Pts
PAOK	3	3	0	10	6	12
Rubin Kazan	3	2	1	11	5	11
TOTTENHAM HOTSPUR	3	1	2	9	4	10
Shamrock Rovers	0	0	6	4	19	0

30 November 2011, Group A

TOTTENHAM HOTSPUR 1 PAOK 2

White Hart Lane, London Att 26,229

Spurs began this game sluggishly and, just three minutes in, William Gallas conceded possession on the halfway line to the away side's Giorgos Fotakis. From the resulting move Dimitris Salpingidis headed PAOK in front. Five minutes later it was 2-0 as Stefanos Athanasiades thumped home from close range, sending the lively and very loud throng of Greek supporters wild. Cue mass waving of shirts above heads. Luka Modric pulled one back from a penalty just before half-time, and with PAOK down to 10 men after a harsh sending off, Spurs stepped up their game in the second half. But PAOK held firm. It was only the fourth White Hart Lane defeat in the club's rich European history, and Spurs were now relying on other results going their way to qualify. Harry Redknapp said afterwards, "We're not going to be in the last 32."

Gomes, Gallas, Bassong, Corluka, Lennon, Modric, Rose (Bale), Livermore, Pienaar (Walker), Defoe, Kane (Falqué)

15 December 2011, Group A

SHAMROCK ROVERS 0 TOTTENHAM HOTSPUR 4

Tallaght Stadium, Dublin Att: 7,500

The trip to Dublin meant Spurs had played in England, Scotland, Wales (Swansea in the league) and Ireland in a single season. But they needed a five-goal swing in goal difference and a defeat for Rubin Kazan to qualify. At half-time it seemed possible. Spurs were three goals up – Stephen Pienaar opening the scoring before Andros Townsend and Jermain Defoe struck. Rubin were a goal and a man down in Greece. But news of a Rubin equaliser early in the second half dampened any lingering hopes. Rovers put on a brave display, restricting Spurs to a single further goal, grabbed by Harry Kane on the stroke of time. The *Daily Telegraph's* Ian Chadband observed that Harry Redknapp "did not even bother to bring more than three outfield substitutes". Redknapp said: "We just had a bad 15 minutes against PAOK at home. Otherwise, everything had gone to plan."

Cudicini, Kaboul, Assou-Ekotto (Falqué), Kranjcar, Rose, Livermore, Sandro, Townsend, Pienaar, Giovani, Defoe (Kane)

Above left: Luka Modric can't believe it as a Spurs goal is disallowed and the team lose at home to PAOK

Above right: Jermain Defoe finds the net in Dublin and is congratulated by fellow scorer Andros Townsend but it's not enough to see Spurs progress in the Europa League

IN CONVERSATION WITH
GARETH BALE & MICHAEL DAWSON

As club football entered a new age with the advent of the Champions League, Spurs looked to a new generation of stars to continue the club's fine traditions. It had been nearly 50 years since Spurs had last graced Europe's premier competition – and in the early 21st century it was exciting young players like Gareth Bale and Michael Dawson who would add thrilling and memorable new chapters to the glory glory nights story.

The club had been pushing to get into the Champions League for a while – and just when it seemed that dream might be realised came the infamous West Ham game in 2006 when several players succumbed to illness before the match. Spurs needed to win in order to get fourth spot and qualify.

What are your memories of that weekend?
Michael Dawson I was rough as a dog. I wish I'd been at home that night instead of in the hotel. We had our usual routine, a pre-match evening meal, and we went to our rooms. I woke up in the night and I thought "I don't feel too good". I was sick and I phoned the doctor and said, "Look, I don't think I'll be the only one. It may be something I ate." I went down in the morning and I thought, "I can't play in this game." Had I been the only one I maybe would not have played.

Football is a physical game and our bodies have to be in good condition to run and compete for 90 minutes. Our bodies were in far from good condition. Had we lost fair and square with everyone fit there would have been no complaints, but the way the lads were feeling… Well, to be going into a game like that and miss out on a Champions League place in that way was just – we certainly felt hard done by.

You did get what you deserved in 2010, however. Was Champions League the target that season?
MD Definitely. To be back in Europe in the Europa League is the next best thing, but it's not the Champions League where everyone wants to be; it's the best competition. Champions League nights are special, there's not many better.

As you honed in on that fourth place what was the spirit in the camp like?
MD I can see the Man City game now, second-last league game. It was an unbelievable night. Massive pressure.
Gareth Bale It was like we won the league, wasn't it?
MD Yeah, that night, after the game…
GB Harry [Redknapp] getting drenched!

Inter's Maicon gets close to Gareth Bale at last

MD I think our reaction showed it – the reward for all the hard work.

That sequence of results with wins over Arsenal, Chelsea and then Man City was fantastic – title-winning form?
MD We certainly deserved to be there. I always say at the end of each season you finish where you deserve to be, there's no luck – there's 38 games. You have bits of luck now and again, but it does tend to even itself out, although when you have bad luck and decisions go against you it's not easy to take, but I do believe you finish where you deserve to.

So you were ready for the big time in the Champions League. What did you know about the European heritage of Spurs, the legacy?
MD When you sign and you're part of the club you tend to learn more about the history. When we did what we achieved to get back into Europe after a long time it was great.

What is it that makes European nights at White Hart Lane special?
GB I think it's the crowd, the fact that the fans are right on top of you. The atmosphere is just unbelievable. European nights are just those evenings when the whole crowd is right behind the team and the chants that they sing are even louder.

And was team spirit made stronger for being in Europe?
MD I don't think so, with the squad that we have had it's not something you just switch on or off – every game you go into you've got to be together as a team fighting for one another. Whether it's Europe, Premier League, cup games – whatever it is, you can't just turn on performances whenever you want to because it will backfire.

GARETH BALE
Spurs career:
159 apps, 29 goals
Europe:
23 apps, 5 goals
(Up to 2011/12 season)

MICHAEL DAWSON
Spurs career:
249 apps, 8 goals
Europe:
29 apps, 1 goal
(Up to 2011/12 season)

GB We room on our own, but we always have team meetings, everyone's in each other's rooms all the time. We're very good together – as Daws said we're a close bunch. There are no individual groups or that sort of thing. We're all together and I think that helps the team on the pitch.

As for the campaign itself and that first game against Young Boys, 3-0 down after half an hour: it's safe to say it wasn't quite going according to plan. What was said at half-time?
GB It wasn't really so much what was said at half-time, it was kind of on the pitch after the third goal went in. The surface wasn't great – Astroturf is a lot quicker, it was wet and the ball just travelled quicker.
MD It was crazy.
GB They caught us off guard in a way, but I think after the third goal went in it hit us and we all woke up and battled back from there.
MD Pav's [Roman Pavlyuchenko] goal right at the end in the 83rd minute; we came back to White Hart Lane and we knew, we always believed we could turn things round. With Crouchie [Peter Crouch] getting the early goal and the fans rocking, in the end we got through comfortably, but we weren't feeling like that after 30 minutes of the first leg.

Back at White Hart Lane you did the job. And hearing the Champions League music while waiting in the tunnel – is that the kind of thing that brings it home that you're in it for real?
GB It brings a smile to your face. You watch it on TV every year and the fact that you're playing in it, and the atmosphere – I think that kind of boosted everybody and knowing that we had to win the game anyway gave everyone that extra lift. It made us more hungry.

It was the games against Inter that really put that Spurs team on the map. Everything was going against you in the first leg at the San Siro.
GB We came in at half-time, we just felt we had to go out there and stop getting embarrassed. The main target was to try not to concede too many more and just give all we can. We've got nothing to lose, we're 4-0 down; we just had to go out there and try our best – regain some pride. It was obviously difficult having 10 men as well, but I think we showed in the second half as a team our character and that we were capable of battling back.

For your goals, Gareth – did you think you'd had the beating of them to run at them with pace?
GB In the first half the game was clearly a lot more one-sided, but when we did get the ball in the right areas we were able to get in behind them and get a few shots off, or get some crosses in. I think we always knew that if we got at them, it was possible.

In the second half we got into the right areas. They had been so dominant in the game, but they played so high in the second half it was easier – they sort of switched off because they were 4-0 up and we were able to kind of pounce on them.

> **"WE KNEW WE HAD THE UPPER HAND PSYCHOLOGICALLY OVER INTER – WE ROCKED THEIR BOAT WHEN WE CAME BACK FROM 4-0 DOWN. BUT WHEN THEY CAME TO OUR OWN STADIUM WE FELT WE HAD THE UPPER HAND"**
> GARETH BALE

By the end they were the ones hanging on?
GB Exactly, I think we won the ball back straight after they kicked off after the third but the ref blew up. It would have been close, a couple of more minutes and I think something might have happened.
MD I was at home injured, watching it on television and thinking…
GB "Thank goodness!" [laughs]
MD [laughs] Well I was thinking, "4-0 down, it's not a nice position to be in." No one else is going to help you on that pitch and the lads have to stick together when things aren't going right – because they don't always go right on the football pitch; there's no place for people to be hiding and chucking things in because you just get beaten more.

Whatever was said at half-time, credit to the lads because coming back in that second half and Gaz getting the goals it was unbelievable. And from that night everyone was scared of playing Tottenham Hotspur. That was probably the turning point in the Champions League group stages. When Inter came to White Hart Lane they did *not* fancy coming to us. I don't blame them. At White Hart Lane it was fantastic.

It was indeed an unforgettable night. A lot of older fans who had seen a lot of glory nights games were saying that was one of the best they'd ever seen in terms of the performance, atmosphere and occasion. Can you describe how you were feeling playing in that kind of game?
GB We knew we had the upper hand psychologically over them – we rocked their boat massively when we came back from 4-0 down. But when they came, the reigning European champions to our own stadium, we felt we had the upper hand. Being in a game like that is massive no matter who you are.

IN CONVERSATION WITH
GARETH BALE & MICHAEL DAWSON

We all went out there fully believing we could score; we went out and showed what we were capable of.

MD I was gutted not to be involved, but watching it the atmosphere was special.

Spurs were on fire in the home game right from the off. What were Harry's instructions beforehand? Was there much in the way of detail?

MD "Get it to Gaz! Get it to Lennon," that's all he needed to say, keep it tight and give it to those two! [laughs]

GB He told us just to go out and do what we're best at. That's what he always asked of us. No matter who we were playing, he wanted us to do what we do best. Part of that was to give the ball to me and Azza and run at their full-backs, for the strikers it was to take their shots, the midfielders to be creative. That was always the case, he always wanted us to express ourselves. We always thought if we did that we'd cause any team problems.

The atmosphere was special that night; could you focus?

GB I never really listen to the crowd that much, you are concentrating on the beating the team in front of you. When it's such a vital game that you have to win to keep your chances of qualifying for the knockout stages alive, it's vitally important to maintain that focus. Even when we were winning it was important that we kept the lead as that game was key to us qualifying.

Luis Figo [an Inter ambassador] said after that game that "they killed us" – it was high praise, an indication that that Spurs team had really "arrived".

MD I think that night made Gaz worldwide. Everyone was talking about Gareth Bale – it was as simple as that. We as players at Tottenham and in England knew what he could do, but from that night, wow – it certainly put his name on the big stage.

> **"TO COME TO WHITE HART LANE AND TO KNOCK A TEAM LIKE AC MILAN OUT WAS A GREAT ACHIEVEMENT. IT WAS A WONDERFUL NIGHT AND ONE I'LL CERTAINLY REMEMBER FOR THE REST OF MY LIFE"**
> MICHAEL DAWSON

Gareth, Cliff Jones said he told you, "You are the Welsh wonder, but don't forget I was the original Welsh wonder."

GB [laughs] Whenever I see Cliff I always speak to him, he always has good words to say about me. I was a bit too young to remember him playing, though [laughter]. But I've seen a few clips and from what I've heard, everybody says what a great player he was – and what a Welsh wizard he was. So for him to speak to me like that is a massive honour and something I obviously respect a lot.

Michael Dawson has a night to remember

On to AC Milan – another wonderful result but a different kind of performance. You played almost in an untypical "Spurs" way, very determined and resolute in an overall team display of high quality?

MD The lads had obviously been to the San Siro before. This one was my first game for a while. And what a game to come back to. We knew it was going to be tough, we were set up different to the normal way. We normally go all-out attacking and teams have to get used to how we play, but when you go somewhere like that against the kind of opposition, you perhaps change your style and we did, with two banks of four.

I thought from front to back everyone worked their socks off and did their jobs. Then when Crouchie put the ball in the back of the net it was great. We were holding on at the end, but then to come to White Hart Lane and to knock a team like AC out was a great achievement. It was a wonderful night and one I'll certainly remember for the rest of my life.

You then came up against Real Madrid. What was it that cost you over the two legs?

GB We just wanted to impress, to give our all I think; we wanted to get every ball. Maybe the whole occasion was just so overwhelming for everybody to be playing at the Bernabeu at that stage of the competition, everybody just wanted to impress a bit *too* much rather than play our more natural game.

MD To go to Real Madrid and go a goal down so early that was a massive blow. Sometimes that's not down to experience, it's about a mistake or simply that they do something better than we did. Our aim is to stay in the game, any game when you go away from home, and not let the other team get the upper hand. We did when we let Ade [Emmanuel Adebayor] score that first goal with a header.

To start that way gave them the momentum. They scored a second, then a third and a fourth and it wasn't nice to take. At White Hart Lane it was always going to be an

Gareth Bale and Michael Dawson embrace after victory over AC Milan, 2011

uphill task. Things have changed before, but that was just one task too many. I think overall the Champions League campaign and journey we'd been on, for the majority of our players it was the first time we'd played in it. I thought they did fantastically well and it made us all hungry to do it on a more regular basis. The way we missed out last year [2011/12 season] was devastating but the aim is to get back into it. It's where everyone wants to be playing.

What's the experience of playing in Europe as against the domestic competition – is there a different style?
GB The Premier League is all hustle and bustle and teams defending for their lives; in European competition it's all about attack, it's end-to-end stuff and you don't have to defend for your lives.

Every team I think, in the Champions League, is used to winning most games and playing attacking football. So you don't often get a situation where you have two banks of four just defending. It's usually open and creative football. Most teams are attacking sides and usually the best team from their respective countries. That's why everyone wants to play in it, because it's the best standard of football in the club game and the most entertaining.

A lot is made of the difference between British players in terms of technique with their counterparts. Is that valid?
GB I wouldn't say they are that much more technical. The Premier League is very physical. In Spain it's probably not as physical, but I think it's just different styles of football, really. We see a lot of Brazilians, for example, struggle to play when they come over here.
MD No, but I think it's just style of football – certain styles suit certain kinds of footballer. That's why the Champions League is so interesting – you bring all those styles and players together and it makes for great entertainment.

THE TROPHY CABINET

It's part of the protocol of European ties for the opposing club directors to meet and exchange gifts. Those from Spurs' early campaigns in the 1960s and 1970s were originally displayed in the Oak Room in the old West Stand. Many went into permanent storage when the stand was rebuilt in 1982. Some more notable gifts – the coal truck from Spurs' first European trip to the coal-mining town of Gornik in Poland and the Benfica ship from the 1962 European Cup semi-final – are on display in the Bill Nicholson suite and can be seen on club tours. The other 1960s items, including two case-mounted medals from Slovan Bratislava and Olympique Lyonnais, are seen here for the first time in decades.

The gifts tend to be symbols of the club or the area in which it is based. The vase from Keflavik of Iceland is encrusted with volcanic rocks and the ceramic from Austria Vienna is dancing a waltz. To mark their meeting in the inaugural UEFA Cup in 1972, Wolves presented Spurs with a silver cigar case (the cigars have gone!). In the 1970s and 1980s there was a trend towards ornaments. A red and white glass vase was presented by Anderlecht prior to the 1984 UEFA Cup Final, and a decorative plate by Real Madrid in 1985.

In the Champions League season of 2010/11, Werder Bremen presented a cast iron statue of their city emblem, the Milan clubs engraved silver plates. Inter also presented Spurs with engraved goblets and a miniature silver tray (see p189) which have pride of place at the club's training ground. Spurs reciprocated these gifts with a silver engraved club cockerel.

Pride of place, though, goes to the European trophies Spurs have won – the Cup Winners' Cup and UEFA Cup. Take a browse round Spurs' European trophy cabinet...

EUROPEAN CUP
1961/62

Gornik Zabrze

Feyenoord

Benfica

CUP WINNERS' CUP
1962/63, 1963/64

Slovan Bratislava

CUP WINNERS' CUP
WINNERS 1963

Manchester United

CUP WINNERS' CUP
1967/68

Hajduk Split

Olympique Lyonnais

EUROPEAN TREASURES

UEFA CUP
1971/72

Keflavik

UEFA CUP
WINNERS
1972 & 1984

Nantes

Wolverhampton
Wanderers

UEFA CUP
1972/73 & 1973/74

Grasshoppers Zurich

Lyn Oslo

Aberdeen

UEFA CUP
1973/74

Locomotive Leipzig

Feyenoord

CUP WINNERS' CUP
1981/82 & 1982/83

Eintracht Frankfurt

Bayern Munich

UEFA CUP
1983/84 & 1984/85

Drogheda

Austria Vienna

Hajduk Split

Anderlecht

Bohemians Prague

Real Madrid

CUP WINNERS' CUP
1991/92

SV Stockerau

Porto

UEFA CUP
1999/2000

Kaiserslautern

UEFA CUP
2006/07, 2007/08 & 2008/09

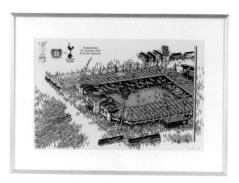

Bayer Leverkusen

Getafe

Udinese

Sevilla

Slavia Prague

Spartak Moscow

Shakhtar Donetsk

CHAMPIONS LEAGUE
2010/11

Young Boys

Inter Milan

FC Twente

EUROPA LEAGUE
2011/2012

Hearts

PAOK

Shamrock Rovers

Werder Bremen

AC Milan

Rubin Kazan

ACKNOWLEDGEMENTS

This book was produced with invaluable assistance and encouragement from the staff of Tottenham Hotspur Football Club, especially John Fennelly.

Thanks also to Victoria Howarth, Rebecca Britain, Gary Jacobson, Jonathan Waite, Gary Belsham and a special mention to Andy Porter and Bob Goodwin for their help and meticulous fact-checking which went beyond the call of duty.

The authors and publishers would also like to thank Cliff Jones, Terry Dyson, Martin Chivers, Phil Beal, Paul Miller, Micky Hazard, Gareth Bale and Michael Dawson for providing such wonderful thoughts and memories for this book.

Thanks also to: Lance Bellers, Jim Duggan, Daphne Edwards, Neville Evans, Alex Fynn, Norman Giller, Richard Havers, Alan Fisher, Mel Gomes, Bernie Kingsley, Bruce Lee, Michael Maynard, Rick Mayston, Julie Welch, Geoff Whitmore, Jonathan Wilson and the staff of Bruce Castle Museum.

Special thanks to Richard Cracknell.

Last but not least, thanks to all the journalists and photographers who have followed Spurs over land and sea, and European travelling companions old and new.

Photography
Action Images: p6-7, 11(2), 28-9, 34, 36-7, 52, 57, 59, 64, 65r, 69, 70(2), 71, 72, 73b, 74, 76-7, 80-1, 83b, 84-5, 86, 87(2), 88(2), 90, 91, 93, 94-5, 96, 97, 98, 99, 100, 101, 107t, 109(2), 111, 113, 114-9(12), 121c, 122-3, 132-3, 135, 136-7, 144, 153b, 154, 158t, 158-9, 175r, 177, 182b, 183bl, 184-5(3), 186-7, 188(2), 189, 190(2), 191, 194, 197(2), 199, 200, 201, 202, 203r, 206, 207, 208, 210-1, 212, 213(2), 214(2), 215, 216-7, 218, 220, 221, 222l, 223r, 224-5(2), 228, 229, 231t, 232-3(3), 234(2), 236-7(4), 239(2), 242, 243, 244, 245(2), 246-9(5)

Getty Images: Back cover, back flap, p4, 8, 9, 13r, 14-5, 18, 18-9, 23, 25, 28l+r, 28r, 31r, 32-3, 35, 38, 39, 40, 43(2), 54-5, 58, 61(2), 65l, 68, 73t, 74-5, 78-9, 79b, 102l, 106-7, 126, 131, 140, 141(2), 142, 146, 150(2), 151, 152, 152-3, 155, 158c+b, 164, 165, 166, 171, 172, 175l, 178, 181t, 182t, 192-3, 195, 196, 203l, 204-5, 209, 219, 222-3, 230, 231b, 235, 238(2), 240-1

Colorsport: p10r, 66-7, 78, 82-3, 102-3, 104-5, 105b, 107b, 121l, 125, 130-1, 145, 149, 156-7
PA Photos: Front cover, p10l, 16, 17, 20(2), 20-1, 22, 24, 26, 40-41, 44-5, 50-1, 63, 128, 138
Professional Sport: p124(2), 126-7, 162-3, 167, 168, 169
Offside: p13l, 105t, 121r, 129l, 170
Rex Features: p46-7, 49, 53, 134, 173
Charles Whitmore: p46 (3)
Aubrey Morris collection: p42(2)
The Times / NI Syndication: 31t

All official matchday penants and gifts are courtesy of THFC, photographed by Paul Downes at 3 Objectives Photography.

Additional memorabilia courtesy of Neville Evans and Bob Goodwin.

Thanks to everyone who helped with photograhy especially Chris Gregory and Mark Platt at Action Images, Damian Dent at Getty Images, Andy Cowie at Colorsport, Mark Leech at Offside, Tommy Hindley at Professional Sport, Edd Griffin at Rex Features, Clare Hindson and Laura Wagg at PA Photos and Paul Downes at 3 Objectives Photography.

In association with Action Images, the photographic partner of Tottenham Hotspur FC